D0988001

discover
BARCELONA

BRENDAN SAINSBURY
DAMIEN SIMONIS

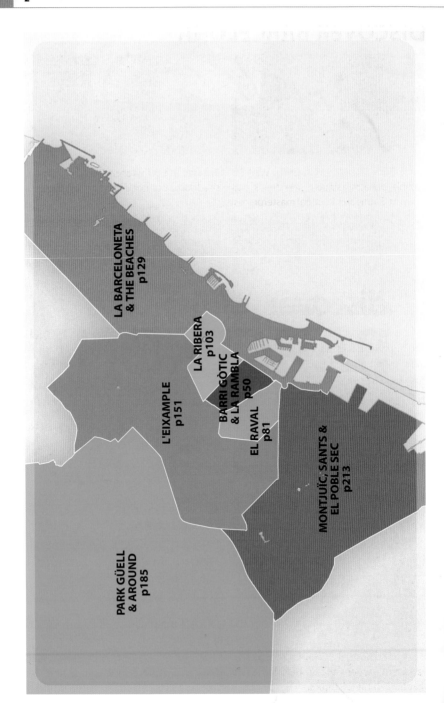

DISCOVER BARCELONA

Barri Gòtic & La Rambla (p50) Walk La Rambla, penetrate sinuous side streets, and gawp at Gothic architectural masterpieces.

El Raval (p81) This once seedy quarter has shed *some* but not *all* its edge.

La Ribera (p103) Experience a culinary and nightlife renaissance in the Old City's trendiest neighbourhood.

La Barceloneta & the Beaches (p129) Fresh seafood meets blond beaches and cutting-edge modernism on the city's waterfront.

L'Eixample (p151) Modernisme rules in Barça's 19th-century 'extension', crowned by Gaudí's La Sagrada Família

Park Güell & Around (p185) Gaudí's gardens fold into the lofty hills and green spaces of Tibidabo.

Montjuïc, Sants & El Poble Sec (p213) Parks and gardens still embellish the hill that hosted the Olympics.

Day Trips (p237) Taste wine, see Roman ruins and explore monastic shrines in Catalonia's hinterland.

↘CONTENTS

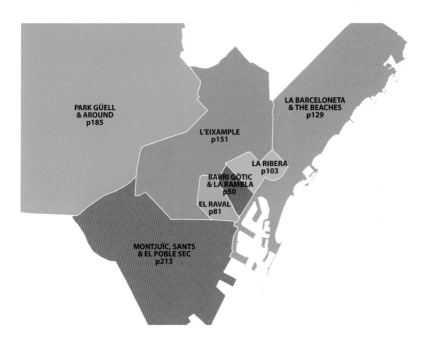

PARK GÜELL
& AROUND
p185

LA BARCELONETA
& THE BEACHES
p129

L'EIXAMPLE
p151

LA RIBERA
p103

BARRI GÒTIC
& LA RAMBLA
p50

EL RAVAL
p81

MONTJUÏC, SANTS
& EL POBLE SEC
p213

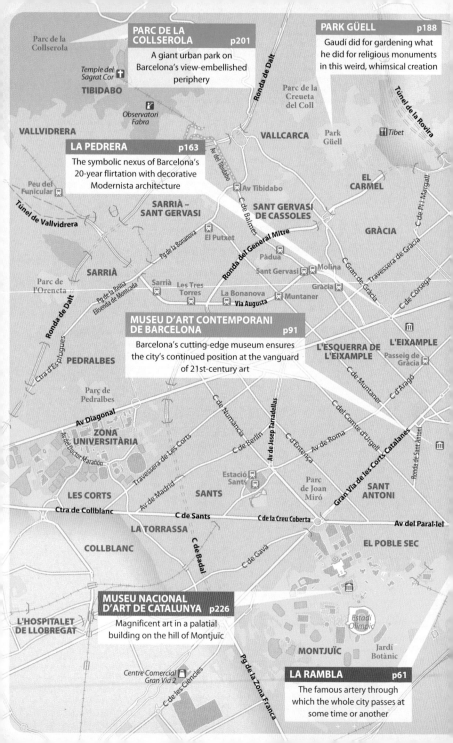

PARC DE LA COLLSEROLA p201

A giant urban park on Barcelona's view-embellished periphery

PARK GÜELL p188

Gaudí did for gardening what he did for religious monuments in this weird, whimsical creation

LA PEDRERA p163

The symbolic nexus of Barcelona's 20-year flirtation with decorative Modernista architecture

MUSEU D'ART CONTEMPORANI DE BARCELONA p91

Barcelona's cutting-edge museum ensures the city's continued position at the vanguard of 21st-century art

MUSEU NACIONAL D'ART DE CATALUNYA p226

Magnificent art in a palatial building on the hill of Montjuïc

LA RAMBLA p61

The famous artery through which the whole city passes at some time or another

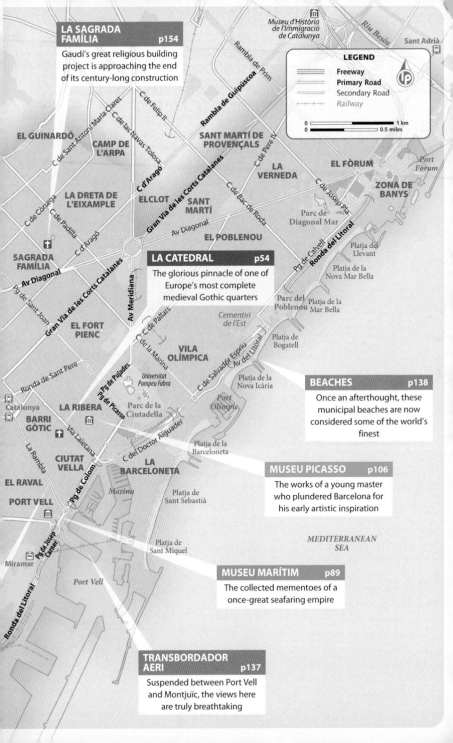

LA SAGRADA FAMÍLIA p154

Gaudí's great religious building project is approaching the end of its century-long construction

Museu d'Història de l'Immigració de Catalunya

Riu Besòs

Sant Adrià

LEGEND

Freeway
Primary Road
Secondary Road
Railway

0   1 km
0   0.5 miles

EL GUINARDÓ

C de Sant Antoni Maria Claret

C de las Navas-Tolosa

CAMP DE L'ARPA

C de Felip II

Rambla de Prim

Rambla de Guipúscoa

SANT MARTÍ DE PROVENÇALS

C de Pere IV

LA VERNEDA

EL FÒRUM

Port Fòrum

ZONA DE BANYS

LA DRETA DE L'EIXAMPLE

C de Còrsega

C de Padilla

C d'Aragó

C d'Aragó

ELCLOT

SANT MARTÍ

Gran Via de les Corts Catalanes

C de Bac de Roda

C de Josep Pla

Parc de Diagonal Mar

SAGRADA FAMÍLIA

Av Diagonal

EL POBLENOU

Av Diagonal

Pg de Calvell

Ronda del Litoral

Platja del Llevant

Platja de la Nova Mar Bella

Pg de Sant Joan

Gran Via de les Corts Catalanes

LA CATEDRAL p54

The glorious pinnacle of one of Europe's most complete medieval Gothic quarters

Av Meridiana

Parc del Poblenou

Platja de la Mar Bella

EL FORT PIENC

C de Pallars

C de la Marina

Cementiri de l'Est

Platja de Bogatell

VILA OLÍMPICA

C de Salvador Espriu

Av del Litoral

Ronda de Sant Pere

Universitat Pompeu Fabra

Platja de la Nova Icària

BEACHES p138

Once an afterthought, these municipal beaches are now considered some of the world's finest

Catalunya

BARRI GÒTIC

Pg de Pujades

Pg de Picasso

LA RIBERA

Via Laietana

Parc de la Ciutadella

Port Olímpic

CIUTAT VELLA

Pg de Colom

LA BARCELONETA

C del Doctor Aiguader

Platja de la Barceloneta

MUSEU PICASSO p106

The works of a young master who plundered Barcelona for his early artistic inspiration

EL RAVAL

La Rambla

Marina

Platja de Sant Sebastià

PORT VELL

MEDITERRANEAN SEA

Pg de Josep Carner

Miramar

Platja de Sant Miquel

Port Vell

Ronda del Litoral

MUSEU MARÍTIM p89

The collected mementoes of a once-great seafaring empire

TRANSBORDADOR AERI p137

Suspended between Port Vell and Montjuïc, the views here are truly breathtaking

↘ THIS IS BARCELONA

Compact Barcelona is a bright, fiery star lapped by the Mediterranean, a magnet to everyone from art-loving beach bums to business execs with a weakness for sunny downtime. It's a city in motion, constantly reinventing itself.

Barcelona manages the trick of merging past with future into an effervescent present. At its core lies one of Europe's best-preserved Gothic-era medieval city centres. Centuries later, that priceless heritage lent Gaudí and co the historical foundation and inspiration for some of their zaniest architectural creations. Their adventurousness is in the city's DNA, and local and international architects continue to unleash their unfettered fantasies here. As a skyline symbol, Gaudí's La Sagrada Família has stiff competition in Jean Nouvel's shimmering Torre Agbar.

The heady mix of Gothic monuments and contemporary skyscrapers is accompanied by a bevy of world-class museums that take you from the wonders of giant Romanesque frescos to the playfulness of Joan Miró, from pre-Columbian South American gold to early Picasso.

MARTIN HUGHES

All that culture fuels the appetite and at times the entire city seems to be out to lunch (or dinner). Thousands of restaurants offer an incredible palette for the palate, from traditional Catalan cooking to the last word in 21st-century *nueva cocina española* kookiness. A plethora of tippling establishments and dance clubs also spreads in a hedonistic arc across the entire city – drop into century-old taverns or glam it up in bright new seaside bars.

Shoppers, meanwhile, may never make it to a museum. Phalanxes of one-off boutiques compete with armies of global-brand-name stores.

> 'local and international architects continue to unleash their unfettered fantasies'

Barcelonins have a reputation for hard work, but everywhere you look people seem to be having fun. On the waterfront, rollerbladers glide past domino-playing pensioners, sun-seekers, windsurfers and sailors. Skateboarders practise their art in motion outside the Macba, temple to contemporary creation, and mountain-bikers blaze trails in the Collserola park.

Barcelona is an intoxicating ride. One visit is unlikely to be enough.

↘ BARCELONA'S TOP
25 EXPERIENCES

1

↘ VISIT LA SAGRADA FAMÍLIA

It is Spain's most visited sight – and the blinking thing isn't even finished!
For many, that is part of the attraction. If you've been to Barcelona before,
you've probably already visited Antoni Gaudí's La Sagrada Família (p161)
church. But that was last time, wasn't it? A work in progress, it is never quite
the same.

↘ STROLL LA RAMBLA

2

Perhaps the best time to wander down **La Rambla** (p61) is at dawn on a crisp sunny day. The street cleaners have been through, the revellers are all tucked up in bed and everything is strangely quiet. Come back a few hours later to see the international multitudes and the odd *barcelonin*.

3

↘ DECIPHER MODERNISME

If there is a part of town where you should always keep an eye skyward, **L'Eixample** (p151) is it. As you wander the grid of streets between Passeig de Sant Joan and Carrer de Muntaner, your eyes fall upon the splendid and whimsical facades of the countless buildings raised by Modernista architects between 1885 and 1914.

1 DAMIEN SIMONIS; 2 CHRIS MELLOR; 3 KIMBERLEY COOLE

1 La Sagrada Família (p161); 2 La Rambla (p61); 3 Roof of La Pedrera (p163)

⬈ ASCEND MONTJUÏC

4

Barcelona is one of the noisier cities in Europe, and there's no better antidote to the grinding decibel assault of traffic, road works, sirens and blaring music than a lazy day of strolling amid the beauty and serenity of soothing gardens (p223), all the while gazing back on the urban madness below.

5

⬈ PRECOCIOUS PICASSO

For a portrait of the artist as a young man, head to the Museu Picasso (p113), which safeguards perhaps the world's best collection of the master's early work. Picasso lived in Barcelona between the ages of 15 and 23, allowing the seedy nocturnal habitats of the Ciutat Vella to seep into his work.

↘ ADMIRE ROMANESQUE ART

For many Catalans, Catalonia is not Spain, but a nation with its own proud history. The Museu Nacional d'Art de Catalunya (p226), encased in the grand Palau Nacional (National Palace), proves the point, a one-stop immersion course in the world of Catalan art. The highlight is the immense Romanesque collection.

6

4 DIEGO LEZAMA; 5 KRZYSZTOF DYDYNSKI; 6 NEIL SETCHFIELD

4 Jardí Botànic, Montjuïc (p225); 5 Museu Picasso (p113); 6 Museu Nacional d'Art de Catalunya (p226)

ESGLÉSIA DE SANTA MARIA DEL MAR

Blessed in 1384, the church (p116) of Our Lady of the Sea is one of the purest examples of Catalan Gothic, generously broad and bereft of the baubles that characterise Gothic temples of other climes. It was raised in record time, a mere 59 years, and is remarkable for its architectural harmony.

7

8

↘ PARK GÜELL

What a fine flop! It started in 1900 as the dream of a *barcelonin* magnate, Eusebi Güell, for an English-style 'garden city' for the hoity-toity, and ended up as an enchanting park (p195) for the hoi polloi. Its inspired, if a little tortured, architect: none other than Antoni Gaudí.

↘ BECOME A FOOTBALL FAN

9

For the sports-minded, little can match the spectacle of a football match at FC Barcelona's Camp Nou (p196), one of the best sports stadiums in the world. Come with 99,999 others for a big game, and the athletic genius of Lionel Messi et al will have you falling off the edge of your seat.

7 SUNE WENDELBOE; 8 ALFREDO MAIQUEZ; 9 KRZYSZTOF DYDYNSKI

7 Església de Santa Maria del Mar (p116); 8 Dragon sculpture at Park Güell (p195); 9 Camp Nou (p196)

10

↘ MUSEU MARÍTIM

This site has been a museum (p89) since the 1940s and is one of the most fascinating in the city. On display are vessels and models of all types, representing all epochs from sail to steam. Climb aboard the life-sized replica of Don Juan of Austria's elaborately adorned 16th-century galley, and imagine life at sea.

↘ UNCOVER EL RAVAL

11

Of the old town districts, El Raval (p81) is the grittiest and perhaps the sexiest. Long a slum and still edgy in parts, it's perfect for a night of bar-crawling. Bohemians and out-of-towners, tourists and touts, artists and characters who might have just stepped from the pages of a Carlos Ruiz Zafón novel: they're all here.

⬊ MERCAT DE LA BOQUERIA

This temple of temptation, known as **La Boqueria** (p62), is one of Europe's greatest permanent produce fairs. Restaurant chefs, homemakers and tourists all compete to get a look at the day's goods. A perennial highlight is the Illa del Peix (Fish Block), a series of stands creaking beneath the weight of tonnes of fresh, glistening seafood.

⬊ ESCAPE TO TIBIDABO

Come to the mountain. An old-style family outing, the trip to the city's highest peak, Tibidabo (512m), bursts with nostalgia. The panoramic vistas are themselves a fine reward; the amusement-park rides are a retro trip to fun parks of yore. A **funicular** (p199) whisks you to the top, from where you can see the whole city.

14

↘ WANDER THROUGH GRÀCIA

Gràcia (p193) bubbles with life. A separate town until 1897, its warren of straight, narrow streets and lanes opens here and there onto a series of busy squares. Swirl around with the locals in Modernista markets, down-to-earth produce stalls, or cycle between bars and eateries and around the shop-and-restaurant-lined Carrer de Verdi.

➘ NIGHTLIFE

Opera, football, gay clubs, live music – oh yeah, and a few bars, too; Barcelona's nightlife is legendary and spins on numerous hubs. In town there's the gentrified buzz of El Born and its tawdry antidote, El Raval (p100), while further out lies the frenetic clubbing scene of L'Eixample (p181) and surprisingly trendy Gràcia (p210).

15

14 PE FORSBERG/ALAMY; 15 DIEGO LEZAMA

14 Rack of free bicycles, Gràcia (p193); 15 Clubbing at Elephant (p211)

↘ SEAFOOD IN LA BARCELONETA

Barcelona gastronomy is a lush combo of highly individualistic regional cuisine, rampant experimentalism and chefs who are the culinary equivalents of Picasso and Miró. In stark contrast, there's the simplicity of the seafood restaurateurs in **La Barceloneta** (p143) who have been knocking out the same fresh uncomplicated fish formulas for decades.

16

⇘ OLYMPIC NOSTALGIA

As a party host extraordinaire, Barcelona earned the title of 'world class city' during the 1992 Olympics, a competition affectionately remembered as one of the greatest sporting events of the modern era. The beautifully preserved Olympic facilities (p224) – many refurbished after their use in the 1929 International Exhibition – speckle the greenery of Montjuïc.

⇘ MARVEL AT MIRÓ

Picasso was born in Màlaga, and Dalí hailed from Figueres, but surrealist visionary Joan Miró was a true dyed-in-the-wool *barcelonin*. As a revolutionary artist and proud Catalan, Miró etched much of his legacy on the city, including the illustrious Fundació Joan Miró (p224), to which he donated a large selection of his work.

16 GUY MOBERLY; 17 PASCALE BEROUJON; 18 NEIL SETCHFIELD

16 Calamari, Catalonia-style; 17 Anella Olímpic and Torre Calatrava (p224); 18 Fundació Joan Miró (p224)

⤢ FESTES DE LA MERCÈ

In this city of festivals, Barcelona's **celebration** (p49) of its patron saint in September is possibly its most raucous affair. If you survive the parade of giants and the head-swimmingly abundant bottles of *cava* (Catalan 'champagne'), pull into Plaça de Jaume, where reckless locals stand on each other's shoulders in attempts to create the tallest human tower.

19

20

🢆 MUNICIPAL BEACHES

An afterthought until the 1980s, Barcelona's rejuvenated beaches (p138) have become one of the city's finest selling points, luring recreationists who might otherwise have headed south to the Costa del Sol or west to the Caribbean. Indeed, recent surveys have rated La Barceloneta's famous scimitars of sand alongside Sydney's and Cape Town's.

19 DAMIEN SIMONIS; 20 JEAN-PIERRE LESCOURRET

19 Feste de la Mercè (p49); 20 A beach at La Barceloneta (138)

21

↘ EL BORN BOUTIQUES

As reinventions go, once-decrepit El Born is up there with New York's Lower East Side as the ghetto that made good. A time traveller from the 1980s would have trouble today recognising this compact pocket of La Ribera, with its cool bars, trendy restaurants, and – for haters of modern chain stores – chic indie boutiques (p125).

↘ NIGHT AT THE OPERA

22

It might have burnt down twice in the past 150 years, but there's no torching the flame-resistant legacy of one of Spain's finest opera houses. The splendiferous Gran Teatre del Liceu (p78) has been knocking out Puccini arias longer than – well – Puccini. Go shopping, invest in some fine clothes and book your ticket.

⟍ CAVA IN THE PENEDÈS

23

While the French sip Dom Pérignon, the Catalans tipple a little less haughtily on their *cava*, made from grapes grown, picked and matured not 30km from Barcelona's city limits. Although you can drink a good bottle of sparkling wine anywhere in Catalonia, there's nothing like sampling it within sight of the **Penedès'** (p245) placid vineyards.

24

⟍ RIDE THE CABLE CAR

From sea to escarpment in three spectacular stages, Barcelona's 80-year-old **Transbordador Aeri** (p137) cable car ascends the hill of Montjuïc from Port Vell like a bird in flight. Vertigo-eschewing riders get a Google Earth view of the city and its refurbished waterfront along the way.

21 El Born boutique (p125); 22 Gran Teatre del Liceu (p78); 23 *Cava* (p259) bottle and glass; 24 Transbordador Aeri (p137)

↘ WATERFRONT PROMENADE

Barcelona's waterfront is abuzz these days, not just with fit *barcelonins* jogging, biking, blading and bantering their way through the afternoon siesta, but with a slew of ambitious architectural projects that have created a new Barcelona apart from the Gothic city of lore. Head to supermodern **El Fòrum** (p140) to view the newest additions.

25

25 GUY MOBERLY

25 Photovoltaic panel at El Fòrum (p140)

BARCELONA'S TOP ITINERARIES

ESSENTIAL & ESOTERIC

THREE DAYS
BARRI GÓTIC TO MONTJUÏC

It's a common dilemma. You're on a limited schedule but you don't want to spend all your time gawping at the obvious. This itinerary allows you to join the multitudes on La Rambla and also dip beneath the radar in some far weirder curiosities.

❶ BARRI GÓTIC

Start day one with an easily recognisable must-see, the rambunctious **La Rambla** (p61). Numerous city icons have plied this famous walkway, from Orwell to Picasso. Eschew the crowds afterwards for a furtive glance inside the **Museu de l'Eròtica** (p67), a slew of saucy secrets, not all of them blush-inducing.

❷ EL RAVAL

Once spurned by discerning tourists, El Raval is a reformed character. After lunch squeeze in a visit to one of its numerous refurb jobs, the **Museu Marítim** (p89), modern testament to Barcelona's erstwhile position as a giant maritime power. Take a walk on the wild side by burrowing into the seedier Barri Xinès next, mingling with the oddballs over dinner in **Mama i Teca** (p96) and late-night drinkers in **Kentucky** (p99).

❸ LA RIBERA

La Ribera's rebirth began two decades earlier than El Raval's, meaning its heavyweight sights tend to jump out at you. Providing a perfect premiere on day two is the textbook Gothic **Església de Santa Maria del Mar** (p116), queen bee in an already impressive Gothic city. Less known but clamouring for attention is the 2005-vintage

MARTIN HUGHES

View from the Museu Nacional d'Art de Catalunya (p226), Montjuïc

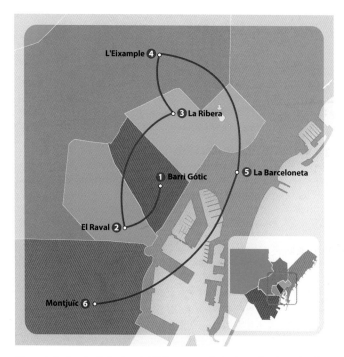

Mercat de Santa Caterina (p117), a surrealistic throwback to the days of Modernisme's sky's-the-limit creativity.

❹ L'EIXAMPLE

Only crazies or extreme contrarians leave Barcelona without seeing Gaudí's **Sagrada Família** (p161), but you can pose as a minor heretic on day two by sparing half your time to admire the life and work of a lesser known Catalan renaissance man in the **Fundación Joan Brossa** (p168).

❺ LA BARCELONETA

Spend the morning of day three in Barcelona's favourite seaside haunt. The biggest don't-miss sight here is the **Transbordador Aeri** (p137), a cable car important not just for its views, but for its role in zapping you up to the next stop – Montjuïc. Before doing so, find time to investigate the ever-changing landscape of **El Fórum** (p140).

❻ MONTJUÏC

The big hill's essential sight is the **Museu Nacional d'Art de Catalunya** (p226) with its incomparable collection of Romanesque art. Before mixing with the swarms, find time for a quick diversion around the spacey cacti that embellish the often overlooked **Jardins de Mossèn Costa i Llobera** (p223).

FOOD & DRINK

FOOD & DRINK

THREE DAYS
MERCAT DE LA BOQUERIA TO PENEDÈS VALLEY

Barcelonins approach cooking the way they approach art: with fiery panache. Adventurous gastronomes will be in heaven while the more cautious can seek comfort in traditional Catalan restaurants, many of which have been around for generations.

❶ MERCAT DE LA BOQUERIA

It ought to be imperative to start any food excursion by casting an eye over the raw ingredients, which in Barcelona means paying a visit to the city's premier food **market** (p62). A favourite stomping ground for chefs and conjurers, weekend cooks and hungry-looking tourists, Boqueria is the overture for most of the city's culinary ambitions.

❷ EL BORN

Food-wise El Born is Barcelona's most concentrated and 'happening' food district. You can warm up here with gourmet tapas in **Cal Pep** (p121), go traditional in **Pla de la Garsa** (p122), or sample Japanese fusion cuisine in **Ikibana** (p122).

❸ EL RAVAL

Save your best drinking nights for El Raval. You can get a feel for the *barrio*'s distinct multiculturalism in **Bar Aurora** (p98). **Kentucky** (p99) emphasises the quarter's weird and wackier side, while **London Bar** (p100) is a blast from the past where Picasso and Hemingway once kept the seats warm before moving on to Gay Paris. Pencil in a late-morning recovery in **Granja Viader** (p98), where hot chocolate and pastries work wonders on hard-to-shift hangovers.

JEAN-PIERRE LESCOURRET

Mercat de la Boqueria (p62)

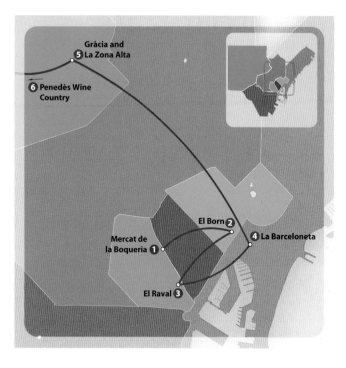

❹ LA BARCELONETA

Hold the fancy foams and foie gras. La Barceloneta is where the city rustles up simple, no-nonsense seafood not far from where it was caught. **Restaurant 7 Portes** (p144) is king of the old-school joints, with humongous portions, while **Can Majó** (p144) is so close to the beach you'll risk getting sand in your shoes – and soup!

❺ GRÀCIA AND LA ZONA ALTA

This suburban hideaway is a latent culinary surprise and a rather varied one at that. To get both ends of the spectrum hit noisy salt-of-the-earth **El Glop** (p206) and come back on another day to sample the refined atmosphere of **Restaurante Evo** (p208), perched 105m above the ground in a Star Trek–like dome.

❻ PENEDÈS VALLEY

Get out more; see a bit of the countryside. And this being Catalonia there's no reason you can't take the culinary theme with you. The Penedès is *cava* country, producing Spain's less snobby version of champagne. Base yourself in **Sant Sadurní d'Anoia** (p245) and visit the well-known **Freixenet winery** (p246) before finishing off with a meal at **Cal Ton** (p247).

BARCELONA'S TOP ITINERARIES

ART & ARCHITECTURE

ART & ARCHITECTURE
FIVE DAYS
BARRI GÓTIC TO TARRAGONA

This tour starts as a Gothic thriller, doffs a cap to Gaudí and Picasso, then immerses you in the weird surrealist domain of Joan Miró. If you ever doubted the range and ambition of Barcelona's art and architecture, start walking.

❶ BARRI GÓTIC

If you needed one adjective to describe Barcelona's atmosphere, it would probably be 'Gothic', though the city's story actually begins with the Romans. Start day one with this subterranean walk through the Museu d'Història de Barcelona (p63), which brings ancient Latin washing habits to life with baths, laundries and shops. Should your interest be piqued divert to the Temple Romà d'August (p70), but you can't take the Gothic out of the Barri Gótic for long. The best genus of the style is undoubtedly the Catedral (p64), a decorative ecclesial triumph that would get far more glory if it wasn't for the small matter of Gaudí and that *other* church.

❷ MUSEU D'ART CONTEMPORANI DE BARCELONA

Shelve Gaudí on the afternoon of day one and move over to El Raval where architecture is overtaken by the contemporary art in a sleek modern museum (p91), usually 'guarded' by large posses of skilful skateboarders.

KRZYSZTOF DYDYNSKI

Vault detail, Església de Santa Maria del Mar (p116)

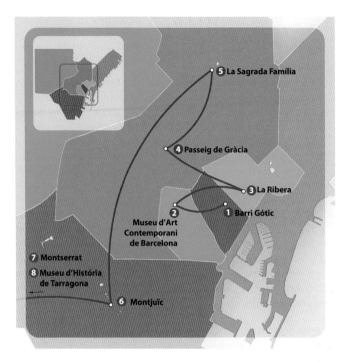

❸ LA RIBERA

Extend the Gothic immersion on day two by paying your respects to the **Església de Santa Maria del Mar** (p116), then follow up with the **Museu Picasso** (p113), housed in five more impressive medieval buildings. Once inside you'll need to zap your brain forward 600 hundred years to appreciate the young master in his fast-evolving early career.

❹ PASSEIG DE GRÀCIA

It's impossible to wander too far in Barcelona without bumping into Gaudí. Resist no longer on day three by heading to the Passeig de Gràcia, where two of his career-defining buildings regularly turn the heads of shoppers and tourists. **La Pedrera** (p163), aka Casa Milà, is a lesson in how to avoid straight lines, while **Casa Batlló** (p165), on the so-called 'Manzana de la Discordia', goes head to head with Gaudí's talented contemporaries, Domènech i Montaner and Puig i Cadafalch.

❺ LA SAGRADA FAMÍLIA

Roll the drums, turn on the stage lights and get ready for Spain's most visited **church** (p161). This one-of-a-kind religious monument is as unique as the Giza pyramids and as shimmeringly beautiful as the

Taj Mahal. It's also a good decade from completion, ensuring that no two visits are the same.

❻ MONTJUÏC

Need a break from Gaudí? Head for the hill of Montjuïc for an even more modern and, arguably, more ground-breaking *barcelonin* artist: Joan Miró. The **Fundació Joan Miró** (p224) has the artist's huge personality stamped all over it, probably because he donated a large body of the foundation's work himself. Art and architecture mix sublimely in the **Museu Nacional d'Art de Catalunya** (p226), whose palatial exterior is emulated by the exquisite collection of Romanesque art inside.

❼ MONTSERRAT

On day four take your artistic quest out of town. The Montserrat Mountains guard the famous **Monestir de Montserrat** (p240), a twice-rebuilt Benedictine monastery where art and architecture are eccentrically combined amid basilicas, chapels and the **Museu de Montserrat** (p242), where you'll spot the odd Picasso amid strange mummified reptiles.

❽ MUSEU D'HISTÓRIA DE TARRAGONA

The story ends on day five where it started, with the Romans, who, if they arrived back in Catalonia today, would be mighty surprised to see their former capital usurped by the bolshie 'barbarians' of Barcelona. You can linger long in this **museum** (p248) which doubles as an archaeological site with its Amfiteatre Romà and walkable Passeig Arqueològic.

MUSEU NACIONAL D'ART DE CATALUNYA, BARCELONA. CALVERAS/MÉRIDA/SAGRISTÀ

Museu Nacional d'Art de Catalunya (p226)

⬎ PLANNING YOUR TRIP

BARCELONA'S BEST...

MUSEUMS

- **Museu Picasso** (p113) Finest ensemble of the 'great one's' youthful etchings.
- **Museu d'Art Contemporani de Barcelona** (p91) Proof of Barcelona's place at the cutting edge of contemporary art.
- **Fundació Joan Miró** (p224) World's biggest Miró collection, in the city of his birth.
- **Museu Nacional d'Art de Catalunya** (p226) Fine Romanesque art collection in even finer neobaroque palace.

VIEWPOINTS

- **Tibidabo** (p201) Ascend the old church or new tower for an even better view.
- **Castell de Montjuïc** (p223) Strategically positioned fortress atop Montjuïc hill.

- **La Sagrada Família** (p161) Head up one of the towers for bird's-eye rooftop views.
- **Transbordador Aeri** (p137) Grab the cable car over the restored Port Vell up to Montjuïc.

GOTHIC MASTERPIECES

- **La Catedral** (p64) Contemplate the incredible decoration on the northwest facade.
- **Església de Santa Maria del Mar** (p116) Catalan Gothic at its purest and most refined.
- **Museu Marítim** (p89) Under these Gothic arches once lay one of the largest shipyards in Europe.
- **Església de Sants Just i Pastor** (p69) Often neglected example of early Gothic ecclesial architecture.

NEIL SETCHFIELD

Palau de la Música Catalana (p115)

PARKS

- **Parc de la Ciutadella** (p118) This city centre air-hole acts like an asthma inhaler between long bouts of Barcelona sightseeing.
- **Parc de la Collserola** (p201) Find your own private space in Europe's largest municipal park.
- **Montjuïc** (p223) Parks and gardens lace these lofty vantage points around the Castell de Montjuïc.
- **Park Güell** (p195) In which Gaudí turned his hand to landscape gardening.

CATALAN RESTAURANTS

- **Agut** (p73) There's art on the walls *and* on the plates in this labyrinthine Gothic classic.
- **Pla de la Garsa** (p122) Amid the experimentalist avant-gardism of El Born, good Catalan cooking remains.
- **Can Majó** (p144) Simple but effective seafood on Barceloneta's beachfront.
- **Casa Calvet** (p175) Creative food in Gaudí-designed interior.

DESIGN HOTELS

- **Hotel Neri** (p72) Old meets off-the-wall in the sympathetically restored Neri.
- **Casa Camper** (p92) Funky Raval hotel owned by Mallorcan shoe company.

- **Grand Hotel Central** (p120) Tranquillity in La Ribera is no oxymoron in this supersoundproofed place.
- **Hotel Omm** (p170) You'll be left wondering if Dalí designed this kooky L'Eixample nook.

MODERNISME

- **La Pedrera** (p163) Gaudí's famous head-turner on busy Passeig de Gràcia.
- **La Sagrada Família** (p161) Spain's most popular visitor attraction – come and see why.
- **Palau de la Música Catalana** (p115) Music turned to glass and stone.
- **Casa Amatller** (p165) The dark horse of the Manzana de la Discordia.

UNEXPECTED SPOTS

- **Observatori Fabra** (p202) Book for dinner under the stars in this Zona Alta observatory.
- **Museu Romàntic** (p244) Peer at hundreds of antique dolls in this Sitges mansion – not all of them pretty.
- **El Rey de la Magia** (p128) Century-old magic shop that materialises like something out of a Carlos Ruiz Zafón novel.
- **Sinagoga Mayor** (p70) Inspect Roman and medieval ruins in a synagogue reclaimed for posterity in the 1990s.

THINGS YOU NEED TO KNOW

AT A GLANCE

- **ATMs** Omnipresent.
- **Credit cards** Visa and MasterCard widely accepted.
- **Currency** Euro.
- **Electricity** Two round-pin plugs, 220V.
- **Language** Spanish and Catalan; English often understood.
- **Tipping** 5% to 10% for good service
- **Visas** Not required for most nationalities.

ACCOMMODATION

- **Hotels** Running the gamut of budgets and facilities from one to five stars.
- **Boutique/Design hotels** Luxurious personalised hotels with special design features.
- **Hostals** Family-run budget hotels with more modest facilities.

ADVANCE PLANNING

- **Three months before** Check cheap flight deals; arrange your plans around any interesting local events and festivals.
- **One month before** Research different neighbourhoods; choose and book accommodation.
- **One week before** Look into airport transfers and city transport links.
- **One day before** Check any restaurants that may need advance booking.

BE FOREWARNED

- **Petty theft** Be on guard in the city centre, on public transport and around the main sights.
- **Monday closures** Many museums and other tourist sites close on Mondays.
- **Dining** The Spanish dine late; dinner generally starts at 9pm. Adjust your body clock to accommodate.

COSTS

- **€80 per day** Stay in a budget-range *hostal* or hotel, dine economically, select cheap or free sights and travel by foot.
- **€80 to €300 per day** Stay in a midrange hotel, leave room for the odd splurge on food, tick off a few museums, and get a day-pass for the bus/metro.
- **More than €300 per day** Stay top-end, check out Barcelona's avant-garde eating scene, hit the nightlife, and get a taxi back to your accommodation.

EMERGENCY NUMBERS

- **Ambulance** (☎ 061)
- **Fire brigade** (Bombers; ☎ 080, 085)
- **Policía Nacional** (National Police; ☎ 091)
- **Guàrdia Civil** (Civil Guard; ☎ 062)

GETTING AROUND

- **Bus** Large, comprehensive and cheap service covering all of the city and its suburbs.

- **Metro** Wide-reaching underground train network with 11 colour-coded lines and 164 stations.
- **Funicular railway** Two special inclined railways allow access to the hills of Montjuïc and Tibidabo.
- **Cable car** Runs from Port Vell up to Montjuïc.
- **Foot** The tight grid of the Ciutat Vella is easily accessed on foot. Many streets are pedestrian only.

GETTING THERE & AWAY

- **Air** Barcelona's international airport is 12km from the city centre, with direct flights to Europe, North and South America, and Asia.
- **Train** High-speed AVE trains link Barcelona with Madrid and Valencia. The Elipsos Trenhotel *Joan Miró* runs overnight to Paris.

- **Bus** Regular efficient coaches run to all major Spanish cities.

TECH STUFF

- **Wi-fi** Widely available in hotels and cafes and at the airport. Sometimes, but not always, free.
- **Mobile (cell) phones** GSM 900/1800. Check ahead with your local service provider regarding access. North American phones will only work if they're GSM/GPRS compatible. European/Australian phones should work but you'll need to get them 'unlocked' in a Spanish phone shop for a small fee.
- **SIM cards** Can be purchased with prepaid time for dual- and tri-band mobile phones that aren't code-blocked. Passport required for purchase.
- **Internet cafes** Widely available, often in *locutorios* (public phone centres).

ALFREDO MAIQUEZ

Facade of Hotel Omm (p170)

PLANNING YOUR TRIP

THINGS YOU NEED TO KNOW

⬇ TRAVEL SEASONS

- **Easter and Christmas** The busy periods; finding accommodation can be more difficult.
- **Spring** Many festivals are celebrated between March and June.
- **High summer** In August tourists flock in, and most Spanish take their vacations.

⬇ WHAT TO BRING

- **Phrasebooks** Both Catalan and Spanish phrasebooks will come in handy.
- **Small laptop** For easy wi-fi connections.
- **Bathing costume** Welcome to a historic city with first-class beaches.
- **Plug adaptor** For visitors from outside continental Europe.
- **Camera** For innumerable stunning vistas.

⬇ WHEN TO GO

- **May** Most pleasant month of year climatically – clear and fresh.
- **August** Main tourist season, warm beaches, and two important festivals in Gràcia.
- **September** Catalonia's national holiday and city's biggest festival: Festes de la Mercè.

KARL BLACKWELL

Sculpture by artist Rebecca Horn, La Barceloneta

GET INSPIRED

BOOKS

- **The Shadow of the Wind** (Carlos Ruiz Zafón, 2001) With a twisting, turning plot that uses post–civil war Barcelona as a vivid backdrop, Catalan-native Zafón's classic has sold millions.
- **Homage to Catalonia** (George Orwell, 1937) One of Orwell's best books provides an on-the-spot commentary of the city at one of the most volatile moments of its history during the civil war.
- **The Time of the Doves** (Mercè Rodoreda, 1962) Arguably the most influential Catalan novel of all time, this seminal book tells the story of a young woman's struggle to reach maturity against the backdrop of civil war Barcelona.
- **Homage to Barcelona** (Colm Tóibin, 1990) Easy-to-digest travelogue of the city by the noted Irish writer.

FILMS

- **All About My Mother** (1999, director Pedro Almodóvar) Almodóvar's most decorated film is the story of a mother who travels to Barcelona to find the father of her recently deceased son.
- **Vicky Cristina Barcelona** (2008, director Woody Allen) Allen does for Barcelona what he did for New York in *Manhattan* (ie idolises it on screen) and helps Penelope Cruz win an Oscar.

- **Land and Freedom** (1995, director Ken Loach) Follows a British Communist Party member fighting for the POUM Militia during the civil war.
- **La Teta y la Luna** (1994, Bigas Luna) Part of the Barcelona-born director's Iberian Trilogy, this off-the-wall movie tackles a boy's obsession with women's breasts.

MUSIC

- **Joan Manuel Serrat** Acclaimed troubadour and king of Nueva Canción; key track 'Mediterráneo'.
- **The Pinker Tones** Electronic alternative pop band; key track 'The Whistling Song'.
- **Sopa de Cabra** Ultimate Catalan rock band; key track 'Si et Quedes amb Mi'.
- **Luís Llach** Hugely popular Catalan-language singer; key song 'Laura'.

WEBSITES

- **Barcelona Tourism** (www.barcelonaturisme.cat) Official Barcelona tourism website.
- **Catalonia Tourism** (www.catalunyaturisme.com) Official Catalonia tourism website with a broader regional focus.
- **Lonely Planet** (www.lonelyplanet.com) Up-to-date hotel and restaurant reviews plus Thorn Tree travel forum.
- **What Barcelona** (www.whatbarcelona.com) Easy-to-navigate travel site.

CALENDAR

| JAN | FEB | MAR | APR |

DAMIEN SIMONIS

A float in the Good Friday procession

JANUARY

REIS/REYES　　　　　　**6 JAN**
Christmas comes a couple of weeks later for Spanish children, as presents are traditionally distributed for the Epifanía (Epiphany). The evening before, children delight in the Cavalcada dels Reis Mags (Three Kings' Parade), with floats, music, and bucketloads of sweets chucked into the scrambling crowds.

FESTES DELS TRES TOMBS
　　　　　　　　　　17 JAN
A key part of the festival of Sant Antoni Abat is this Feast of the Three Circuits, a parade of horse-drawn carts (St Anthony is the patron saint of domestic animals) near the Mercat de Sant Antoni.

FEBRUARY–MARCH

FESTES DE SANT EULALÍA
Coinciding with the Carnaval (below) is this festival of Barcelona's first patron saint, Sant Eulália. The Ajuntament organises numerous activities, from concerts to big parades featuring people dressed as *mulasses* (strange mulelike creatures).

CARNESTOLTES/CARNAVAL
Barcelona's carnival is colourful enough but the real fun happens in Sitges (see p243), where the gay community stages gaudy parades and party-goers let rip.

FESTIVAL DE JAZZ
A major season of jazz concerts (www .jazzterrassa.org) from mid-February to mid-March in the nearby city of Terrassa.

MARCH–APRIL

DIVENDRES SANT/VIERNES SANTO (GOOD FRIDAY)

Taste Andalucían Easter with processions from Església de Sant Agustí featuring a float of the Virgin of the Macarena, robed members of religious fraternities and barefoot penitent women dragging crosses and chains.

DIA DE SANT JORDI   23 APR

Catalonia celebrates St George – men give women a rose and women give men a book (it's also Dia del Llibre, Book Day).

FERIA DE ABRIL DE CATALUNYA

A long history of immigration from Andalucía has resulted in imported traditions such as the ebullient spring feria (free day), which closely apes the

Brazilian drummer, Dia de Sant Jordi

mother of all ferias in Seville. Tents are set up in El Fórum, where high-spirited revellers drink sherry, dress up in polka-dot dresses and dance flamenco till the fishermen come home.

MAY–JUNE

L'OU COM BALLA

The curious 'Dancing Egg' is an empty eggshell that bobs on top of the flower-festooned fountain in La Catedral's cloister to mark the feast of Corpus Christi (the Thursday after the eighth Sunday after Easter Sunday).

PRIMAVERA SOUND

For three days in late May and/or early June the Parc del Fòrum hosts international DJs and musicians (www.primaverasound.com). A winter version, Primavera Club, takes place in early December.

Castellers (human pyramid)

PLANNING YOUR TRIP

CALENDAR

| JAN | FEB | MAR | APR |

DAMIEN SIMONIS

Festes de la Mercè, Platja de la Mar Bella

SÓNAR

Sónar (www.sonar.es) is Barcelona's celebration of electronic music and Europe's biggest such event. See big names and experimental acts.

DIA DE SANT JOAN (FEAST OF ST JOHN THE BAPTIST)   24 JUN

The night before this feast day, people celebrate Berbena de Sant Joan (St John's Night), aka La Nit del Foc (Night of Fire), with drinking, dancing, bonfires and fireworks.

GREC

Grec is the city's premier performing arts festival, encompassing music, dance and theatre. It takes its name from the open-air Teatre Grec on the slopes of Montjuïc, once the exclusive venue for the performances, though in recent years they have spread to other parts of the city. Grec lasts for six weeks from mid-June to the end of July.

AUGUST

FESTES DE SANT ROC

For four days in mid-August, Plaça Nova in the Barri Gòtic becomes the scene of parades, a *correfoc* (fire race), a market, traditional music, and magic shows for kids.

FESTA MAJOR DE GRÀCIA

Around 15 August, this knees-up in the Gràcia area (www.festamajorde gracia.cat) features a competition for the best-decorated street. Enjoy feasting, bands and drinking.

FESTA MAJOR DE SANTS

The district of Sants launches its own weeklong version of decorated mayhem hard on Gràcia's heels, around 24 August.

PLANNING YOUR TRIP

CALENDAR

⬎ SEPTEMBER

FESTES DE LA MERCÈ
Barcelona's biggest party (www.bcn
.cat/merce), with *castellers, sardanes*
(folk dancing), *gegants* (giants), *cap-
grossos* (big heads), a *correfoc* and
Barcelona Acció Musical (www.bcn
.cat/bam, in Catalan), a huge live-
concert series. See also p26.

DIADA DE CATALUNYA   11 SEP
This date has different connotations
elsewhere in the world but in Catalonia
it is celebrated as the Catalan National
Holiday, commemorating the fall of
Barcelona to the Bourbon monarchy
of Philip V in 1714 during the Spanish
War of Succession. The sometimes solemn celebrations are marked by floral
tributes, concerts and often political
demonstrations. The holiday was established in 1980, soon after the death
of Franco.

FESTA MAJOR DE LA BARCELONETA
A neighbourhood party, this time
in the tight-knit Barceloneta district, meaning there's good seafood,
flashy fireworks and plenty of sailor-
inspired jigs. This being Spain, the
all-night dancing is de rigueur. The
revelries occupy the last week of
September.

⬎ NOVEMBER

FESTIVAL INTERNACIONAL DE JAZZ DE BARCELONA
For most of the month, the big
venues across town (from l'Auditori
down) host a plethora of international jazz acts (www.theproject.es).
At the same time, a more homespun
jazz fest takes place in bars across the
Old City.

DAMIEN SIMONIS

Mounted brass band, Festes de la Mercè

↘ BARRI GÒTIC &
LA RAMBLA

BARRI GÒTIC & LA RAMBLA

BARRI GÒTIC & LA RAMBLA

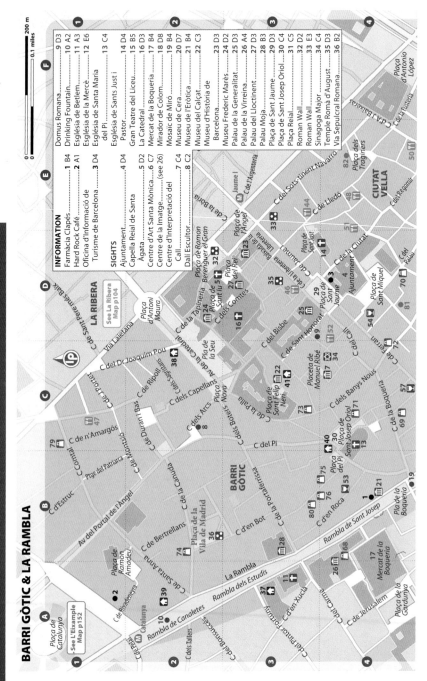

INFORMATION
Farmàcia Clapés....................1 B4
Hard Rock Café......................2 A1
Oficina d'Informació de
Turisme de Barcelona.........3 D4

SIGHTS
Ajuntament...........................4 D4
Capella Reial de Santa
Àgata..................................5 D2
Centre d'Art Santa Mònica....6 C7
Centre de la Imatge..........(see 26)
Centre d'Interpretació del
Call.....................................7 C4
Dalí Escultor........................8 C2
Domus Romana....................9 D3
Drinking Fountain...............10 A2
Església de Betlem...............11 A3
Església de la Mercè............12 E6
Església de Santa Maria
del Pi.................................13 C4
Església de Sants Just i
Pastor...............................14 D4
Gran Teatre del Liceu..........15 B5
La Catedral..........................16 D3
Mercat de la Boqueria.........17 B4
Mirador de Colom................18 D8
Mosaic de Miró....................19 B4
Museu de Cera.....................20 D7
Museu de l'Eròtica...............21 B4
Museu del Calçat.................22 C3
Museu d'Història de
Barcelona..........................23 D3
Museu Frederic Marès..........24 D2
Palau de la Generalitat........25 D3
Palau de la Virreina.............26 A4
Palau del Lloctinent............27 D3
Palau Moja..........................28 B3
Plaça de Sant Jaume............29 D3
Plaça de Sant Josep Oriol....30 C4
Plaça Reial..........................31 C5
Roman Wall.........................32 D2
Roman Wall.........................33 E3
Sinagoga Major...................34 C4
Temple Romà d'August........35 D3
Via Sepulcral Romana.........36 B2

200 m
0.1 miles

See La Ribera
Map p104

See L'Eixample
Map p152

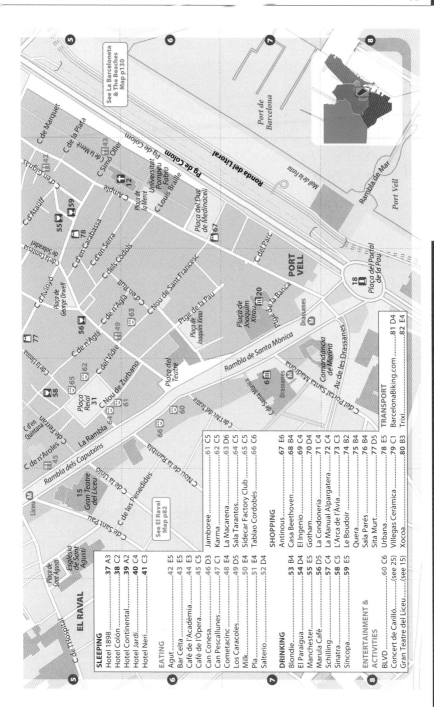

BARRI GÒTIC & LA RAMBLA

See La Barceloneta
& The Beaches
Map p130

Port de
Barcelona

Rambla de Mar

Port Vell

See El Raval
Map p82

EL RAVAL

HIGHLIGHTS

1 | LA CATEDRAL

While most cities make do with *one* great religious monument, Barcelona hoards two. The Catedral de la Santa Creu i Santa Eulàlia emulates Gaudí's La Sagrada Família; it's a riot of Gothic and gargoyles, high altars and murky crypts, Catalan legends and 13 resident geese. Like many Spanish churches it is a hybrid – the 14th-century shell has been overlaid by a 19th-century neo-Gothic facade – a factor that makes it all the more fascinating and enigmatic.

↘ OUR DON'T MISS LIST

❶ CHOIR

The late-14th-century *coro*, in the middle of the central nave, was exquisitely sculpted from timber. The coats of arms on the stalls belong to members of the Barcelona chapter of the Order of the Golden Fleece – Emperor Carlos V presided over the order's meeting here in 1519. Take the time to look at the craft up close; the Virgin Mary and Child depicted on the pulpit are especially fine.

❷ ROOFTOP VIEW

With so much going on inside it's easy to forget the outside. The roof is notable not just for the views of medieval Barcelona but also for the opportunity to evaluate the cathedral's huge footprint from above. Access to the higher echelons is gained via a lift from the Capella de les Animes del Purgatori, near the northeast transept.

Clockwise from top: Cloister of La Catedral (p64); Interior of apse; La Catedral's exterior illuminated at night; Main facade; Choir stalls in central nave

CLOCKWISE FROM TOP: NEIL SETCHFIELD; JOHN ELK III; BILL WASSMAN; MARTIN LLADO; KRZYSZTOF DYDYNSKI

BARRI GÒTIC & LA RAMBLA

HIGHLIGHTS

❸ GEESE

The Tower of London has ravens; Barcelona's Catedral has geese. The 13 birds in the leafy *claustre* (cloister) supposedly represent the age of Santa Eulàlia at the time of her martyrdom and have, generation after generation, been squawking here since medieval days. They make fine watchdogs!

❹ CRYPT

Here lies the hallowed tomb of Santa Eulàlia, one of Barcelona's two patron saints, and more affectionately known as Laia. The reliefs on the alabaster sarcophagus, executed by Pisan artisans, recount some of her tortures and, along the top strip, the removal of her body to its present resting place.

❺ BAPTISMAL FONT

Columbus purportedly kidnapped two dozen North American Indians from the Caribbean island of Hispaniola after his first voyage and brought them back to Spain. Only six survived the journey and, legend has it, they were bathed in holy water at this font just left from the main entrance.

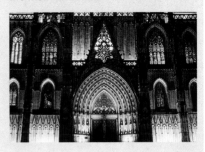

⬎ THINGS YOU NEED TO KNOW

Costs Entry to the cathedral is free but there are three paying areas inside: the Sala Capitular (€2), the Choir (€2.20) and the roof (€2.20) **Top tip** During the daily 1-5pm 'special visit', it is much quieter **Afterwards** Pop across the road to the Palau Episcopal (Bishop's Palace) **See p64 for more information**

HIGHLIGHTS

2

↘ STROLLING LA RAMBLA

From the air **La Rambla** (p61) looks like a green snake slithering its way through the urban disquiet of the Ciutat Vella. At ground level it's more of a 24-hour jamboree, a benchmark street that has become a byword for almost every other tree-lined urban avenue on the planet. Change into your walking shoes, hit the central walkway and *dar un paseo* (go for a stroll) with everyone else.

3

↘ MERCAT DE LA BOQUERIA

Just when you thought you'd seen every piece of art Barcelona could muster, you end up in this pulsating **market** (p62), where the eye-catching fruit displays look as if they've been concocted by greengrocers posing as Picasso. La Boqueria is the city's oldest and most atmospheric market, a noisy mélange of history, heritage and street theatre. Not surprisingly, it's also one of the biggest tourist magnets.

⬑ MIRADOR DE COLOM

Barcelona makes its claim on the Columbus legend with this sinuous **monument** (p69). The enigmatic explorer came here after his first voyage to the Americas and was received by his financial backers. Ruminate on his much-disputed historical legacy while being transported by lift to the monument's eagle's-eye lookout.

⬑ PLAÇA REIAL

Car-free and highly recuperative after the narrow, sometimes seedy, streets of the Ciutat Vella, **Plaça Reial** (p68) is where you can come up for air after hours of Gothic exploration. Though ostensibly relaxed, the square is a crossroads for pretty much everyone during the daytime. After dark it's a hidden hive of cool candlelit restaurants and clubs.

⬑ MUSEU D'HISTÒRIA DE BARCELONA

More subterranean adventure trail than stash of dusty exhibits, this highly original **museum** (p63) offers a visual history lesson through a bewildering array of mansions, chapels, courtyards and vaults. Look for Gothic and baroque town houses, the hall where Columbus met Ferdinand and Isabella, Roman shops, and wine stores.

2 KRZYSZTOF DYDYNSKI; 3 KIMBERLEY COOLE; 4 CHRISTOPHER GROENHOUT; 5 MARTIN MOOS; 6 GUY MOBERLY

2 La Rambla (p61); 3 Mercat de la Boqueria (p62); 4 Mirador de Colom (p69); 5 Cafe on Plaça Reial (p68); 6 Museu d'Història de Barcelona (p63)

BARRI GÒTIC WALKING TOUR

With Plaça de la Vila de Madrid as a launching pad, this historical trajectory goes from Roman to Romanesque, Gothic, baroque and back to Roman, finishing amid the walls and gateways of Centre Cívic Pati Llimona. Allow 30 minutes for the 1.5km.

❶ ROMAN TOMBS

On Plaça de la Vila de Madrid is a sunken garden with various **Roman tombs** (Via Sepulcral Romana; p70), plus a small explanatory museum. It was customary to line highways leading out of cities with tombs, and it is believed this road connected Roman Barcino with the Via Augusta, which linked Rome and Cádiz.

❷ ESGLÉSIA DE SANTA ANNA

In a tranquil square just off busy Carrer de Santa Anna lies this rarely visited **church**. It dates from the 12th century, but little remains of the original Romanesque structure. The Gothic cloister is a shady haven (if you can get in – it's open only sporadically).

❸ PALACE WALLS OF GUIFRÉ EL PELÓS

Stroll along Carrer de n'Amargós and muse on the plaque at No 8, which claims that the **palace garden walls** of the first Count of Barcelona, Guifré el Pelós (Wilfred the Hairy), stood here. Carrer de n'Amargós was the first street in Barcelona to get gas lighting.

❹ ELS QUATRE GATS

Around the corner from the supposed site of Wilfred's palace is a Modernista icon. 'The Four Cats', a colourful if mediocre **restaurant**, started life as Casa Martí (1896), built by Puig i Cadafalch. From 1897 to 1903, it was *the* hang-out for Modernista artists and other bohemians.

❺ LA CATEDRAL

Don't come this far without at least stealing a glance at the **Catedral** (p64), accessible by diverting briefly down Avenida de la Catedral into Pla de la Seu. The wondrous northwest facade doesn't look 500 years newer than the rest of the building, so skilful were the integration techniques of the 19th-century craftspeople.

❻ ESGLÉSIA DE SANT FELIP NERI

The baroque facade of the **Església de Sant Felip Neri** (completed in 1752) has been shattered by the impact of machine-gun fire. One story says that pro-Franco troops carried out summary executions here shortly after they marched into the city in 1939. An eerie silence hangs over the square.

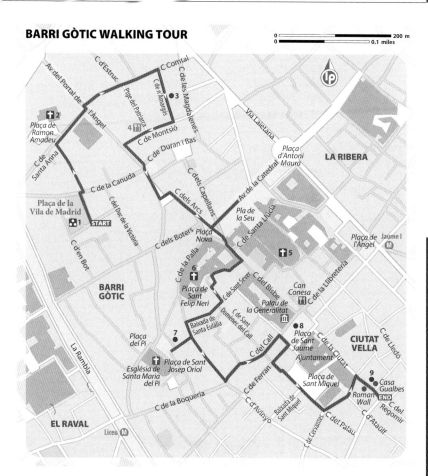

❼ PALAU DE FIVELLER

Just opposite the silent stone flank of the **Església de Santa Maria del Pi** (p68), stands **Palau de Fiveller**, a one-time private mansion dating from 1571. The facade dates from the 18th century.

❽ PLAÇA DE SANT JAUME

In this old town square you can compare the Gothic merits of the **Ajuntament** (p66) and **Palau de la Generalitat** (p66). Then head to the local lunch spot **Can Conesa** (p74), on Carrer de la Llibreteria.

❾ CENTRE CÍVIC PATI LLIMONA

Remains of Roman Barcino's city gate and of the 3rd- and 4th-century **city wall** line Carrer de Regomir. To get a closer look, enter the **Centre Cívic Pati Llimona**. At No 13 stands a 15th-century mansion, **Casa Gualbes**.

BEST...

⤴ GOTHIC MASTERPIECES

- **La Catedral** (p64) Behold the northwest facade.
- **Església de Sants Just i Pastor** (p69) City's oldest Gothic fountain.
- **Església de Santa Maria del Pi** (p68) Huge 10m rose window.
- **Saló del Tinell** (p63) Banqueting hall of former Royal Palace.
- **Palau de la Generalitat** (p66) Catalan seat of government.

⤴ ESOTERIC SHOPS

- **Xocoa** (p79) Addictive chocolate haven.
- **La Condoneria** (p79) No translation required.
- **El Ingenio** (p80) First stop for fancy-dress parties.
- **Le Boudoir** (p80) Lingerie and erotica.
- **L'Arca de L'Àvia** (p80) Vintage clothes back in fashion.

⤴ TRAFFIC-FREE HAVENS

- **Avinguda de la Catedral** (p64) Stop and admire the Gothic gargoyles.
- **Plaça Reial** (p68) Take a breather from the labyrinth.
- **Plaça de Sant Jaume** (p66) Reflect on great architecture.
- **La Rambla** (p61) The ultimate in urban walkways.
- **Plaça de Sant Josep Oriol** (p67) Listen to the buskers.

⤴ RAMBLA PAUSES

- **Drinking fountain** (p61) Drink from here and it's said you'll return to the city.
- **Mercat de la Boqueria** (p62) Quintessential food market.
- **Palau de la Virreina** (p61) Eye-catching rococo splendour.
- **Gran Teatre del Liceu** (p78) One of Europe's great opera houses.
- **Mirador de Colom** (p69) Columbus guards the sea entrance.

JEAN-PIERRE LESCOURRET

Plaça Reial (p68)

DISCOVER BARRI GÒTIC & LA RAMBLA

Everyone walks La Rambla during a Barcelona stay. Visitors outnumber locals, but that just adds to the colour. In just a 1.25km strip you'll find bird stalls, flower stands, buskers, bars, historic shops, grand buildings, a pungent produce market, pickpockets, prostitutes, bored police and a veritable UN of paraders. Once a sewage ditch lined by medieval walls, La Rambla marks the southwest flank of what in the 20th century was dubbed the Barri Gòtic (Gothic Quarter).

This is where the Romans set up shop 2000 years ago. At its heart, the city and Catalan governments face each other on Plaça de Sant Jaume, where the forum was. Nearby are sprinkled Gothic mansions, the cathedral, an underground slice of ancient Barcelona and leftover Roman walls. To the square's north and west, shoppers revel along Avinguda del Portal del Àngel and Carrer de la Boqueria. To the southeast, between crowded Carrer de Ferran and the port, narrow lanes are festooned with bars and eateries.

SIGHTS

LA RAMBLA

Ⓜ Catalunya, Liceu or Drassanes

Flanked by narrow traffic lanes and plane trees, the middle of La Rambla is a broad pedestrian boulevard, crowded every day until the wee hours with a cross-section of *barcelonins* and out-of-towners. Dotted with cafes, restaurants, kiosks and newsstands, and enlivened by buskers, pavement artists, mimes and living statues, La Rambla rarely allows a dull moment.

The initial stretch from Plaça de Catalunya is **La Rambla de Canaletes**, named after a turn-of-the-20th-century **drinking fountain**, the water of which supposedly emerges from what were once known as the springs of Canaletes. It used to be said that *barcelonins* 'drank the waters of Les Canaletes'. Nowadays, people claim that anyone who drinks from the fountain will return to Barcelona, which is not such a bad prospect. This is the traditional meeting point for happy FC Barcelona fans when they win cups and competitions.

The second stretch, **La Rambla dels Estudis** (Carrer de la Canuda to Carrer de la Portaferrissa) is also called La Rambla dels Ocells (birds) because of its twittering bird market.

Just north of Carrer del Carme, the **Església de Betlem** was constructed in baroque style for the Jesuits in the late 17th and early 18th centuries to replace an earlier church destroyed by fire in 1671. Fire was a bit of a theme for this site: the church was once considered the most splendid of Barcelona's few baroque offerings, but leftist arsonists torched it in 1936.

La Rambla de Sant Josep, named after a former monastery dedicated to St Joseph, runs from Carrer de la Portaferrissa to Plaça de la Boqueria and is lined with verdant flower stalls, which give it the alternative name La Rambla de les Flors.

The **Palau de la Virreina** (La Rambla de Sant Josep 99) is a grand 18th-century rococo mansion (with some neoclassical elements) housing an arts/entertainment information and ticket office run by the Ajuntament (town hall). In a series of exhibition rooms, including the bulk of the 1st floor, it houses the **Centre de la Imatge** (☎ 93 316 10 00; www.bcn.cat/virreinacentredela imatge), scene of rotating photo exhibitions; admission prices and opening hours vary.

Across La Rambla at No 118 is an equally rare example of a more pure neoclassical pile, **Palau Moja**, which houses government offices, the Generalitat's bookshop and exhibition space. Its clean, classical lines are best appreciated from across La Rambla.

Next, you are confronted by the bustling sound, smell and tastefest of the **Mercat de la Boqueria**. It is possibly La Rambla's most interesting building, not so much for its Modernisme-influenced design (it was actually built over a long period, from 1840 to 1914, on the site of the former St Joseph monastery) as for the action of the food market.

At Plaça de la Boqueria, where four side streets meet just north of Liceu Metro sta-

tion, you can walk all over a Miró – the colourful **Mosaïc de Miró** in the pavement, with one tile signed by the artist.

La Rambla dels Caputxins (aka La Rambla del Centre), named after another now nonexistent monastery, runs from Plaça de la Boqueria to Carrer dels Escudellers. The latter street is named after the potters' guild, founded in the 13th century, whose members lived and worked here (their raw materials came principally from Sicily). On the western side of La Rambla is the **Gran Teatre del Liceu** (p78).

Further south on the eastern side of La Rambla dels Caputxins is the entrance to the palm-shaded **Plaça Reial** (p68). Below this point, La Rambla gets seedier, with the occasional strip club and peep show. The final stretch, **La Rambla de Santa Mònica**, widens to approach the **Mirador de Colom** (p69), overlooking Port Vell. La Rambla here is named after the Convent de Santa Mònica, which once stood on the western flank of the street and has since been converted into

KRZYSZTOF DYDYNSKI

Drinks stall, Mercat de la Boqueria

an art gallery and cultural centre, the **Centre d'Art Santa Mònica** (☎ 93 567 11 10; www.artssantamonica.cat; La Rambla de Santa Mònica 7; admission free; ☽ 11am-9pm Tue-Sun & holidays; Ⓜ Drassanes).

MUSEU D'HISTÒRIA DE BARCELONA

☎ 93 256 21 00; www.museuhistoria.bcn.cat; Carrer del Veguer; adult/under 7yr/senior & student €7/free/5, from 4pm 1st Sat of month and from 3pm Sun free; ☽ 10am-2pm & 4-7pm Tue-Sat Oct-Mar, 10am-8pm Tue-Sat Apr-Sep, 10am-8pm Sun, 10am-3pm holidays; Ⓜ Jaume I Leap back into Roman Barcino with a subterranean stroll and then stride around parts of the former Palau Reial Major (Grand Royal Palace) on Plaça del Rei (King's Sq, the former palace's courtyard), among the key locations of medieval princely power in Barcelona, in what is one of Barcelona's most fascinating museums.

Enter through **Casa Padellàs**, just south of Plaça del Rei. Casa Padellàs was built for a 16th-century noble family in Carrer dels Mercaders and moved here, stone by stone, in the 1930s. It has a courtyard typical of Barcelona's late-Gothic and baroque mansions, with a graceful external staircase up to the 1st floor. Today it leads to a restored Roman tower and a section of Roman wall (whose exterior faces Plaça Ramon de Berenguer el Gran), as well as a section of the house set aside for temporary exhibitions (these can be visited independently to the rest of the museum for €2).

Below ground is a remarkable walk through about 4 sq km of excavated Roman and Visigothic Barcelona. After the display on the typical Roman *domus* (villa), you reach a public laundry (outside in the street were containers for people to urinate into, as the urine was used as disinfectant). You pass more laundries

and dyeing shops, a 6th-century public cold-water bath and more dye shops. As you hit the Cardo Minor (a main street), turn right then left and reach various shops dedicated to the making of *garum*. This paste, a fave food across the Roman Empire, was made of mashed-up fish intestines, eggs and blood. Further on are fish-preserve stores.

Next come remnants of a 6th- to 7th-century church and episcopal buildings, followed by winemaking stores, with ducts for allowing the must to flow off and ceramic, round-bottomed *dolia* for storing and ageing wine. Ramparts then wind around and upward, past remains of the gated patio of a Roman house, the medieval Palau Episcopal (Bishops' Palace) and into two broad vaulted halls with displays on medieval Barcelona.

You eventually emerge at a hall and ticket office set up on the north side of Plaça del Rei. To your right is the **Saló del Tinell**, the banqueting hall of the royal palace and a fine example of Catalan Gothic (built 1359–70). Its broad arches and bare walls give a sense of solemnity that would have made an appropriate setting for Fernando and Isabel to hear Columbus' first reports of the New World.

As you leave the *saló* you come to the 14th-century **Capella Reial de Santa Àgata**, the palace chapel. Outside, a spindly bell tower rises from the northeast side of Plaça del Rei. Inside, all is bare except for the 15th-century altarpiece and the magnificent *techumbre* (decorated timber ceiling).

Head down the fan-shaped stairs into Plaça del Rei and look up to observe the **Mirador del Rei Martí** (lookout tower of King Martin), built in 1555, long after the king's death. It is part of the Arxiu de la Corona d'Aragón and so the magnificent views over the old city are now enjoyed only by a privileged few.

BARRI GÒTIC & LA RAMBLA

SIGHTS

Vault detail, La Catedral

⬎ LA CATEDRAL

Approached from the broad Avinguda de la Catedral, Barcelona's central place of worship presents a magnificent image. The richly decorated main (northwest) facade, laced with gargoyles and the stone intricacies you would expect of northern European Gothic, sets it quite apart from other churches in Barcelona. The facade was actually added in 1870 (and is receiving a serious round of restoration), although it is based on a 1408 design. The rest of the building was built between 1298 and 1460. The other facades are sparse in decoration, and the octagonal, flat-roofed towers are a clear reminder that, even here, Catalan Gothic architectural principles prevailed.

The interior is a broad, soaring space divided into a central nave and two aisles by lines of elegant, slim pillars. The cathedral was one of the few churches in Barcelona spared by the anarchists in the civil war, so its ornamentation, never overly lavish, is intact.

You may visit La Catedral in one of two ways. In the morning or afternoon, entrance is free and you can opt to visit any combination of the choir stalls, chapter house and roof. To visit all three areas, it costs less to enter for the so-called 'special visit' between 1pm and 5pm.

Things you need to know: ☎ 93 342 82 60; www.website.es/catedralbcn, in Catalan & Spanish; Pla de la Seu; admission free, special visit €5; ☯ 8am-12.45pm & 5.15-8pm Mon-Sat, special visit 1-5pm Mon-Sat, 2-5pm Sun & holidays; Ⓜ Jaume I

From Plaça del Rei, it's worth taking a detour northeast to see the two best surviving stretches of Barcelona's **Roman walls**, which once boasted 78 towers (as much a matter of prestige as of defence). One is on the southwest side of Plaça Ramon de Berenguer Gran, with the Capella Reial de Santa Àgata atop.

The other is a little further south, by the northern end of Carrer del Sots-tinent Navarro.

PALAU DEL LLOCTINENT

Carrer dels Comtes; admission free; ⏲ 10am-7pm; Ⓜ Jaume I

The southwest side of Plaça del Rei is taken up by this palace, built in the 1550s as the residence of the Spanish *lloctinent* (viceroy) of Catalonia and later converted into a convent. From 1853, it housed the Arxiu de la Corona d'Aragó, a unique archive with documents detailing the history of the Crown of Aragón and Catalonia – this impressive archive started in the 12th century and reaches the 20th. Gracefully restored in 2006, the palace's courtyard is worth wandering through. Have a look upwards from the main staircase to admire the extraordinary timber *artesonado*, a sculpted ceiling made to seem like the upturned hull of a boat. It was done in the 16th century by Antoni Carbonell.

MUSEU FREDERIC MARÈS

☎ 93 256 35 00; www.museumares.bcn.es; Plaça de Sant Iu 5-6; Ⓜ Jaume I

Closed for renovation until 2011, this eclectic collection is housed in what was once part of the medieval Palau Reial Major, on Carrer dels Comtes. Frederic Marès i Deulovol (1893–1991) was a rich sculptor, traveller and obsessive collector. He specialised in medieval Spanish sculpture, huge quantities of which are displayed in the basement and on the ground and 1st floors – including some lovely polychrome wooden sculptures of the Crucifixion and the Virgin.

The top two floors hold a mind-boggling array of knick-knacks, from toy soldiers and cribs to scissors and 19th-century playing cards, and from early still cameras to pipes and fine ceramics. A room that once served as Marès' study and library is now crammed with sculpture. The shady courtyard houses a pleasant summer cafe (Cafè de l'Estiu) and a series of interactive screens that allow visitors to get an idea of the collection while the museum remains closed.

Museu Frederic Marès

PLAÇA DE SANT JAUME

Ⓜ Jaume I

In the 2000 or so years since the Romans settled here, the area around this square (often remodelled), which started life as the forum, has been the focus of Barcelona's civic life. Facing each other across it are the Palau de la Generalitat (seat of Catalonia's regional government) on the north side and the Ajuntament (town hall) to the south. Both have fine Gothic interiors, which, unfortunately, the public can enter only at limited times.

Founded in the early 15th century on land that had largely belonged to the city's by then defunct Jewish community to house Catalonia's government, the **Palau de la Generalitat** (☷ free guided visit 10am-1pm 2nd & 4th weekend of month, open doors 23 Apr, 11 Sep & 24 Sep) was extended over the centuries as its importance (and bureaucracy) grew. For weekend visits, you need to book online at www.gencat.cat. Click on *Guia Breu de la Generalitat,* then on *Visites guiades al Palau de la Generalitat* under *Activitats* to reach the booking form.

Marc Safont designed the original Gothic main entrance on Carrer del Bisbe. The modern main entrance on Plaça de Sant Jaume is a late-Renaissance job with neoclassical leanings. If you wander by in the evening, squint up through the windows into the **Saló de Sant Jordi** (Hall of St George) and you will get some idea of the sumptuousness of the interior.

If you *do* get inside, you're in for a treat. Normally you will have to enter from Carrer de Sant Sever. The first rooms you pass through are characterised by low vaulted ceilings. From here you head upstairs to the raised courtyard known as the **Pati dels Tarongers**, a modest Gothic orangery (opened about once a month for concert performances of the palace's chimes). The 16th-century **Sala Daurada i de Sessions**, one of the rooms leading off the patio, is a splendid meeting hall lit up by huge chandeliers. Still more imposing is the Renaissance Saló de Sant Jordi, whose murals were added last century – many an occasion of pomp and circumstance takes place here. Finally, you descend the staircase of the Gothic **Pati Central** to leave by what was, in the beginning, the building's main entrance.

Facing the Palau de la Generalitat, and otherwise known as the Casa de la Ciutat, the **Ajuntament** (☎ 010; admission free; ☷ 10am-1pm Sun) has been the seat of city power for centuries. The Consell de Cent, from medieval times the city's ruling council, first sat here in the 14th century, but the building has lamentably undergone many changes since the days of Barcelona's Gothic-era splendour.

Only the original, now disused, entrance on Carrer de la Ciutat retains its Gothic ornament. The main 19th-century neoclassical facade on the square is a charmless riposte to the Palau de la Generalitat. Inside, the **Saló de Cent** is the hall in which the town council once held its plenary sessions. The broad vaulting is pure Catalan Gothic and the *artesonado* ceiling demonstrates fine work. In fact, much of what you see is comparatively recent. The building was badly damaged in a bombardment in 1842 and has been repaired and tampered with repeatedly. The wooden neo-Gothic seating was added at the beginning of the 20th century, as was the grand alabaster *retablo* (retable, or altarpiece) at the back. To the right you enter the small **Saló de la Reina Regente**, built in 1860, where the Ajuntament now sits. To the left of the Saló de Cent is the **Saló de les Croniques** – the murals here recount Catalan exploits in Greece and the Near East in Catalonia's empire-building days.

LOOK DIE BILDAGENTUR DER FOTOGRAFEN GMBH/ALAMY

Wax figures in the Museu de Cera

↘ IF YOU LIKE...

If you like the ephemera in the **Museu Frederic Marés** (p65) you'll enjoy these other off-the-wall museums:

- **Museu del Calçat** (Footwear Museum; ☎ 93 301 45 33; Plaça de Sant Felip Neri 5; admission €2.50; ⊙ 11am-2pm Tue-Sun; Ⓜ Jaume I) This obscure museum is home to everything from Egyptian sandals to dainty ladies' shoes of the 18th century. The museum and cobblers' guild, which has its roots in the city's medieval past, were moved here shortly after the civil war.
- **Museu de Cera** (☎ 93 317 26 49; www.museocerabcn.com; Passatge de la Banca 7; adult/under 5yr/senior, student & 5-11yr €12/free/7; ⊙ 10am-10pm daily Jun-Sep, 10am-1.30pm & 4-7.30pm Mon-Fri, 11am-2pm & 4.30-8.30pm Sat, Sun & holidays Oct-May; Ⓜ Drassanes) Inside this late-19th-century building, you can stand, sit and lounge about with 300 wax figures. Frankenstein is here, along with a rather awkward-looking Prince Charles with Camilla. In the same hall and grouped willy-nilly are Hitler, Bill Clinton, Mussolini, Che Guevara, Fidel Castro, General Franco and head of the former Catalan government-in-exile Josep Taradellas.
- **Museu de l'Eròtica** (Erotica Museum; ☎ 93 318 98 65; www.erotica-museum.com; La Rambla de Sant Josep 96; adult/senior & student €9/8; ⊙ 10am-9pm Jun-Sep, 10am-8pm Oct-May; Ⓜ Liceu) Observe what naughtiness people have been getting up to since ancient times in this museum, with lots of Kama Sutra and 1920s flickering porn movies. The museum caters to all tastes.

PLAÇA DE SANT JOSEP ORIOL & AROUND

Ⓜ Liceu

This small plaza is the prettiest in the Barri Gòtic. Its bars and cafes attract buskers and artists and make it a lively place to hang out. The plaza is surrounded by quaint streets, many of which are dotted with appealing cafes, restaurants and shops.

BARRI GÒTIC & LA RAMBLA

SIGHTS

Sunday market, Plaça Reial

PASCALE BEROUJON

Looming over the square is the flank of the **Església de Santa Maria del Pi** (🕙 9.30am-1pm & 5-8.30pm Mon-Fri, 9.30am-1pm & 4-8.30pm Sat, 9.30am-2pm & 5-8.30pm Sun & holidays), a Gothic church built in the 14th to 16th centuries. The bulk of it was completed in 1320–91. With its 10m diameter, the beautiful rose window above its entrance on Plaça del Pi is claimed by some to be the world's biggest. The interior of the church was gutted when leftists ransacked it in the opening months of the civil war in 1936 and most of the stained glass is modern. Perhaps one happy result of the fire was the destruction of the 19th-century, neo-Gothic seating, which therefore had to be replaced by the 18th-century baroque original.

PLAÇA REIAL & AROUND

Ⓜ Liceu

Just south of Carrer de Ferran, near its La Rambla end, Plaça Reial is a traffic-free plaza whose 19th-century neoclassical facades are punctuated by numerous eateries, bars and nightspots. It was created on the site of a convent, one of several destroyed along La Rambla (the strip was teeming with religious institutions) in the wake of the Spain-wide disentailment laws that stripped the Church of much of its property. The lamp posts by the central fountain are Antoni Gaudí's first known works in the city.

The southern half of the Barri Gòtic is imbued with the memory of Picasso, who lived as a teenager with his family in Carrer de la Mercè, had his first studio in Carrer de la Plata (now a rather cheesy restaurant) and was a regular visitor to a brothel at Carrer d'Avinyó 27. That experience may have inspired his 1907 painting *Les Demoiselles d'Avignon*.

GRAN TEATRE DEL LICEU

☎ 93 485 99 14; www.liceubarcelona.com; La Rambla dels Caputxins 51-59; admission with/without guide €8.70/4; 🕙 guided tour 10am, unguided visits 11.30am, noon, 12.30pm & 1pm; Ⓜ Liceu

If you can't catch a night at the opera, you can still have a look around one of Europe's greatest opera houses, known to locals as the Liceu. Smaller than Milan's La

Scala but bigger than Venice's La Fenice, it can seat up to 2300 people in its grand horseshoe auditorium.

Built in 1847, the Liceu launched such Catalan stars as Josep (aka José) Carreras and Montserrat Caballé. Fire virtually destroyed it in 1994, but city authorities were quick to get it back into operation. Carefully reconstructing the 19th-century auditorium and installing the latest in theatre technology, technicians brought the Liceu back to life in October 1999. You can take a 20-minute quick turn around the main public areas of the theatre or join a one-hour guided tour.

On the guided tour you are taken to the grand foyer, with its thick pillars and sumptuous chandeliers, and then up the marble staircase to the **Saló dels Miralls** (Hall of Mirrors). These both survived the 1994 fire and the latter was traditionally where theatregoers mingled during intermission. With mirrors, ceiling frescos, fluted columns and high-and-mighty phrases in praise of the arts, it all exudes a typically neobaroque richness worthy of its 19th-

century patrons. You are then led up to the 4th-floor stalls to admire the theatre itself.

MIRADOR DE COLOM

☎ 93 302 52 24; Plaça del Portal de la Pau; lift adult/under 4yr/senior & 4-12yr €2.50/free/1.50; ☺ 9am-8.30pm Jun-Sep, 10am-6.30pm Oct-May; Ⓜ Drassanes

High above the swirl of traffic on the roundabout below, a pigeon-poop-coiffed Columbus keeps permanent watch, pointing vaguely out to the Mediterranean (to his home town of Genoa?). Built for the Universal Exhibition in 1888, the monument allows you to zip up 60m in the lift for bird's-eye views back up La Rambla and across the ports of Barcelona.

ESGLÉSIA DE SANTS JUST I PASTOR

☎ 93 301 74 33; www.basilicasantjust.cat, in Catalan; Plaça de Sant Just 5; admission free; ☺ 11am-2pm & 5-9pm Wed-Fri, 5-9pm Sat, 10am-1.30pm Sun, 11am-2pm & 5-8pm Tue; Ⓜ Liceu or Jaume I

This somewhat neglected, single-nave church, with chapels on either side of the

BARRI GÒTIC & LA RAMBLA

SIGHTS

Gran Teatre del Liceu

MARTIN HUGHES

buttressing, was built in 1342 in Catalan Gothic style on what is reputedly the site of the oldest parish church in Barcelona. Inside, you can admire some fine stained-glass windows. In front of it, in a pretty little square that was used as a film set (a smelly Parisian marketplace) in 2006 for *Perfume: The Story of a Murderer*, is what is claimed to be the city's oldest Gothic fountain.

CENTRE D'INTERPRETACIÓ DEL CALL
☎ 93 256 21 00; www.museuhistoria.bcn.cat; Placeta de Manuel Ribé; admission free; ☾ 10am-2pm Wed-Fri, 11am-6pm Sat, 11am-3pm Sun & holidays; Ⓜ Jaume I or Liceu
Once a 14th-century house of the Jewish weaver Jucef Bonhiac, this small visitors' centre is dedicated to the history of Barcelona's Jewish quarter, the Call. Glass sections in the ground floor allow you to inspect Mr Bonhiac's former wells and storage space. The house, also known as the Casa de l'Alquimista (Alchemist's House), hosts a modest display of Jewish artefacts, including ceramics excavated in the area of the Call, along with explanations and maps of the one-time Jewish quarter.

SINAGOGA MAJOR
☎ 93 317 07 90; www.calldebarcelona.org; Carrer de Marlet 5; admission €2 donation; ☾ 10.30am-6pm Mon-Fri, 10.30am-3pm Sat & Sun; Ⓜ Liceu
When an Argentine investor bought a run-down electrician's store with an eye to converting it into central Barcelona's umpteenth bar, he could hardly have known he had stumbled onto the remains of what could be the city's main medieval synagogue (some historians cast doubt on the claim). Remnants of medieval and Roman-era walls remain in the small vaulted space that you enter from the street. Also remaining are tanners' wells installed in the 15th

century. The second chamber has been spruced up for use as a synagogue. A remnant of late-Roman-era wall here, given its orientation facing Jerusalem, has led some to speculate that there was a synagogue here even in Roman times. A guide will explain what is thought to be the significance of the site in various languages.

TEMPLE ROMÀ D'AUGUST
Carrer del Paradis; admission free; ☾ 10am-8pm Tue-Sun, 10am-3pm holidays Apr-Sep, 10am-2pm & 4-7pm Tue-Sat, 10am-8pm Sun, 10am-3pm holidays Oct-Mar; Ⓜ Jaume I
Opposite the southeast end of La Catedral, narrow Carrer del Paradis leads towards Plaça de Sant Jaume. Inside No 10, itself an intriguing building with Gothic and baroque touches, are four columns and the architrave of Barcelona's main Roman temple, dedicated to Caesar Augustus and built to worship his imperial highness in the 1st century AD. You are now standing on the highest point of Roman Barcino, Mont Tàber (a grand total of 16.9m, unlikely to induce altitude sickness). You may well find the door open outside the listed hours. Just pop in.

VIA SEPULCRAL ROMANA
☎ 93 256 21 00; www.museuhistoria.bcn.cat; Plaça de la Vila de Madrid; admission €2; ☾ 10am-8pm Tue-Sun, 10am-3pm holidays Apr-Sep, 10am-2pm & 4-7pm Tue-Sat, 10am-8pm Sun, 10am-3pm holidays Oct-Mar; Ⓜ Catalunya
Along Carrer de la Canuda, a block east of the top end of La Rambla, is a sunken garden where a series of Roman tombs lies exposed. The burial ground stretches along either side of the road that led northwest out of Barcelona's Roman predecessor, Barcino. Roman law forbade burial within city limits and so everyone, the great and humble, were generally buried along roads leading out of cities. A smallish display in

NEIL SETCHFIELD

Via Sepulcral Romana

Spanish and Catalan by the tombs explores the Roman road and highway system, burial and funerary rites and customs.

DOMUS ROMANA

☎ 93 256 21 00; www.museuhistoria.bcn.cat; Carrer de la Fruita 3; ⊙ 10am-3pm Sat, Sun & holidays; Ⓜ Liceu

The remains of a Roman *domus* (town house) have been unearthed. The house (and vestiges of three small shops) lay close to the Roman forum and the owners were clearly well off. Apart from getting something of an idea of daily Roman life through these remains, the location also contains six medieval grain silos installed at the time the Jewish quarter, the Call, was located in this area. The whole is housed in the mid-19th century Casa Morell. So, in an unusual mix, one gets a glimpse of three distinct periods in history in the same spot.

ESGLÉSIA DE LA MERCÈ

Plaça de la Mercè; Ⓜ Drassanes

Raised in the 1760s on the site of its Gothic predecessor, the baroque Església de la Mercè is home to Barcelona's most celebrated patron saint. It was badly damaged during the civil war. What remains is quite a curiosity. The baroque facade facing the square contrasts with the Renaissance flank along Carrer Ample. The latter was actually moved here from another nearby church that was subsequently destroyed in the 1870s.

DALÍ ESCULTOR

Carrer dels Arcs 5; admission €8; ⊙ 10am-10pm; Ⓜ Liceu

One of the best things about this collection is its superb location in the Reial Cercle Artístic (Royal Art Circle) building just near La Catedral. This somewhat hyped display offers 60-odd little-known sculptures by a man, Salvador Dalí, who was largely renowned for his paintings. Documents, sketches and photos by and of the artist complete the picture. If you can't visit his **museum-mausoleum** in Figueres, this is no substitute, but does provide some clues to the life and work of the mustachioed maestro.

SLEEPING

La Rambla is lined with hotels, *pensiones* and fleapits, and in the labyrinth of the Barri Gòtic are scattered countless others. Many of the smaller joints are nothing special, catering to an at times rowdy party crowd. But there are some real gems, too.

HOTEL 1898   Hotel €€€

☎ 93 552 95 52; www.hotel1898.com; La Rambla 109; d €295-388; Ⓜ Liceu; Ⓟ ⌗ 🖥 🛜 🚇

The former Compañía de Tabacos Filipinas (Philippines Tobacco Company) has been resurrected as a luxury hotel. Some of the rooms are smallish but deluxe rooms and suites have their own terraces, and all combine modern comfort and elegance, with hardwood floors and tasteful furniture. Etro toiletries await in the bathrooms. Some of the suites (up to €1600) have access to a private indoor pool, while all guests can use the outdoor one.

HOTEL NERI   Design Hotel €€

☎ 93 304 06 55; www.hotelneri.com; Carrer de Sant Sever 5; d from €235; Ⓜ Liceu; ⌗ 🖥 🛜

Occupying a beautifully adapted, centuries-old building, which backs on to the quiet Plaça de Sant Felip Neri, this is a tranquil stop. The sandy stone and timber furnishings lend the building a sense of history but the rooms have a slick feel, with cutting-edge technology, including plasma-screen TVs and infra-red lights in the stone-clad designer bathrooms. Choose from a menu of sheets and pillows, or sun yourself, shower and order a drink on the roof deck.

HOTEL COLÓN   Hotel €€

☎ 93 301 14 04; www.hotelcolon.es; Avinguda de la Catedral 7; s/d from €105/195; Ⓜ Jaume I; ⌗ 🖥

The privileged position opposite the cathedral lends this hotel special grace. A range of rooms (142 in all), from mod-

est singles to diaphanous doubles and suites, offers elegant accommodation. Decoration varies considerably (from hardwood floors to carpet) and the top-floor superior rooms with terrace are marvellous (and go for about €300).

HOTEL CONTINENTAL   Hotel €€

☎ 93 301 25 70; www.hotelcontinental.com; Rambla 138; s/d €87/97; Ⓜ Catalunya; ⌗ 🖥

You can imagine being here in 1937, when George Orwell returned from the front line during the Spanish Civil War, and Barcelona was tense with factional strife. Rooms at the Continental are a little spartan, but have romantic touches such as ceiling fans, brass bedsteads and frilly bedclothes. You will pay €20 more for a double with a balcony overlooking La Rambla. Take breakfast in bed… or head down to the buffet any time – it's open 24 hours.

HOTEL JARDÍ   Hotel €€

☎ 93 301 59 00; www.hoteljardi-barcelona .com; Plaça de Sant Josep Oriol 1; d €65-95; Ⓜ Liceu; ⌗

The 'Garden Hotel' has no garden but several attractive doubles with balcony overlooking one of the prettiest squares in the city. If you can snare one of them, it is well worth climbing up the stairs. If you can't get a room with a view, you are better off looking elsewhere.

EATING

First things first: skip the strip. La Rambla is fine for people watching, but no great shakes for the palate. Instead venture off into the streets that wind into the Barri Gòtic and your tum will be eternally grateful. Inside the medieval labyrinth, choices abound. If you had to pinpoint any one area, it would be the half of the *barri* (neighbourhood) between Plaça de Sant Jaume and the waterfront, especially towards Via Laietana. On and around Carrer de la Mercè a huddle of old-time tapas bars survives, down dirty and simple, as if caught in a time warp in postwar Spain.

PLA
Fusion €€

☎ 93 412 65 52; www.elpla.com; Carrer de la Bellafila 5; meals €45-50; ⌚ dinner; Ⓜ Liceu; ✂

You could be forgiven for thinking you have waltzed into a dark designer cocktail bar. Actually it's a medieval den (with a huge stone arch) of devious culinary mischief, where the cooks churn out such temptations as *daus de tonyina poc feta a la flama, verduretes i una salsa de cassis i citronella* (lightly flamed tuna cubes with vegetables and a cassis and lemongrass sauce). It has a tasting menu for €29 Sunday to Thursday.

COMETACINC
Fusion €€

☎ 93 310 15 58; www.cometacinc.com; Carrer del Cometa 5; meals €35; ⌚ dinner daily; Ⓜ Jaume I; ✂

In this grand medieval space, the kitchen constantly produces a changing menu that criss-crosses all boundaries. The elegant candle-lit wooden tables over two floors set an intimate mood for, say, some *tonyina vermella a la brasa amb confitura agre-dolça de albercoc* (charcoal-grilled red tuna with chutney). It also has a fair range of tapas.

AGUT
Catalan €€

☎ 93 315 17 09; Carrer d'en Gignàs 16; meals €35; ⌚ dinner Tue-Sat, lunch Sun Sep-Jul; Ⓜ Jaume I; ✂

Deep in the Gothic labyrinth lies this classic eatery. A series of cosy dining areas is connected by broad arches while, high up, the walls are tightly lined by artworks. There's art in what the kitchen serves up too, from the oak-grilled meat to a succulent variety of seafood offerings, like the *cassoleta de rap a l'all cremat amb cloïsses* (monkfish with browned garlic and clams).

CAFÈ DE L'ACADÈMIA
Catalan €€

☎ 93 319 82 53; Carrer de Lledó 1; meals €30-35; ⌚ Mon-Fri; Ⓜ Jaume I; ✂

Expect a mix of traditional dishes with the occasional creative twist. At lunchtime, local Ajuntament (town hall) office workers

XAVIER MENDIOLA

Pla restaurant

pounce on the *menú del día* (for €14, or €9.80 at the bar). In the evening it is rather more romantic, as soft lighting emphasises the intimacy of the timber ceiling and wooden decor. Offerings range from *chuletón* (huge T-bone steak) for two to *guatlla farcida de foie d'ànec i botifarra amb salsa de ceps* (quail stuffed with duck foie gras and sausage with a mushroom sauce).

LOS CARACOLES Spanish €€
☎ 93 302 31 85; www.los-caracoles.es; Carrer dels Escudellers 14; meals €30-35; ☽ daily; Ⓜ Drassanes; ✗
Run by the fifth generation of the Bofarull family, 'The Snails' started life as a tavern in 1835 and is one of Barcelona's best-known, if somewhat touristy, restaurants. Several interlocking rooms (consider asking for the small medieval-looking banquet room), with centuries of history seemingly greased into the tables and garlic-clad walls, may well distract you from the rotisserie chickens and snails that are the house specialities. Locals still dine here and the ambience alone makes it worth dropping by, if only for a drink or two at the bar.

CAN PESCALLUNES Catalan €€
☎ 93 318 54 83; Carrer de les Magdalenes 23; meals €25-30; ☽ Mon-Fri; Ⓜ Jaume I
A muted sort of place the 'House of the Moon-Fisher' may be, and decoratively stuck in another era, but the family that run this Catalan eatery is no slouch in the kitchen. Expect generous and well-prepared servings of steak tartare or *bacallà amb samfaina* (cod with *samfaina* sauce). The first courses are equally good.

BAR CELTA Galician €€
☎ 93 315 00 06; Carrer de la Mercè 16; meals €20-25; ☽ noon-midnight Tue-Sun; Ⓜ Drassanes
This bright, rambunctious bar-cum-restaurant specialises in *pulpo* (octopus)

and other sea critters such as *navajas* (razor clams). It does a good job: even the most demanding Galician natives give it the thumbs up. Sit at the zinc bar and order a bottle of Ribeiro and the traditional Galician *tazas* (little white cups).

MILK Bar-Restaurant €
☎ 93 268 09 22; www.milkbarcelona.com; Carrer d'en Gignàs 21; meals €15-20; ☽ brunch 11am-4pm Thu-Sun; Ⓜ Jaume I
Known to many as a cool cocktail spot, the Irish-run Milk's key role for Barcelona night owls is providing morning-after brunches. Avoid direct sunlight and tuck into pancakes or salmon eggs Benedict in the penumbra. Anyone for a triple whammy hamburger or a Milk's fry-up? Get some hair of the dog with cocktails at €5 to €7.

CAN CONESA Snacks €
☎ 93 310 57 95; Carrer de la Llibreteria 1; rolls & toasted sandwiches €3-5; ☽ Mon-Sat; Ⓜ Jaume I
Locals, especially lunching workers from the Ajuntament and Generalitat, have been lining up for the succulent *entrepans* (filled rolls), toasted sandwiches and other snacks since the 1950s.

CAFÈ DE L'ÒPERA Cafe €
☎ 93 302 41 80; La Rambla 74; ☽ 9am-3am; Ⓜ Liceu; ✗
Opposite the Gran Teatre del Liceu is La Rambla's most intriguing cafe. Operating since 1929, it is pleasant enough for an early evening libation or coffee and croissants. Upstairs offers elevated seats above the busy boulevard. Tempted by the *cafè de l'Òpera* (coffee with chocolate mousse)?

SALTERIO Cafe €
Carrer de Sant Domènec del Call 4; ☽ 2pm-1am Mon-Sat; Ⓜ Jaume I
If it got any mellower here, with its gentle Middle Eastern music and low whispering,

DIEGO LEZAMA

Barri Gòtic lanes

you'd nod off. The wait for the mint tea is worth it – it's filled with real mint, as good as in Morocco.

DRINKING

La Rambla holds little interest, so leave it to those content to settle for expensive pints, and plunge into the narrow streets and back alleys of the lower end of the Barri Gòtic. Check out Carrer dels Escudellers, Carrer Ample (and the parallel Carrer d'en Gignàs and Carrer del Correu Vell) and the area around Plaça Reial.

BLONDIE   Bar

www.blondie-bcn.com; Carrer d'en Roca 14; ⏰ 7pm-2am Sun-Thu, 7pm-3am Fri & Sat; Ⓜ Liceu

Long a dark little dive that had slowly sunk into oblivion, this simple, backstreet bar has subtle, multicoloured lighting, Estrella Galicia beer (the country's crispest lager) and something of a conspiratorial air. Italian run, it lures folk for happy hour from 7pm to 10pm. You could find yourself locked in until 4am.

EL PARAIGUA   Bar

☎ 93 302 11 31; www.elparaigua.com; Carrer del Pas de l'Ensenyança 2; ⏰ 10am-midnight Sun-Thu, 11am-2.30am Fri & Sat; Ⓜ Liceu

A tiny chocolate box of dark tinted Modernisme, the 'Umbrella' has been serving up drinks since the 1960s. The turn-of-the-20th-century decor was transferred here from a shop knocked down elsewhere in the district and cobbled back together to create this cosy locale. Take a trip in time from Modernisme to medieval by heading downstairs to the brick and stone basement bar area. Part of the walls date to the 11th century.

MANCHESTER   Bar

☎ 663 071748; www.manchesterbar.com; Carrer de Milans 5; ⏰ 7pm-2.30am Sun-Thu, 7pm-3am Fri & Sat; Ⓜ Liceu

A drinking den that has undergone several transformations down the years now treats you to the sounds of great Manchester bands, from the Chemical Brothers to Oasis, but probably not the Hollies. It has a pleasing rough-and-tumble feel, with tables jammed in every which way. Cocktails cost €4 from 7pm to 10pm.

MARULA CAFÈ — Bar

☎ 663 071748; www.marulacafe.com; Carrer dels Escudellers 49; ☿ 11pm-5am Sun-Thu, 11pm-5.30am Fri & Sat; Ⓜ Liceu

A fantastic new funk find in the heart of the Barri Gòtic, Marula will transport you to the 1970s and the best in funk and soul. James Brown fans will think they've died and gone to heaven. It's not, however, a monothematic place and occasionally the DJs slip in other tunes, from breakbeat to house. Samba and other Brazilian dance sounds also penetrate here.

SCHILLING — Bar

☎ 93 317 67 87; Carrer de Ferran 23; ☿ 10am-2.30am Mon-Thu, 10am-3am Fri & Sat, noon-2am Sun; Ⓜ Liceu

A gay-friendly favourite with a classy low-lit feel. Perch at the bar, take a little table or slink out the back to the lounges, while various snacks are served up. Whatever you choose, it's a congenial place for a drink and some knowing eye contact.

SINATRA — Bar

☎ 93 412 52 79; Carrer de les Heures 4-10; ☿ 6pm-2.30am Sun-Thu, 6pm-3am Fri & Sat; Ⓜ Liceu

Lurking back a block from boisterous Plaça Reial is this no less raucous location. It's largely patronised by foreigners (Spanish-speaking staff are hard to locate!) who flop into splotchy cowhide-pattern lounges, perch on long stools beneath the mirror ball and sip Desperados beer while listening to '80s tracks.

SÍNCOPA — Bar

Carrer d'Avinyó 35; ☿ 6pm-2.30am; Ⓜ Liceu

Lovers of self-conscious grunge will want to pop in here for the mellow music and conversation. It's a saunter from Plaça de George Orwell (or Plaça del Trippy to those who hang around here taking drugs).

ENTERTAINMENT & ACTIVITIES

BLVD — Club

☎ 93 301 62 89; www.boulevardcultureclub .com; La Rambla 27; ☿ midnight-6am Mon-Sat May-Sep, Thu-Sat Oct-Apr; Ⓜ Drassanes

Flanked by striptease bars (in the true spirit of the lower Rambla's old days), this place has undergone countless reincarnations. The culture in this club is what a long line-up of DJs brings to the (turn)table. With three different dance spaces, one of them upstairs, it has a deliciously tacky feel, pumping out anything from 1980s hits to house (especially on Saturdays in the main room). There's no particular dress code.

KARMA — Club

☎ 93 302 56 80; www.karmadisco.com, in Spanish; Plaça Reial 10; admission €8; ☿ midnight-5.30am Tue-Sun; Ⓜ Liceu

Sick of the metallic sounds of the new century? What about some good, mainstream indie music (during the week)? At weekends it becomes unpredictable, with anything from rock to 1980s disco fever. The odd Madonna track even pops up. A golden oldie in Barcelona, tunnel-shaped Karma is small and becomes quite tightly packed with a good-natured crowd of locals and out-of-towners.

LA MACARENA — Club

☎ 637 416647; Carrer Nou de Sant Francesc 5; admission up to €5; ☿ midnight-5am; Ⓜ Drassanes

You simply won't believe this was once a tile-lined Andalucian flamenco musos' bar. Now it is a dark dance space, of the kind where it is possible to sit at the bar, meet people around you and then stand up for a bit of a shake to the DJ's electro and house offerings, all within a couple of square metres.

SIDECAR FACTORY CLUB Live Music

☎ 93 302 15 86; www.sidecarfactoryclub.com; Plaça Reial 7; admission €7-15; ☾ 10pm-5am Mon-Thu, 10pm-6am Fri & Sat; Ⓜ Liceu

With its entrance on Plaça Reial, you can come here for a meal before midnight or a few drinks at ground level (which closes by 3am at the latest), or descend into the red-tinged, brick-vaulted bowels for live music most nights. Just about anything goes here, from UK indie through to country punk, but rock and pop lead the way. Most shows start at 10pm (Thursday to Saturday). DJs take over at 12.30am to keep you dancing until dawn.

JAMBOREE Live Music & Club

☎ 93 319 17 89; www.masimas.com/jamboree; Plaça Reial 17; admission €5-15; ☾ 9.30pm-6am; Ⓜ Liceu

Since long before Franco said *adiós* to this world, Jamboree had been bringing joy to the jivers of Barcelona, with headline jazz and blues acts of the calibre of Chet Baker and Ella Fitzgerald. Nowadays, concerts usually start around 11pm, although 9pm sessions are also frequent, and after all the live stuff finishes at about 2am, Jamboree takes on a different hue, as a club. Sounds under the low arches range fairly inevitably from hip hop through funk to R&B.

CONCERT DE CARILLÓ

Classical Music & Opera

www.gencat.net/presidencia/carillo; Palau de la Generalitat, Plaça de Sant Jaume; admission free; ☾ noon first Sun of month Oct-Jul & 9pm various days in Jul; Ⓜ Jaume I

Some 5000kg of bronze in 49 bells (a carillon) swings into action for monthly 'concerts' in the seat of the Catalan government, allowing spectators a rare chance to get inside. In the pretty Gothic Pati dels Tarongers, an internal terrace lined with orange trees at the heart of the building, the audience is treated to a midday performance of just about anything, from classical through bossa nova, all with bells on. There are no reservations.

Sign for Jamboree

NEIL SETCHFIELD

GRAN TEATRE DEL LICEU
Classical Music & Opera

☎ 93 485 99 00; www.liceubarcelona.com;
La Rambla dels Caputxins 51-59; ⌚ box office
2-8.30pm Mon-Fri & 1hr before show Sat & Sun;
Ⓜ Liceu

Barcelona's grand old opera house, restored after fire in 1994, is one of the most technologically advanced theatres in the world. To take up a seat in the grand auditorium, returned to all its 19th-century glory but with the very latest in acoustic accoutrements, is to be transported to another age. Red plush seating and stage curtains stand in regal contrast to the glistering gold of the five tiers of boxes. Tickets can cost anything from €7 for a cheap seat behind a pillar to €200 plus for a well-positioned night at the opera.

SALA TARANTOS   Flamenco
☎ 93 319 17 89; www.masimas.net; Plaça
Reial 17; admission from €7; ⌚ performances
8.30pm, 9.30pm & 10.30pm daily; Ⓜ Liceu
Since 1963, this basement locale has been the stage for some of the best flamenco to pass through or come out of Barcelona.

You have to keep your eye on the place because top-class acts are not a daily diet. For lower-grade stuff, a half-hour *tablao* takes place three times a night.

TABLAO CORDOBÉS   Flamenco
☎ 93 317 57 11; www.tablaocordobes.com;
La Rambla 35; show €37, with dinner €60-68;
⌚ shows 8.15pm, 10pm & 11.30pm; Ⓜ Liceu
This *tablao* is typical of its genre and has been in business since 1970. Artists perform on a tiny hardwood stage with a vaulted backdrop that is supposed to make us think of Granada's El Alhambra. Generally, tourists book for the dinner and show, although you can skip the food and just come along for the performance (about 1¼ hours). Some great names have come through here, so it is not always cheese.

SHOPPING
A handful of interesting shops dot La Rambla, but the real fun starts inside the labyrinth. Young fashion on Carrer d'Avinyó, a mixed bag on Avinguda del Portal de l'Àngel, some cute old shops on

DIEGO LEZAMA

Sita Murt boutique

Carrer de la Dagueria and lots of exploring in tight old lanes awaits.

SALA PARÉS   Art
☎ 93 318 70 20; www.salapares.com; Carrer del Petritxol 5; Ⓜ Liceu

Picasso had works on sale here a century ago in what is one of the city's most venerable and still-dynamic private galleries. In business since 1877, the gallery has maintained its position as one of the city's leading purveyors of Catalan art, old and contemporary.

QUERA   Books
☎ 93 318 07 43; Carrer del Petritxol 2; ☾ 10am-8pm Tue, 10am-1.30pm & 4.30-8pm Wed-Sat; Ⓜ Liceu

Crammed into a tiny bookshop is a treasure trove of travel material, mostly on Catalonia and the Pyrenees. It specialises in maps and guides, including a host of stuff for walking, and has been in business since 1916.

VILLEGAS CERÀMICA   Ceramics
☎ 93 317 53 30; www.villegasceramica.net; Carrer Comtal 31; Ⓜ Urquinaona

For some curious ceramics that have nothing to do with traditional wares, poke your head in here. Arresting items include owl's-head clocks (in which the eyes move back and forth), pottery statues of stretched human figures, Barcelona taxis, ceramic wall-hangings and loads of other original items.

XOCOA   Chocolate
☎ 93 301 11 97; www.xocoa-bcn.com; Carrer del Petritxol 11-13; Ⓜ Liceu

Shield your eyes from the ultrabright rose-and-white decor and prepare yourself for a different kind of chocolate. Carefully arranged inside this den of dental devilry are ranks and ranks of original chocolate bars, chocolates stuffed with sweet stuff,

gooey pastries and more. It has eight other branches scattered about town.

LA CONDONERIA   Condoms
☎ 93 302 77 21; Plaça de Sant Josep Oriol 7; Ⓜ Liceu

Run out of kinky coloured condoms? Need a fresh batch of lubricant? Pick up these vital items and a host of bedside novelties and naughty bits here.

GOTHAM   Design
☎ 93 412 46 47; www.gotham-bcn.com; Carrer de Cervantes 7; Ⓜ Jaume I

Look back with fondness at the furniture and lights, which date back to at least the 1960s, and in some cases the '30s. Much of it is restored and given a bright, decorative once-over. Retro design freaks will fall in love with this place.

SITA MURT   Fashion
☎ 93 301 00 06; www.sitamurt.com; Carrer d'Avinyó 18; Ⓜ Liceu

A Catalan fashion company, Sita Murt produces light and sexy women's fashion for summer, and striding-out outfits for the girl about town in winter. Much of it is aimed at a night out rather than a day in the office.

URBANA   Fashion
☎ 93 269 09 20; Carrer d'Avinyó 46; ☾ 11am-3pm & 4.30-9pm Mon-Sat; Ⓜ Liceu

Colourful, fun city clothes, shoes and accessories await boys and girls in this easygoing store with Basque Country origins. It offers a variety of brands of urban threads, like Supremebeing, Rocketdog and Matilda.

ANTINOUS   Gay & Lesbian
☎ 93 301 90 70; www.antinouslibros.com, in Spanish; Carrer de Josep Anselm Clavé 6; Ⓜ Drassanes

Gay and lesbian travellers may want to browse in this spacious and relaxed gay bookshop, which also has a modest cafe out the back. This is the place for porn mags, postcards of muscle-bound fellows and an awful lot of highbrow lit on homosexual issues mixed in with rather lower-brow lit to groan to.

LE BOUDOIR   Lingerie & Erotica
☎ 93 302 52 81; www.leboudoir.net; Carrer de la Canuda 21; Ⓜ Catalunya
Need to spice up the bedroom situation? Stroll around this sensual shop, where anything from lacy, racy underwear to exuberant sex toys is available. Transparent handcuffs might be fun, or perhaps a bit of slap and tickle with a whip and mask?

EL INGENIO   Masks & Costumes
☎ 93 317 71 38; www.el-ingenio.com; Carrer d'en Rauric 6; Ⓜ Liceu
In this whimsical fantasy store you will discover giant Carnaval masks, costumes, theatrical accessories and other fun things. You can pick up some 'devil's batons' to do a little fiery juggling, a monocycle or clown make-up.

CASA BEETHOVEN   Music
☎ 93 301 48 26; La Rambla de Sant Josep 97; Ⓜ Liceu
This isn't any old sheet-music shop. In business since 1880 and with an air more of a museum than of a store, Casa Beethoven's customers have included Montserrat Caballé, Josep Carreras and Plácido Domingo. It keeps up with the times, however, and you're as likely to find music by Metallica as by Mozart. On Saturdays small concerts are sometimes held.

LA MANUAL ALPARGATERA   Shoes
☎ 93 301 01 72; www.lamanual.net; Carrer d'Avinyó 7; Ⓜ Liceu
The bright white shopfront is a local landmark. Everyone from the Pope to Michael Douglas has ordered a pair of *espadrilles* (rope-soled canvas shoes or sandals) from this store, which holds its own against Nike and co. It also does a line in sun hats and bags.

L'ARCA DE L'ÀVIA
Vintage Clothes & Accessories
☎ 93 302 15 98; Carrer dels Banys Nous 20; Ⓜ Liceu
Grandma's chest is indeed full of extraordinary remembrances from the past, when young ladies used to put together a trousseau of clothes and other items for their wedding. You might find anything from old silk kimonos to wedding dresses from the 1920s. Some items sold here wound up being used in the film *Titanic*.

EL RAVAL

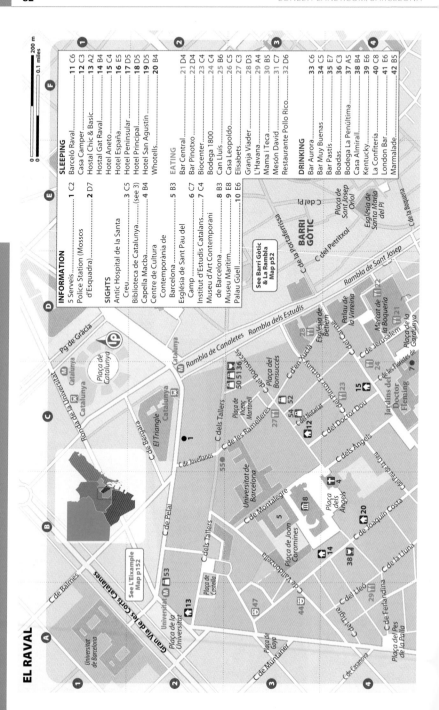

INFORMATION

5 Serveis.............................**1** C2
Police Station (Mossos
  d'Esquadra).....................**2** D7

SIGHTS

Antic Hospital de la Santa
  Creu................................**3** C5
Biblioteca de Catalunya.....(see 3)
Capella Macba....................**4** B4
Centre de Cultura
  Contemporània de
  Barcelona.........................**5** B3
Església de Sant Pau del
  Camp..............................**6** C7
Institut d'Estudis Catalans...**7** C4
Museu d'Art Contemporani
  de Barcelona.....................**8** B3
Museu Marítim...................**9** E8
Palau Güell.......................**10** E6

SLEEPING

Barceló Raval.....................**11** C6
Casa Camper.....................**12** C3
Hostal Chic & Basic............**13** A2
Hostal Gat Raval................**14** B4
Hotel Aneto......................**15** C4
Hotel España.....................**16** E5
Hotel Peninsular................**17** D5
Hotel Principal...................**18** D5
Hotel San Agustín..............**19** D5
Whotells............................**20** B4

EATING

Bar Central........................**21** D4
Bar Pinotxo.......................**22** D4
Biocenter..........................**23** C4
Bodega 1800......................**24** C4
Can Lluís...........................**25** B6
Casa Leopoldo...................**26** C5
Elisabets...........................**27** C3
Granja Viader.....................**28** D3
L'Havana...........................**29** A4
Mama i Teca......................**30** B5
Mesón David......................**31** C7
Restaurante Pollo Rico.........**32** D6

DRINKING

Bar Aurora.........................**33** C6
Bar Muy Buenas.................**34** C5
Bar Pastís..........................**35** E7
Boadas..............................**36** C3
Bodega La Penúltima...........**37** A5
Casa Almirall......................**38** B4
Kentucky...........................**39** E6
La Confitería......................**40** C8
London Bar........................**41** E6
Marmalade........................**42** B5

See Barri Gòtic & La Rambla p52

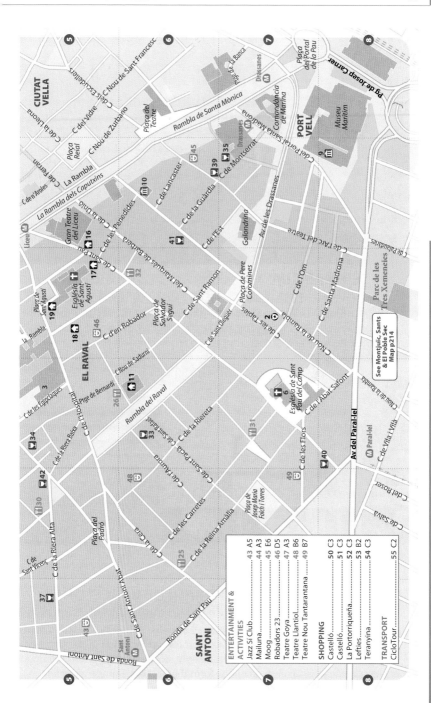

See Montjuïc, Sants & El Poble Sec Map p214

HIGHLIGHTS

1

⬐ MUSEU MARÍTIM

For a break from the art and architecture of the Ciutat Vella, dip into this snapshot of seafaring history. The Gothic Museu Marítim (p89) is more than the usual stash of naval ephemera – Barcelona is Europe's largest Mediterranean port, with a maritime legacy surpassed only by Venice's. Despite an ongoing sprucing-up campaign the museum retains its prize exhibit: a replica of a 16th-century Spanish flagship.

2

⬐ MUSEU D'ART CONTEMPORANI DE BARCELONA

Usually referred to by its acronym Macba, this modern museum (p91), set on Plaça de Ángels (a hangout for local skateboarders), is stuffed with over seven decades' worth of modern art. This is the place to view the cutting edge of the contemporary scene in rooms flooded with natural light, courtesy of huge south-facing windows. Catalan and Spanish paintings form the backbone of the collection.

EL RAVAL

HIGHLIGHTS

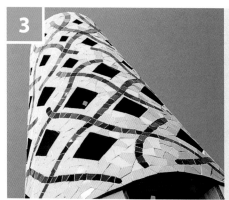

⇲ PALAU GÜELL

Mega-rich industrialist Eusebi Güell and Modernista architect Gaudí are as synonymous with Barcelona as they are with each other. This gilded **mansion** (p92), with its toadstool chimneys and gabled frontage, captures Gaudí in a youthful, less flamboyant incarnation. Art fiends flock here to gain an insight into a genius in the making.

⇲ BARS

Long infamous for its seedy nightlife and louche drinking holes, El Raval's abundant **bars** (p98) have been sanitised in recent years, replicating what happened in La Ribera's El Born district in the 1990s. Nonetheless, the neighbourhood still retains 'edge', along with enough grungy, open-all-night places to keep any Hemingway-emulating barfly happy for weeks.

⇲ ETHNIC FOOD

Sitting in one of the most exciting parts of town, El Raval's still-evolving **restaurant scene** (p95) is characterised by diverse ethnic make-up and a hungry army of students. To meet the local need, the district's traditional eating houses have been complemented in recent years by vegetarian self-service joints, juice bars and the odd classy candlelit nook.

2 BRENT WINEBRENNER; 3 MACBA., RAFAEL VARGAS, 2010; 4 & 5 NEIL SETCHFIELD; 6 PETER FORSBERG/ALAMY

1 Museu Marítim (p89); 2 Museu d'Art Contemporani de Barcelona (p91); 3 Roof detail, Palau Güell (p92); 4 London Bar (p100), El Raval district; 5 Outdoor restaurant in El Raval district

WINING & DINING WALKING TOUR

This nine-stop eating-and-drinking sojourn starts in L'Havana restaurant (a good lunch spot) and ends 2.5km later in the famous London Bar. In between you can survey snippets of Modernista architecture, grab the odd snack and indulge in a couple of beers or cocktails.

❶ L'HAVANA

A long way from the notorious food shortages of Cuba, L'Havana (p96) is actually a specialist Catalan restaurant that has been knocking out fine local food since the 1940s. You can load up for the impending walk with a meat- or fish-based lunch in a dining area flecked with Modernista embellishments.

❷ CASA ALMIRALL

Long run by the Almirall family, who opened it in the mid-19th century, this corner tavern (p99) on Carrer de Joaquín Costa preserves much of its Modernista decor, especially in the picture windows opening on to the street, and in the counter and display cabinet.

❸ MARMALADE

Another misleading name. Don't come expecting a British breakfast spread at Marmalade (p100). Instead, there is a trendy dark bar where cool people come to sip cocktails. Things getting kicking after 7pm-ish so it may be a question of logging the location and returning later.

❹ BAR MUY BUENAS

You'll recognise similarly sinuous curves as you enter Bar Muy Buenas (p98), on Carrer del Carme. Opened as a milk bar in the late 19th century, it retains much of its original decoration. It's a welcoming, cosy spot for a tipple and snacks.

❺ LA CONFITERÍA

On Carrer de Sant Pau, past the Romanesque church, drop by La Confitería (p100), once a barber shop and then confectioner's. It was lovingly restored for its reconversion into a bar in 1998. Most of the elements, including facade, bar counter and cabinets, are the real deal.

❻ RESTAURANT POLLO RICO

Hungry again already? Pollo Rico (p97) is good for its large but economically priced portions of chicken and chips served by waiters who know the meaning of 'quick service'. It's also a good place to listen into the local conversation and pick up what's happening at street level.

WINING & DINING WALKING TOUR

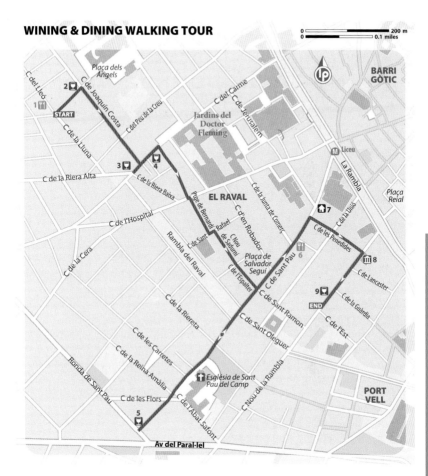

EL RAVAL

WINING & DINING WALKING TOUR

❼ HOTEL ESPAÑA

If you don't care for chicken, try the moderately priced Catalan fare at this recently renovated **hotel** (p94). The famous dining rooms are part of the 1903 design by Domènech i Montaner, and there is a magnificent alabaster fireplace designed by Eusebi Arnau.

❽ PALAU GÜELL

You should not miss El Raval's Modernista star and one of Gaudí's earlier big commissions, **Palau Güell** (p92).

❾ LONDON BAR

The **London Bar** (p100) displays Modernista decor and is run by the family of the waiter who founded it in 1910. In its heyday, it stayed open 24 hours and attracted the likes of Picasso and Miró for countless swift beers.

EL RAVAL

BEST...

BEST...

⇘ WATERING HOLES

- **London Bar** (p100) Erstwhile Picasso and Miró hangout.
- **Antic Hospital de la Santa Creu** (p90) Studenty bar in a tropical garden.
- **Carrer de Sant Pau** (p98) Energetic street in Raval's edgiest neighbourhood.
- **Jazz Sí Club** (p100) Jamming musician's workshop.
- **Boadas** (p99) Opened by the man who invented the daiquirí.

⇘ MUSEUMS

- **Museu Marítim** (p89) Seafaring museum in Gothic shipyards.
- **Museu del Llibre Frederic Marès** (p90) Library inside Antic Hospital de la Santa Creu.
- **Museu d'Art Contemporani de Barcelona** (p91) Modern art in postmodern building.
- **Casa de Convalescència de Sant Pau** (p91) Hospice that operated from the 17th to the 20th century.
- **Capella Macba** (p91) Contemporary art in a Gothic chapel.

⇘ CATALAN EATERIES

- **Granja Viader** (p98) Bar-deli renowned for its hot chocolate.
- **Elisabets** (p96) No-nonsense neighbourhood nosh.
- **Mama i Teca** (p96) Local cod and steak place.
- **L'Havana** (p96) No Cuban food, just Catalan classics.
- **Casa Leopoldo** (p96) Featured in the novels of Manuel Vázquez Montalbán.

⇘ ODD STUFF

- **Kentucky** (p99) American kitsch bar.
- **Teatre Llantiol** (p101) Off-the-wall Brit-inspired performances.
- **Teranyina** (p102) Textile workshop with loom courses.
- **Biocenter** (p98) Top restaurant in veggie eat-street.
- **Palau Güell** (p92) Flamboyant Gaudí creation.

DISCOVER EL RAVAL

El Raval (and especially its lower half, known as the Barri Xinès, or Chinese Quarter, an odd name that means 'red-light district') was long an old-city slum and all-round louche quarter. To some extent it still is. It is doubtless the most colourful of the three Ciutat Vella (Old City) districts, home to a strong migrant community (mostly Pakistanis and North Africans) and still a haunt for down-and-outs, prostitutes and the occasional drug dealer. At the same time, the opening of the Macba contemporary art gallery, CCCB cultural centre, and enormous philosophy and history faculties of the Universitat de Barcelona have injected new life. New housing has gone up around La Rambla del Raval, where a luxury hotel is also nearing completion.

The massive arrival of local students and tourists has further transformed the district. Classic bars and restaurants have been joined by all manner of sparkling new places, some snooty, some grungy. Awaiting discovery are a Romanesque church and one of Gaudí's early commissions.

SIGHTS

MUSEU MARÍTIM

☎ 93 342 99 20; www.mmb.cat; Avinguda de les Drassanes; adult/under 7yr/senior & student €2.50/free/1.25, 3-8pm Sun free; ☺ 10am-8pm; Ⓜ Drassanes; ☞

Venice had its Arsenal and Barcelona the Reials Drassanes (Royal Shipyards), from which Don Juan of Austria's flagship galley was launched to lead a joint Spanish-Venetian fleet into the momentous Battle of Lepanto against the Turks in 1571.

These mighty Gothic shipyards are not as extensive as their Venetian counterparts but they're an extraordinary piece of civilian architecture nonetheless. Today the broad arches shelter the Museu Marítim, the city's seafaring-history museum and one of the most fascinating museums in town.

Barcelona's shipyards were, in their heyday, among the greatest in Europe. Begun in the 13th century and completed by 1378, the long, arched bays (the highest arches reach 13m) once sloped off as slipways directly into the water, which lapped the seaward side of the Drassanes until at least the end of the 18th century.

The centre of the shipyards is dominated by a full-sized replica (made in the 1970s) of Don Juan of Austria's flagship. A clever audiovisual display aboard the vessel brings to life the ghastly existence of the slaves, prisoners and volunteers (!) who at full steam could haul this vessel along at 9 knots. They remained chained to their seats, four to an oar, at all times. Here they worked, drank (fresh water was stored below decks, where the infirmary was also located), ate, slept and went to the loo.

Fishing vessels, old navigation charts, models and dioramas of the Barcelona waterfront make up the rest of this engaging museum. The museum was being largely overhauled at the time of writing. While this work continues, only Don Juan's flagship and a limited selection of the museum's objects can be seen.

ANTIC HOSPITAL DE LA SANTA CREU

☎ 93 270 23 00; www.bnc.cat; Carrer de l'Hospital 56; Ⓜ Liceu

Behind the Mercat de la Boqueria stands what was, in the 15th century, the city's main hospital. The restored Antic Hospital de la Santa Creu (Former Holy Cross Hospital) today houses the **Biblioteca de Catalunya** (Library of Catalonia; admission free; ☿ 9am-8pm Mon-Fri, 9am-2pm Sat), as well as the **Institut d'Estudis Catalans** (Institute for Catalan Studies).

The library is the single most complete collection of documents (estimated at around three million) tracing the region's long history. The hospital, which was begun in 1401 and functioned until the 1930s, was considered one of the best in Europe in its medieval heyday.

Entering from Carrer de l'Hospital, you find yourself in a delightfully bedraggled, vaguely tropical garden that is home to bums, earnest students on a break and a cheerful **bar-cafe**. Off the garden lies the entrance to the prestigious Massana conservatorium and, up a sweep of stairs, the library. You can freely visit the most impressive part, the grand reading rooms beneath broad Gothic stone arches, where you can also see temporary displays of anything from old records to medieval monastic hymnals.

Otherwise, it is possible to join a tour on 23 April (Sant Jordi) and one day late in September (the date changes), when the entire building throws itself open for guided visits.

The guided visit takes you through the library's public areas and others usually closed to the public, such as the **Museu del Llibre Frederic Marès**, a former private ward in the hospital, whose bright tile decoration of the stations of the cross was done in the 17th century. Marès donated 1500 documents and books to the library, some of which are on display. Antoni Gaudí wound up in the Via Crucis ward in 1926 after being run over by a tram; he died here.

As you are approaching the complex down a narrow lane from Carrer del Carme or, alternatively, from Jardins del Doctor Fleming (the little park with swings), you

KRZYSZTOF DYDYNSKI

The church of the Antic Hospital de la Santa Creu

EL RAVAL

RICHARD CUMMINS

La Ola, by Jorge Oteiza, at the Museu d'Art Contemporani de Barcelona

SIGHTS

🡢 MUSEU D'ART CONTEMPORANI DE BARCELONA

The ground and 1st floors of this great white bastion of contemporary art are generally given over to exhibitions from the gallery's own collections (some 3000 pieces centred on three periods: post-WWII; around 1968; and the years since the fall of the Berlin wall in 1989, right up until the present day). You may see works by Antoni Tàpies, Joan Brossa, Paul Klee, Miquel Barceló and a whole raft of international talent, depending on the theme(s) of the ever-changing exposition. The gallery also presents temporary visiting exhibitions and has an extensive art bookshop. Outside, the spectacle is as intriguing as inside. While skateboarders dominate the space south of the museum (considered one of Europe's great skateboard locations), you may well find Pakistani kids enjoying a game of cricket in Plaça de Joan Coromines.

Across the main skateboard-infested square, the renovated 400-year-old Convent dels Àngels houses the Capella Macba, where the Macba regularly rotates selections from its permanent collection. The Gothic framework of the one-time convent-church remains intact.

Things you need to know: Museu d'Art Contemporani de Barcelona (Macba; ☎ 93 412 08 10; www.macba.cat; Plaça dels Àngels 1; adult/concession €7.50/6; 🕙 11am-8pm Mon & Wed, 11am-midnight Thu & Fri, 10am-8pm Sat, 10am-3pm Sun & holidays late Jun-late Sep, 11am-7.30pm Mon & Wed-Fri, 10am-8pm Sat, 10am-3pm Sun & holidays late Sep-late Jun; Ⓜ Universitat); Capella Macba (Plaça dels Àngels; Ⓜ Universitat)

arrive at the entrance to the institute, which sometimes opens its doors for expositions. If it happens to be open, wander into what was once the 17th-century Casa de Convalescència de Sant Pau, which housed recovering patients from the hospital. At first, it was host to just seven men and five women. By the end of the 17th century, there were 200 beds and 400 mattresses. In addition to this, patients received meat and desserts (which is more than many might have hoped for outside). The hospice operated until the early 20th century. The building, which centres on a cloister, is richly decorated with ceramics (especially the entrance vestibule).

PALAU GÜELL
☎ 93 317 39 74; www.palauguell.cat; Carrer Nou de la Rambla 3-5; admission free; ☼ 10am-2.30pm Tue-Sat; Ⓜ Drassanes

Welcome to the early days of Gaudí's fevered architectural imagination. This extraordinary Modernista mansion, one of the few major buildings of that era raised in Ciutat Vella, gives an insight into its maker's prodigious genius. He built it just off La Rambla in the late 1880s for his wealthy and faithful patron, the industrialist Eusebi Güell. Although a little sombre compared with some of his later whims, it is still a characteristic riot of styles (Gothic, Islamic, art nouveau) and materials. After the civil war, the police occupied it and tortured political prisoners in the basement.

Up two floors are the main hall and its annexes (closed for renovation at the time of writing). The hall is a parabolic pyramid – each wall an arch stretching up three floors and coming together to form a dome. The roof is a mad Gaudíesque tumult of tiled colour and fanciful design in the building's chimney pots.

Picasso – who, incidentally, hated Gaudí's work – began his Blue Period in 1902 in a studio across the street at Carrer Nou de la Rambla 10. Begging to differ with Señor Picasso, Unesco declared the Palau, together with Gaudí's other main works (La Sagrada Família, p161; Casa Batlló, p165; La Pedrera, p163; Park Güell, p195; Casa Vicens; and Colònia Güell crypt, p230) a World Heritage Site.

The ground floor and basement reopened to the public in early 2008 after renovation. When the rest will open is unclear.

ESGLÉSIA DE SANT PAU DEL CAMP
☎ 93 441 00 01; Carrer de Sant Pau 101; admission free; ☼ cloister 10am-1pm & 4-7pm Mon-Sat; Ⓜ Paral·llel

Back in the 9th century, when monks founded the monastery of Sant Pau del Camp (St Paul in the Fields), it was a good walk from the city gates amid fields and gardens. Today, the church and cloister, erected in the 12th century and partly surrounded by the trees of a small garden, are located on a fairly down-at-heel street and surrounded by dense inner-city housing. The church's doorway bears rare Visigothic sculptural decoration, predating the Muslim invasion of Spain.

SLEEPING

You're right in the thick of things when staying in this mildly wild side of the old town. Accommodation options are broad, from fleapits on dodgy lanes through to the latest in designer comfort.

CASA CAMPER   Design Hotel €€€
☎ 93 342 62 80; www.casacamper.com; Carrer d'Elisabets 11; s/d €228/255; Ⓜ Liceu; ✗ ⊠ ⌨

An original designer hotel in the middle of El Raval, Casa Camper belongs to the Mallorcan shoe company of the same name. The massive foyer looks more like a contemporary art museum entrance, but the rooms are the real surprise. Slip into your Camper slippers and contemplate the Vinçon furniture. Across the corridor from your room (which faces hanging gardens) is a separate, private sitting room with balcony, TV and hammock. You can contemplate the city from the rooftop.

WHOTELLS
Hostal €€

☎ 93 443 08 34; www.whotells.com; Carrer de Joaquín Costa 28; apt from €230; Ⓜ Universitat;

Decked out with Muji furniture and very comfortable, these apartments can sleep four to six people and give a sense of being at home away from home. Prices fluctuate enormously in response to demand. Cook up a storm in the kitchen with products bought in the nearby La Boqueria market, or flop in front of the

LCD TV. They have other apartment buildings in L'Eixample and La Barceloneta.

BARCELÓ RAVAL
Design Hotel €€

☎ 93 320 14 90; www.barceloraval.com; Rambla del Raval 17-21; d €150-210; Ⓜ Liceu;

As part of the city's plans to pull up the El Raval district's bootstraps, this oval-shaped designer hotel tower makes a 21st-century splash. The rooftop terrace offers fabulous views and the B-Lounge bar-restaurant is the toast of the town for meals and cocktails. Three classes of room all offer slick appearance (lots of white

EL RAVAL

SLEEPING

KAS/IMAGE BROKER

Centre de Cultura Contemporània de Barcelona

◤ IF YOU LIKE...

If you like the deft artwork at the Museu d'Art Contemporani de Barcelona (p91), you'll also appreciate the exhibitions at the Centre de Cultura Contemporània de Barcelona (CCCB; ☎ 93 306 41 00; www.cccb.org; Carrer de Montalegre 5; 2 exhibitions adult/under 16yr/senior & student €6/free/4.50, 1 exhibition €4.50/free/3.40, free 1st Wed of month, 8-10pm Thu, 3-8pm Sun; ⏲ 11am-8pm Tue, Wed & Fri-Sun, 11am-10pm Thu; Ⓜ Universitat).

This complex of auditoriums, exhibition spaces and conference halls opened in 1994 in what had been the former 18th-century Casa de la Caritat hospice. The courtyard alone, with its vast glass wall on one side, is spectacular. Behind the front facade there is 4500 sq metres of exhibition space hosting a constantly changing program of exhibitions and events.

NEIL SETCHFIELD

Cloister of the Església de Sant Pau del Camp (p92)

and contrasting lime greens or ruby-red splashes of colour), Nespresso machine and iPod loaders.

HOTEL SAN AGUSTÍN · Hotel €€

☎ 93 318 16 58; www.hotelsa.com; Plaça de Sant Agustí 3; s €123-144, d €171; Ⓜ Liceu; ✖ 🖥 🛜
This former 18th-century monastery opened as a hotel in 1840, making it the city's oldest (it's undergone various refits since then!). The location is perfect – a quick stroll off La Rambla on a curious square. Rooms sparkle, and are mostly spacious and light-filled. Consider an attic double (€134) with sloping ceiling and bird's-eye views.

HOTEL PRINCIPAL · Hotel €€

☎ 93 318 89 70; www.hotelprincipal.es; Carrer de la Junta del Comerç 8-12; s/d/tr €105/120/160; Ⓜ Liceu; Ⓟ ✖ 🖥 🛜
This hotel has clean-lined rooms complete with parquet floors, hairdryers and original art depicting Barcelona. All 110 rooms, spread across three adjoining buildings, have double glazing and flat-screen TVs, and you can sink into a deckchair to sun-

bathe on the roof. For €170, it has a big room with private terrace.

HOTEL ESPAÑA · Hotel €€

☎ 93 318 17 58; www.hotelespanya.com; Carrer de Sant Pau 9-11; s €96, d €118-145; Ⓜ Liceu; ✖
Best known for its eccentric Modernista restaurants, in which architect Domènech i Montaner, sculptor Eusebi Arnau and painter Ramón Casas had a hand, this hotel has been given an overhaul and offers clean, straighforward rooms in a building that still manages to ooze a little history. In the 1920s it was a favourite with bullfighters.

HOSTAL CHIC & BASIC · Hostal €€

☎ 93 302 51 83; www.chicandbasic.com; Carrer de Tallers 82; s €60, d €93-114; Ⓜ Universitat; ✖ 🖥
The theme colour is predominantly white, with exceptions like the screaming orange fridge in the communal kitchen and chill-and-basic area where you can make yourself a cuppa or sandwich. Rooms are also themed lily white, from the floors to the sheets. Finishing touches

include the plasma-screen TVs and the option of plugging your iPod or MP3 player into your room's sound system. The street can get noisy.

HOSTAL GAT RAVAL
Hostal €€

☎ 93 481 66 70; www.gataccommodation.com; Carrer de Joaquín Costa 44; d €82, s/d without bathroom €58/74; Ⓜ Universitat; ⊠ 🖳 🛜
There's pea-green and lemon-lime decor in this hip 2nd-floor *hostal* located on a bar-lined lane dominated by resident migrants and wandering bands of uni students. The individual rooms are pleasant and secure, but only some have private bathrooms. The staff also run the more upmarket **Hostal Gat Xino** (☎ 93 324 88 33; www.gataccommodation.com; Carrer de l'Hospital 149-155; s/d/ste with terrace €80/115/140; Ⓜ Liceu; ⊠ 🖳 🛜) nearby.

HOTEL PENINSULAR
Hotel €€

☎ 93 302 31 38; www.hpeninsular.com; Carrer de Sant Pau 34; s/d €55/78; Ⓜ Liceu; ⊠ 🖳 🛜
An oasis on the edge of the slightly dicey Barri Xinès, this former convent (which was connected by tunnel to the Església de Sant Agustí) has a plant-draped atrium extending its height and most of its length. The 60 rooms are simple, with tiled floors and whitewash, but mostly spacious and well-kept. There is wi-fi throughout.

HOTEL ANETO
Hotel €

☎ 93 301 99 89; www.hotelaneto.com; Carrer del Carme 38; s/d €45/65; Ⓜ Liceu; ⊠
This budget bargain is in a handy spot on one of the more attractive streets of El Raval's upper half. The best of the 15 rooms are the doubles with the shuttered balconies looking on to the street.

EATING

For contrast alone, El Raval is possibly the most interesting part of the old town. Timeless classics of Barcelona dining are scattered across what was long the old city's poorest *barri* (neighbourhood), and since the late 1990s, battalions of hip new eateries have also sprung up,

GUY MOBERLY

Restaurante Pollo Rico (p97)

especially in the area around the Museu d'Art Contemporani. Some of the cheapest eats in town, full of character, lurk along El Raval's streets. From Carrer de Sant Pau north towards Carrer de Pelai, the university and Ronda de Sant Antoni is where you'll find most of these haunts.

CASA LEOPOLDO   Catalan €€

☎ 93 441 30 14; www.casaleopoldo.com; Carrer de Sant Rafael 24; meals €60; ⏰ lunch & dinner Tue-Sat, lunch Sun Sep-Jul, closed Easter; Ⓜ Liceu; ✕

Long hidden in the slum alleys of El Raval, this was writer Manuel Vázquez Montalbán's favourite restaurant; it figures constantly in the urban wanderings of his detective character, Pepe Carvalho. Several rambling dining areas in this 1929 classic have magnificent tiled walls and exposed beam ceilings. The mostly seafood menu is extensive and the wine list strong.

CAN LLUÍS   Catalan €€

☎ 93 441 11 87; Carrer de la Cera 49; meals €30-35; ⏰ Mon-Sat Sep-Jul; Ⓜ Sant Antoni

Three generations have kept this spick and span old-time classic in business since 1929. Beneath the olive-green beams in the back dining room you can see the spot where an anarchist's bomb went off in 1946, killing the then owner. Expect fresh fish and seafood. The llenguado (sole) is oven cooked in whisky and raisins.

BODEGA 1800   Catalan €€

☎ 93 317 30 79; http://bodega1800.com; Carrer del Carme 31; meals €25-30; ⏰ daily; Ⓜ Liceu

Ricardo loves nothing better than to come up with a new canapé or other delicious, bite-sized snack to offer his tippling guests. He has converted an old wine store into a charming wine bar. Linger at the casks inside his little bottle-lined establishment or in the adjacent arcade and be guided through snack and wine suggestions. Wine, no matter which one you want, goes for €2.50 a glass and snacks €3.50 a pop.

L'HAVANA   Catalan €€

☎ 93 302 21 06; Carrer del Lleó 1; meals €25-30; ⏰ lunch & dinner Tue-Sat, lunch Sun; Ⓜ Sant Antoni

Little has changed in this cavernous, family-run place since it opened in the 1940s. The front dining area, with frosted glass windows, Modernista design touches and spaciously spread tables, is a touch more severe than the better-lit rear area. A great starter is the combinat, with three mussels, a smidge of amanida russa (potato salad), esqueixada and more. Meat and fish options follow, and the calamars farcits (stuffed calamari) are filling. Round off with homemade crema catalana.

MAMA I TECA   Catalan €€

☎ 93 441 33 35; Carrer de la Lluna 4; meals €25-30; ⏰ lunch & dinner Sun-Mon & Wed-Fri, dinner Sat; Ⓜ Sant Antoni

A tiny place with half a dozen tables, Mama i Teca is more a lifestyle than a restaurant. The setting is a multicultural and often rowdy street deep in El Raval. Locals drop in and hang about for a drink, and diners are treated to Catalan treats served without rush. How about bacallà al traginer (cod deep fried in olive oil with garlic and red pepper) or a juicy sirloin steak?

ELISABETS   Catalan €€

☎ 93 317 58 26; Carrer d'Elisabets 2-4; meals €20-25; ⏰ Mon-Sat Sep-Jul; Ⓜ Catalunya

This unassuming restaurant is popular for no-nonsense local fare. The walls are lined with old radio sets and the menú del día (€10.75) varies daily. If you prefer a la carta, try the ragú de jabalí (wild boar stew) and finish with *mel i mató*. Those with a late hunger on Friday nights can probably get a meal here as late as 1am.

BAR CENTRAL
Tapas €

☎ 93 301 10 98; Mercat de la Boqueria; meals €20; lunch Mon-Sat; M Liceu

Hiding out towards the back area of Barcelona's best-known market is this fabulously chaotic lunchtime bar. Marketeers, local workers and the occasional curious tourist jostle for a stool – get there early or be prepared to wait. Order a few generous *raciones*, and make one of them the grilled fish of the day.

BAR PINOTXO
Tapas €

☎ 93 317 17 31; Mercat de la Boqueria; meals €20; 6am-5pm Mon-Sat Sep-Jul; M Liceu

Of the half-dozen or so tapas bars and informal eateries within the market, this one near the La Rambla entrance is about the most popular. Roll up to the bar and enjoy the people-watching as you munch on tapas assembled from the products on sale in the stalls around you.

MESÓN DAVID
Spanish €

☎ 93 441 59 34; Carrer de les Carretes 63; meals €15-20, menú del día €8.50; Tue-Sun; M Paral·lel

With its smoky timber ceiling, excitable waiting staff and generally chaotic feel, this is a tavern the likes of which they don't make any more – a slice of the old Spain. Plonk yourself down on a bench for gregarious dining, such as house specialities *caldo gallego* (sausage broth), and the main course of *lechazo al horno* (a great clump of oven-roasted suckling lamb for €8.90).

RESTAURANTE POLLO RICO
Spanish €

☎ 93 441 31 84; Carrer de Sant Pau 31; meals €15-20; daily; M Liceu;

The 'Tasty Chicken' is true to its name, with fast, cheap, abundant grub. Head upstairs and carve out a space amid the garrulous punters, then rattle off your order to a high-speed waiter. Chicken (quarter chicken and chips costs €4), meat and various other options can be put together to help you fill to bursting. Skip the paella.

EL RAVAL

EATING

DIEGO LEZAMA

Elisabets

EL RAVAL

BIOCENTER
Vegetarian €

☎ 93 301 45 83; http://restaurantebiocenter.es; Carrer del Pintor Fortuny 25; meals €10-15; ⏲ lunch & dinner Mon-Sat, lunch Sun; Ⓜ Catalunya; ☒ 🛜

Head past the coffee bar and the dining area, with its warm exposed brickwork and dark wooden tables, to the kitchen at the back to order your *menú del día* (€9.75 plus drink). A huge *plat combinat* (single dish with several portions) costs €7.95. Top up with as much salad as you can handle. This is one of several options on what has become a bit of a vegetarian street.

GRANJA VIADER
Cafe €

☎ 93 318 34 86; Carrer d'en Xuclà 4; ⏲ 9am-1.45pm & 5-8.45pm Tue-Sat, 5-8.45pm Mon; Ⓜ Liceu

For more than a century, people have flocked down this alley to get to the cups of homemade hot chocolate and whipped cream (ask for a *suís*) ladled out in this classic Catalan-style milk bar-cum-deli. Together with one of the many pastries on display, the offerings here make for the sweet tooth's ideal breakfast. The Viader clan invented Cacaolat, a forerunner of kids' powdered-chocolate beverages.

DRINKING

DRINKING

What happened in the El Born area in the mid-1990s is slowly happening here now – new bars and clubs are opening along the long, slummy alleys. Beside them, some great old harbour-style taverns still thrive – dark, wood panelled and bare except for the odd mirror and vast arrays of bottles behind the bar. Unlike El Born, the lower end of El Raval has a long history of dodginess and the area

around Carrer de Sant Pau retains its edgy feel: drug dealers, pickpockets and prostitutes mingling with the streams of nocturnal hedonists.

BAR AURORA
Bar

☎ 635 902454; Carrer de l'Aurora 7; ⏲ 8am-2.30am Mon-Thu, 8am-3am Fri & Sat, 3pm-midnight Sun; Ⓜ Sant Antoni

Once a dark and crowded early opener, the Aurora has morphed under Italian management into a cheery, laid-back multicoloured spot. Set over a couple of floors with variegated lighting, low music and a good vibe, this place is worth wandering just off the Rambla del Raval as you search for beer or a mixed drink.

BAR MUY BUENAS
Bar

☎ 93 442 50 53; Carrer del Carme 63; ⏲ 9am-2am Mon-Thu, 9am-3am Fri & Sat, 7pm-2am Sun; Ⓜ Liceu

This bar started life as a late-19th-century corner store. The Modernista decor and relaxed company make this a great spot for a quiet mojito. You may catch a little live music or even a poetry reading, and can nibble on a limited menu of Middle Eastern titbits.

BAR PASTÍS
Bar

☎ 93 318 79 80; www.barpastis.com; Carrer de Santa Mònica 4; ⏲ 7.30pm-2am Sun-Fri, 7.30pm-3am Sat; Ⓜ Drassanes

A French cabaret theme (with lots of Piaf in the background) dominates this tiny, cluttered classic. It's been going, on and off, since the end of WWII. You'll need to be in before 9pm to have a hope of sitting, getting near the bar or anything much else. On some nights it features live acts, usually performing French chansons. Tuesday night is Tango night.

BOADAS
Bar

☎ 93 318 88 26; Carrer dels Tallers 1; ⏱ noon-2am Mon-Thu, noon-3am Fri & Sat; Ⓜ Catalunya

One of the city's oldest cocktail bars, Boadas is famed for its daiquiris. The bow-tied waiters have been serving unique drinkable creations since Miguel Boadas opened it in 1933. Miguel was born in Havana, where he was the first bartender at the immortal La Floridita. Boadas specialises in short, intense drinks, such as the house special, the sweetish Boadas, with rum, Dubonnet and curaçao. Joan Miró and Hemingway drank here.

BODEGA LA PENÚLTIMA
Bar

Carrer de la Riera Alta 40; ⏱ 7pm-2am Tue-Thu, 7pm-3am Fri & Sat, 7pm-1am Sun; Ⓜ Sant Antoni

There is a baroque semidarkness about this dark timber and sunset-yellow place, which gives off airs of an old-time wine bar. In Spanish lore, one never drinks *la última* (the last one) as it is bad luck. Rather, it is always the 'second last' *(penúltima)* round. A mixed group crowds into the lumpy lounges around uneven tables at the back or huddles at the bar for endless second-last rounds of wine, beer or cocktails.

CASA ALMIRALL
Bar

☎ 93 318 99 17; Carrer de Joaquín Costa 33; ⏱ 5.30pm-2.30am Sun-Thu, 7pm-3am Fri & Sat; Ⓜ Universitat

In business since the 1860s, this unchanged corner bar is dark and intriguing, with Modernista decor and a mixed clientele. There are some great original pieces in here, like the marble counter, and the cast-iron statue of the muse of the Universal Exposition, held in Barcelona in 1888.

KENTUCKY
Bar

☎ 93 318 28 78; Carrer de l'Arc del Teatre 11; ⏱ 10pm-3am Tue-Sat; Ⓜ Liceu

A haunt of visiting US Navy boys, this exercise in smoke-filled Americana kitsch is the perfect way to finish an evening – if you can squeeze in. All sorts of odd bods from the *barri* and beyond gather. An institution in the wee hours, this place often stays open as late as 5am.

KRZYSZTOF DYDYNSKI

Bar Muy Buenas

LA CONFITERÍA — Bar

☎ 93 443 04 58; Carrer de Sant Pau 128;
🕑 11am-2am; Ⓜ Paral·lel

This is a trip into the 19th century. Until the 1980s it was a confectioner's shop, and although the original cabinets are now lined with booze, the look of the place has barely changed in its conversion into a laid-back bar. A quiet enough spot for a house *vermut* (€3; add your own soda) in the early evening, it fills with theatregoers and partiers later at night.

LONDON BAR — Bar

☎ 93 318 52 61; Carrer Nou de la Rambla 34-36;
🕑 7.30pm-4am Tue-Sun; Ⓜ Liceu

Open since 1909, this Modernista bar started as a hang-out for circus hands and was later frequented by the likes of Picasso, Miró and Hemingway (didn't they have any work to do?). As popular as it was in Picasso's time, this place fills to the brim with punters at the long front bar and rickety old tables. On occasion, you can attend concerts at the small stage right up the back.

MARMALADE — Bar

☎ 93 442 39 66; www.marmaladebarcelona
.com; Carrer de la Riera Alta 4-6; 🕑 7pm-3am;
Ⓜ Sant Antoni

From the street you can see the golden hues of the backlit bar way down the end of a long lounge-lined passageway. To the left of the bar by a bare brick wall is a pool table, popular but somehow out of place in this chic, ill-lit chill den (with attached restaurant). Happy hour (cocktails for €4) is from 7pm to 9pm.

ENTERTAINMENT & ACTIVITIES

MOOG — Club

☎ 93 301 72 82; www.masimas.com/moog;
Carrer de l'Arc del Teatre 3; admission €10;
🕑 midnight-5am; Ⓜ Drassanes

This fun and minuscule club is a standing favourite with the downtown crowd. In the main dance area, DJs dish out house, techno and electro, while upstairs you can groove to a nice blend of indie and occasional classic-pop throwbacks.

DIEGO LEZAMA

Moog

EL RAVAL

ENTERTAINMENT & ACTIVITIES

JAZZ SÍ CLUB
Live Music

☎ 93 329 00 20; www.tallerdemusics.com; Carrer de Requesens 2; admission €5-8; ☼ 6-11pm; Ⓜ Sant Antoni

A cramped little bar run by the Taller de Músics (Musicians' Workshop) serves as the stage for a varied program of jazz through to some good flamenco (Friday nights). Thursday night is Cuban night, Sunday is rock and the rest are devoted to jazz and/or blues sessions. It makes for a mellow start to a long night in El Raval. Concerts start around 9pm but the jam sessions can get going as early as 6.30pm.

ROBADORS 23
Live Music

Carrer d'en Robador 23; ☼ music from 8.30pm Wed; Ⓜ Liceu

On what remains a classic dodgy El Raval street, where a hardy band of streetwalkers, junkies and other misfits hangs out in spite of all the work being carried out to gentrify the area, a narrow little bar has made a name for itself with its Wednesday night gigs. Jazz is the name of the game and the free concerts start at 8.30pm. You'll want to get there earlier for a spot.

TEATRE GOYA
Theatre

☎ 93 343 53 23; www.teatregoya.cat; Carrer de Joaquín Costa 68; admission €23-30; ☼ box office 5.30pm to start of show; Ⓜ Sant Antoni

A classic stage that long had its shutters down, the Goya was reopened to much fanfare in 2009. The program is generally mid- to highbrow, complementing partner theatre, the Teatre Romea. Among the first pieces shown (in Catalan), were Oscar Wilde's *An Ideal Husband* and David Mamet's *November*.

TEATRE LLANTIOL
Theatre

☎ 93 329 90 09; www.llantiol.com; Carrer de la Riereta 7; admission €6-10; Ⓜ Sant Antoni

At this curious place in El Raval all sorts of odd stuff, from concerts and ballads to magic shows, is staged. On Saturdays at 12.30am there is a regular cabaret-variety slot, a bit of a throwback to another era. About once a month you can see stand-up comedy in English here too. Check out the **Giggling Guiri** (www.comedyinspain.com) program for upcoming acts, mostly from the UK. For other occasional UK stand-up comedy acts, keep an eye on www.gloungebcn.com.

TEATRE NOU TANTARANTANA
Theatre

☎ 93 441 70 22; www.tantarantana.com; Carrer de les Flors 22; ☼ box office 1hr before show; Ⓜ Paral·lel

Apart from staging all sorts of contemporary and experimental drama (anything from Harold Pinter to local creations), this cosy theatre (which has room for about 150 spectators) also has a kids' program, including pantomime and puppets. These shows tend to start at 6pm (noon on Sundays). The adult theatre productions are at 9pm Wednesday to Saturday, and 7pm Sunday.

MAILUNA
Spas & Massage

☎ 93 301 20 02; www.mailuna.net, in Spanish; Carrer de Valldonzella 48; 1hr massage €55; ☼ 5-11.30pm Mon, 1-11.30pm Tue-Sat; Ⓜ Universitat

Mailuna is a bit of a wellness universe. Not only does it offer all sorts of massages (Ayurvedic, Swedish, Thai and more), it's also a restaurant, aromatherapy setting, wellness goods store and more. Stop for tea and you'll feel better already.

SHOPPING

The area boasts a handful of art galleries around the Macba, along with a burgeoning secondhand and vintage clothes scene on Carrer de la Riera Baixa. Carrer dels Tallers is one of the city's main music strips.

LA PORTORRIQUEÑA   Coffee
☎ 93 317 34 38; Carrer d'en Xuclà 25;
Ⓜ Catalunya

Coffee beans from around the world, freshly ground before your eyes, has been the winning formula in this store since 1902. It also offers all sorts of chocolate goodies. The street is good for little old-fashioned food boutiques.

LEFTIES   Fashion
☎ 93 317 50 70; Carrer de Pelai 2; ⏲ 10am-9.30pm Mon-Sat; Ⓜ Universitat

Don't mind being seen in last year's Zara fashions? Lefties (ie leftovers) could be the browsing spot for you, with men's, women's and kids' cast-offs from the previous year at silly prices. You could fill a wardrobe with perfectly good middle-of-the-road threads and your bank manager would be none the wiser.

CASTELLÓ   Music
☎ 93 318 20 41; Carrer dels Tallers 3 & 7;
Ⓜ Catalunya

These two shops are part of a large family business that has been going since 1935 and which is said to account for a fifth of the retail record business in Catalonia.

TERANYINA   Textiles
☎ 93 317 94 36; Carrer del Notariat 10;
Ⓜ Catalunya

Artist Teresa Rosa Aguayo runs this textile workshop in the heart of the artsy bit of El Raval. You can join courses at the loom, admire some of the rugs and other works that Teresa has created and, of course, buy them.

LA RIBERA

LA RIBERA

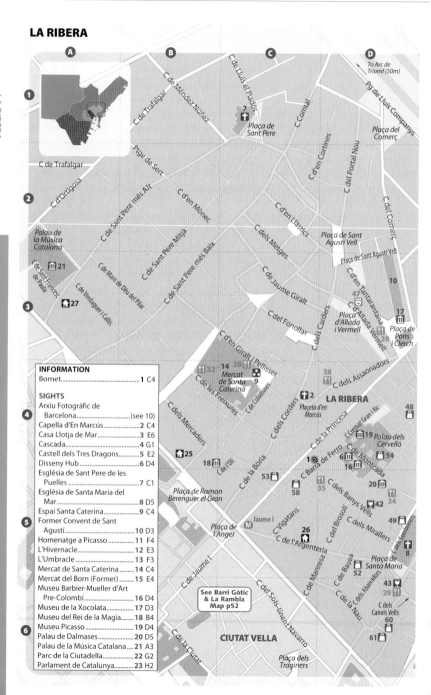

INFORMATION
Bornet..................................1 C4

SIGHTS
Arxiu Fotogràfic de
  Barcelona...........................(see 10)
Capella d'En Marcús.....................2 C4
Casa Llotja de Mar........................3 E6
Cascada...4 G1
Castell dels Tres Dragons.............5 E2
Disseny Hub..................................6 D4
Església de Sant Pere de les
  Puelles..7 C1
Església de Santa Maria del
  Mar..8 D5
Espai Santa Caterina.....................9 C4
Former Convent de Sant
  Agustí..10 D3
Homenatge a Picasso...............11 F4
L'Hivernacle..............................12 E3
L'Umbracle.................................13 F3
Mercat de Santa Caterina........14 C4
Mercat del Born (Former).......15 E4
Museu Barbier-Mueller d'Art
  Pre-Colombí.............................16 D4
Museu de la Xocolata...............17 D3
Museu del Rei de la Magia.......18 B4
Museu Picasso...........................19 D4
Palau de Dalmases....................20 D5
Palau de la Música Catalana....21 A3
Parc de la Ciutadella................22 G2
Parlament de Catalunya..........23 H2

LA RIBERA

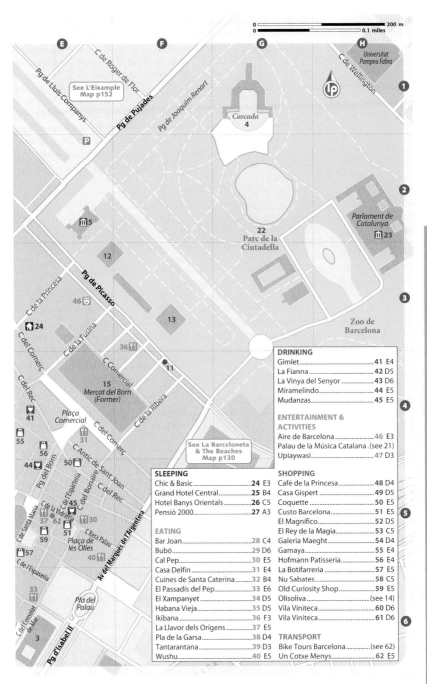

DRINKING

Gimlet	**41** E4
La Fianna	**42** D5
La Vinya del Senyor	**43** D6
Miramelindo	**44** E5
Mudanzas	**45** E5

ENTERTAINMENT & ACTIVITIES

Aire de Barcelona	**46** E3
Palau de la Música Catalana	(see 21)
Upiaywasi	**47** D3

SLEEPING

Chic & Basic	**24** E3
Grand Hotel Central	**25** B4
Hotel Banys Orientals	**26** C5
Pensió 2000	**27** A3

EATING

Bar Joan	**28** C4
Bubó	**29** D6
Cal Pep	**30** E5
Casa Delfin	**31** E4
Cuines de Santa Caterina	**32** B4
El Passadís del Pep	**33** E6
El Xampanyet	**34** D5
Habana Vieja	**35** D5
Ikibana	**36** F3
La Llavor dels Orígens	**37** E5
Pla de la Garsa	**38** D4
Tantarantana	**39** D3
Wushu	**40** E5

SHOPPING

Café de la Princesa	**48** D4
Casa Gispert	**49** D5
Coquette	**50** E5
Custo Barcelona	**51** E5
El Magnífico	**52** D5
El Rey de la Magia	**53** C5
Galeria Maeght	**54** D4
Gamaya	**55** E4
Hofmann Patisseria	**56** E4
La Botifarreria	**57** C5
Nu Sabates	**58** C5
Old Curiosity Shop	**59** E5
Olisoliva	(see 14)
Vila Viniteca	**60** D6
Vila Viniteca	**61** D6

TRANSPORT

| Bike Tours Barcelona | (see 62) |
| Un Cotxe Menys | **62** E5 |

LA RIBERA

HIGHLIGHTS

1   MUSEU PICASSO

Set in five adjacent Gothic-baroque mansions, this art museum showcases Picasso's early career. Works that predate the painter's Cubist reinvention in Paris offer insight into his youthful development. They also emphasise the role that Barcelona has played in influencing the man who, some say, single-handedly reinvented 20th-century art. For late-career fans, a trio of rooms is dedicated to Picasso's reevaluation of Velázquez's *Meninas*.

HIGHLIGHTS

⬎ OUR DON'T MISS LIST

❶ *RETRATO DE LA TÍA PEPA*

This portrait of Picasso's Aunt Pepa (Josefa Ruíz Blasco), done in Málaga in 1896 when the artist was just 14 years old, signifies not just the scope of his precocious talent, but also his coming of age as an artist. It is shockingly realistic, especially compared to his more abstract later work.

❷ *CIÈNCIA I CARITAT*

Knowing what came next, *Science and Charity*, completed when he was 15, appears to be another rather un-Picasso-like painting but it played a key part of his artistic education. Huge in size and scope it depicts a doctor (science) and a nun (charity) sitting beside a sick bed-bound woman. A fine study of social-realism, it was donated to the museum by Picasso three years before his death in 1970.

❸ THE BLUE PERIOD

Room 8 is dedicated to the first significant new stage in Picasso's development, the Blue Period (1901–04), a sombre, lugubrious response to

Clockwise from top: Admiring Picasso; Courtyard of the Museu Picasso; *Las Meninas*

the suicide of his close friend Carlos Casagemas. The nocturnal blue-tinted views of *Terrats de Barcelona* (Rooftops of Barcelona) and *El Foll* (The Madman) are cold and cheerless, yet somehow alive.

❹ LAS MENINAS

From 1954 to 1962 Picasso was obsessed by the idea of 'rediscovering' the greats, in particular Velázquez. In 1957, he made a series of renditions of the latter's masterpiece, *Las Meninas,* now displayed in rooms 12 to 15. It's as though he looked at the original painting through a prism reflecting all the styles he had worked in until then.

❺ CERAMICS

Picasso's role as a ceramicist is less hailed, but the last rooms contain engravings and some 40 ceramic pieces completed throughout the latter years of his unceasingly creative life. Things such as a plate with a fish on it are typical. Imagine dusting something like that off for your next dinner party!

⬎ THINGS YOU NEED TO KNOW

Historical context The museum consists mainly of Picasso's early work up until his Rose Period – there is very little from the Cubist era **Artist involvement** About 1000 of the 3500 items were donated by Picasso himself **Admission** Free on Sundays from 3pm to 8pm See p113 for more information

HIGHLIGHTS

2

↘ EL BORN REBORN

Barcelona rarely stands still, especially in 'El Born', the tight grid of streets south of Carrer de la Princesa that has been transformed into its most *à la mode* neighbourhood. Passeig del Born and the Plaça de Santa María are the hottest strips: trendy boutiques merge with hip bars (p124), specialist shops (p125) and experimental cuisine (p121). The renaissance began in the 1990s but shows no signs of abating.

3

↗ PALAU DE LA MÚSICA CATALANA

Give a talented Modernista architect (Lluís Domènech i Montaner) carte blanche in a music theatre and this is what you get: a splendiferous quasi-palace. Dripping in intricate details, the 1908 palau (p115) is music recreated in stone and stained glass with fine acoustics to match. For the most intimate picture, take a guided tour; for a full musical explosion, attend a performance – preferably Wagner.

LA RIBERA

HIGHLIGHTS

4

ᨈ ESGLÉSIA DE SANTA MARIA DEL MAR

The Barri Gótic might be Barcelona's most quintessential medieval quarter, but you have to roam a few blocks east to view its greatest Gothic monument. This 14th-century church (p116) exhibits the purest manifestation of the Gothic genre. The exterior is rather monastic, but inside the atmosphere is light and airy.

5

ᨈ PARC DE LA CIUTADELLA

For a long time La Ciutadella (p118) was the city's *only* green space, and it still serves as a vital air-hole between immersions in La Ribera and the Ciutat Vella. Aside from offering the standard diversions of walking, jogging and bunking off work for an afternoon siesta, the park hides a zoo, a Gaudíesque fountain and the Catalan parliament.

6

ᨈ MUSEU DE LA XOCOLATA

In a neighbourhood that plays heavily on its gourmet credentials, a chocolate museum (p118) might seem like a rather obvious attraction. Browse a raft of assorted chocolate paraphernalia and learn how the substance has been sinfully tempting us for centuries (and still is, if the queues in the museum shop are anything to go by).

2 DIEGO LEZAMA; 3 NEIL SETCHFIELD; 4 & 5 KRZYSZTOF DYDYNSKI; 6 DIEGO LEZAMA

2 Cafes in the El Born district (p121); 3 Palau de la Música Catalana (p115); 4 Església de Santa Maria del Mar (p116); 5 Parlament de Catalunya (p118), Parc de la Ciutadella; 6 Chocolate drumkit, Museu de la Xocolata

SINS OF GLUTTONY WALK

It's worth committing a few sins to experience this 2.5km amble starting from the Mercat de Santa Caterina and ending up at El Passadís del Pep. Reserve one hour for the full feast. Confessions can be said later, jogging in the Parc de la Ciutadella.

❶ MERCAT DE SANTA CATERINA

A glutton's guide to La Ribera has to begin in this modern version of a 19th-century market (p117). A rival to La Boqueria, its stands overflow with fish, meats, cheeses, countless varieties of olives, olive oil and vinegar specialist Olisoliva (p128), bar-eateries and a good restaurant.

❷ MUSEU DE LA XOCOLATA

Barcelona is awash in specialist chocolate stores, whether traditional *granjas* (milk bars), for thick hot chocolate with a pastry, or modern dens of chocolate delinquency. Where better to get introduced to the history behind this seductive food than the Museu de la Xocolata (p118)?

❸ HOFMANN PASTISSERIA

You've been to the museum, now try eating the stuff. Hofmann Pastisseria (p127) offers gourmet chocolate bars and all sorts of sweet goodies in jars, as well as fresh pastries and custom-ordered cakes.

❹ CASA GISPERT

Welcome to the house of nuts. Since the mid-19th century, Casa Gispert (p127) has been toasting up all sorts of nuts and other goodies. The walls are lined with jars of dried fruit, honeyed hazelnuts and other tasty morsels. Sinful they may be, but there's protein in there somewhere.

❺ LA BOTIFARRERIA

The most startling array of sausages and all sorts of other gourmet goodies are on offer at La Botifarreria (p127). Aromatic cheeses, cold meats, ready-to-eat snacks and more form the colourful armoury. Stash the best cuts in a basket and draft the invites for your next cocktail party.

❻ BUBÓ

Further opportunities for rotting teeth are presented at Bubó (p122). You could appease your conscience with a couple of savoury items first, but resistance to the sweet pastry treats thereafter is futile. Take a seat outside, down one of the mousses, and wait for the sugar rush.

❼ EL MAGNÍFICO

Coffee represents a significant element in Catalan tradition. This magnificent store (p126) offers a range of fine coffees from around the world.

SINS OF GLUTTONY WALK

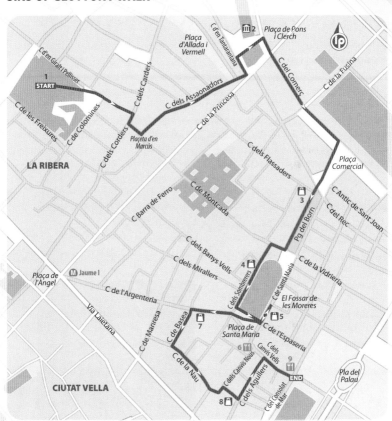

With such high doses of sugar and caffeine in your system, you should be able to muster enough energy to stagger through the last two stops.

❽ VILA VINITECA

Sweets, coffee…surely it's time for a bit of – ahem – wine. To investigate the enormous variety of Catalan and Spanish drops, visit **Vila Viniteca** (p126). Never too arrogant to doff a cap to other producing countries, Vineteca has many foreign wines on hand. It also hosts tasting events.

❾ EL PASSADÍS DEL PEP

After all that picking surely it's time for a proper meal. Handily positioned on the cusp of La Ribera and the seafood district of La Barceloneta lies this refreshingly spontaneous fish **restaurant** (p121). No sign, no printed menu – just fresh, simply prepared fodder plucked from the Med.

LA RIBERA

BEST...

BEST...

⤷ FOOD OBSESSIONS

- Habana Vieja (p123) Eat 'old clothes' in 'Old Havana'.
- Cal Pep (p121) Best tapas bar in Barcelona?
- El Magnífico (p126) One-stop coffee shop.
- Casa Gispert (p127) A nut store – are they serious?
- La Botifarrera (p127) Delectable deli with hams and cheeses.

⤷ ART NOOKS

- Museu Picasso (p113) The master and his (early) works.
- Homenatge a Picasso (p118) Tàpies' homage to the master.
- Disseny Hub (p115) Art in a palace.
- Galeria Maeght (p126) Acclaimed Parisian gallery.
- Museu Barbier-Mueller d'Art Pre-Colombí (p114) Ancient American art.

⤷ EL BORN REHAB

- Chic & Basic (p120) Sympathetically renovated hotel.
- Gamaya (p127) New women's-wear store.
- Passeig de Born bars (p124) Revitalised evening bar scene.
- Fusion food (p121) Pan-Asian meets Med-Asian meets everything else.
- Mercat de Santa Caterina (p117) Nineteenth century market re-opened in 2005.

⤷ NO-COST SIGHTS

- Església de Santa Maria del Mar (p116) Textbook Catalan-Gothic church.
- Arxiu Fotogràfic de Barcelona (p114) The city's history in photos.
- Mercat de Santa Caterina (p117) Recently reincarnated produce market.
- Parc de la Ciutadella (p118) Central city park.
- Església de Sant Pere de les Puelles (p119) Much-altered medieval church.

DIEGO LEZAMA

Alley in the El Born district

DISCOVER LA RIBERA

An integral part of the Barri Gòtic until it was split off by Via Laietana in the early 1900s, La Ribera was medieval Barcelona's economic powerhouse. You'll know you're in what was once one of the wealthiest streets in medieval Barcelona, Carrer de Montcada, when you see the queues outside the centuries-old mansions that constitute the Museu Picasso. In the 12th century, when Barcelona emerged as one of the main Mediterranean trading hubs, Carrer de Montcada was laid out to connect the then waterfront with one of the main roads from the city to Rome.

In medieval times, activity was especially great around Passeig del Born, a short, leafy boulevard behind Barcelona's mightiest Gothic church, Santa Maria del Mar. But the area declined as trading routes closed, and until the early 1990s it was dotted with a handful of sad old bars. Today, the timeless lanes are crammed with restaurants, bars and boutiques.

SIGHTS

CARRER DE MONTCADA

Ⓜ Jaume I

An early example of town planning, this medieval high street was driven down towards the sea from the road that in the 12th century led northeast from the city walls. It would, in time, become the snootiest address in town for the city's merchant class. The bulk of the great mansions that remain today date to the 14th and 15th centuries, although they were often tampered with later. This area was the commercial heartland of medieval Barcelona.

Five of the mansions on the east side of the street have been linked to house the Museu Picasso. Across the road, others house the Museu Barbier-Mueller d'Art Pre-Colombí (p114) and the Disseny Hub (p115). Several other mansions on this street are commercial art galleries where you're welcome to browse. The biggest is the local branch of the prestigious Parisian Galeria Maeght (No 25; see p126) in the 16th-century Palau dels Cervelló. If you can, peek into the baroque courtyard of the originally medieval Palau de Dalmases (☎ 93 310 06 73; ⏰ 8pm-2am Tue-Sat, 6-10pm Sun) at No 20; you can sip wine in the evening while listening to baroque music or operatic snippets.

At the corner of Carrer dels Corders and the northern end of the street, just beyond the 19th-century Carrer de la Princesa, stands a much-meddled-with Romanesque chapel, the Capella d'en Marcús, once a wayfarers' stop on the road northeast out of medieval Barcelona.

MUSEU PICASSO

☎ 93 256 30 00; www.museupicasso.bcn.es; Carrer de Montcada 15-23; adult/senior & under 16yr/student €9/free/6, temporary exhibitions adult/student/seniors & under 16 yr €5.80/2.90/free, free 3-8pm Sun & all day 1st Sun of month; ⏰ 10am-8pm Tue-Sun & holidays; Ⓜ Jaume I

The setting alone, in five contiguous medieval stone mansions, makes the Museu Picasso worth the detour (and the probable queues). The pretty courtyards, galleries and staircases preserved in the first

LA RIBERA

three of these buildings are as delightful as the collection inside is unique. One word of warning: the collection concentrates on the artist's formative years, sometimes disappointing for those hoping for a feast of his better-known later works (best found in Paris).

The permanent collection is housed in Palau Aguilar, Palau del Baró de Castellet and Palau Meca, all dating to the 14th century. The 18th-century Casa Mauri, built over medieval remains (even some Roman leftovers have been identified), and the adjacent 14th-century Palau Finestres accommodate temporary exhibitions.

The collection, which includes more than 3500 artworks, is strongest on Picasso's earliest years, up until 1904, but there is enough material from subsequent periods to give you a deep impression of the man's versatility and genius. Above all, you feel that Picasso is always one step ahead of himself, let alone anyone else, in his search for new forms of expression.

SIGHTS

BAB/IMAGE BROKER

Museu Barbier-Mueller d'Art Pre-Colombí

⤵ IF YOU LIKE...

If you like the Museu Picasso (p113) you might also admire the less-heralded displays at these arty nooks:

- **Museu Barbier-Mueller d'Art Pre-Colombí** (☎ 93 310 45 16; www.barbier-mueller.ch; Carrer de Montcada 14; adult/under 16yr/senior & student €3/free/1.50, 1st Sun of month free; ⊗ 11am-7pm Tue-Fri, 10am-7pm Sat, 10am-3pm Sun & holidays; M Jaume I) Inside the medieval Palau Nadal you can plunge into one of the world's most prestigious collections of pre-Columbian American art. In blacked-out rooms, eerily illuminated artefacts such as jewellery and ceramics flare up through the gloom.
- **Arxiu Fotogràfic de Barcelona** (☎ 93 256 34 20; www.bcn.cat/arxiu/fotografic; Plaça de Pons i Clerch; admission free; ⊗ 10am-7pm Mon-Sat; M Jaume I) On the 2nd floor of the former Convent de Sant Agustí, this modest exhibition space chronicles Barcelona from the late 19th century in photographs.

KRZYSZTOF DYDYNSKI

Mercat de Santa Caterina (p117)

DISSENY HUB

☎ 93 256 23 00; www.dhub-bcn.cat; Carrer de Montcada 12; adult/under 16yr/senior & student €5/free/3, free 3-8pm Sun; ⏱ 11am-7pm Tue-Sat, 11am-8pm Sun, 11am-3pm holidays; Ⓜ Jaume I

The 13th-century Palau dels Marquesos de Llió (which underwent repeated alterations into the 18th century) is now temporary home to part of the city's Disseny (Design) Hub collection of applied arts, which will eventually come together in the centre being built at Plaça de les Glòries Catalanes (due to open in 2011). This building is used for temporary exhibitions, while the permanent collections are housed in the Palau Reial de Pedralbes (p198). Often the exhibition on the ground floor is free, while the more extensive 1st-floor exhibition is what you pay for (admission includes entry to both locations). The building's courtyard, with its cafe-restaurant, makes a delightful stop.

PALAU DE LA MÚSICA CATALANA

☎ 902 475485; www.palaumusica.org; Carrer de Sant Francesc de Paula 2; adult/child/student & EU senior €12/free/10; ⏱ 50min tours every hour 10am-6pm Easter week & Aug, 10am-3.30pm Sep-Jul; Ⓜ Urquinaona

This concert hall is a high point of Barcelona's Modernista architecture. It's not exactly a symphony, but more a series of crescendos in tile, brick, sculpted stone and stained glass.

Built by Domènech i Montaner between 1905 and 1908 for the Orfeo Català musical society, with the help of some of the best Catalan artisans of the time, it was conceived as a temple for the Catalan Renaixença (Renaissance). The palace was built within the cloister of the former Convent de Sant Francesc, and since 1990 it has undergone several major changes.

The *palau,* like a peacock, shows off much of its splendour on the outside. Take in the principal facade with its mosaics, floral capitals and the sculpture cluster representing Catalan popular music. Wander inside the foyer and restaurant areas to admire the spangled, tiled pillars. Best of all is the richly colourful auditorium upstairs, with its ceiling of blue-and-gold stained glass and shimmering skylight that looks like a giant, crystalline, downward-thrusting nipple. Above a bust of Beethoven on the stage towers a wind-blown sculpture of Wagner's Valkyries (Wagner was top of the Barcelona charts at the time it was created). This can only be savoured on a guided tour or by

Església de Santa Maria del Mar

KRZYSZTOF DYDYNSKI

⬎ ESGLÉSIA DE SANTA MARIA DEL MAR

At the southwest end of Passeig del Born stands the apse of Barcelona's finest Catalan Gothic church, Santa Maria del Mar (Our Lady of the Sea). Built in the 14th century, Santa Maria was lacking in superfluous decoration even before anarchists gutted it in 1909 and 1936.

Built with record-breaking alacrity for the time (it took just 59 years), the church is remarkable for its architectural harmony. The main body is made up of a central nave and two flanking aisles separated by slender octagonal pillars, creating an enormous sense of lateral space. This was built as a people's church. The city's porters (*bastaixos*) spent a day each week carrying on their backs the stone required to build the church from royal quarries in Montjuïc. Their memory lives on in reliefs of them in the main doors and stone carvings elsewhere in the church.

Keep an eye out for music recitals, often baroque and classical, here. The uneven acoustics are more than made up for by the setting.

Opposite the church's southern flank, an eternal flame burns brightly over an apparently anonymous sunken square. This was once El Fossar de les Moreres (The Mulberry Cemetery), named after the mulberry trees that grew here, and was originally the site of a Roman cemetery. It's also where Catalan resistance fighters were buried after the siege of Barcelona ended in defeat in September 1714.

Things you need to know: ☎ 93 319 05 16; Plaça de Santa Maria; admission free; ⏰ 9am-1.30pm & 4.30-8pm; Ⓜ Jaume I

attending a performance – either is highly recommended.

The original Modernista creation, now a World Heritage Site, did not meet with universal approval in its day. The doyen of Catalan literature, Josep Pla, did not hesitate to condemn it as 'horrible', but few share his sentiments today. Montaner himself was also in a huff. He failed to attend the opening ceremony in response to unsettled bills. In 2009, the Palau was at the centre of a fraud scandal, as its president, who subsequently resigned, admitted to having siphoned millions of euros of its funds.

Tour tickets can be bought as much as a week in advance by phone or online. Space is limited to a maximum of 55 people.

MERCAT DE SANTA CATERINA

☎ 93 319 17 40; www.mercatsantacaterina.net, in Catalan; Avinguda de Francesc Cambó 16; ⏱ 7.30am-2pm Mon, 7.30am-3.30pm Tue, Wed & Sat, 7.30am-8.30pm Thu & Fri; Ⓜ Jaume I

Come shopping for tomatoes at this extraordinary-looking produce market, built by Enric Miralles and Benedetta Tagliabue to replace its 19th-century predecessor. Finished in 2005, it is distinguished by its kaleidoscopically weird wavy roof, held above the bustling produce stands, restaurants, cafes and bars by twisting slender branches of what look like grey steel trees.

The multicoloured ceramic roof (with a ceiling made of warm, light timber) recalls the Modernista tradition of *trencadís* decoration (a type of mosaic, such as that in Park Güell). Indeed, its curvy design, like a series of Mediterranean rollers, seems to plunge back into an era when Barcelona's architects were limited only by their (vivid) imagination. The market roof bares an uncanny resemblance to that of the Escoles de Gaudí at La Sagrada Família.

The market's 1848 predecessor had been built over the remains of the demolished 15th-century Gothic Monestir de Santa Caterina, a powerful Dominican monastery. A small section of the church foundations is glassed over in one corner as an archaeological reminder (with explanatory panels), the **Espai Santa**

Arc de Triomf (p118), Parc de la Ciutadella

JOHN ELK III

LA RIBERA

SIGHTS

Caterina (admission free; ☾ 8.30am-2pm Mon-Wed & Sat, 8.30am-8pm Thu & Fri).

PARC DE LA CIUTADELLA

Passeig de Picasso; ☾ 8am-6pm Nov-Feb, 8am-8pm Oct & Mar, 8am-9pm Apr-Sep; Ⓜ Arc de Triomf

Come for a stroll, picnic, visit to the zoo or to inspect Catalonia's regional parliament, but don't miss a visit to this, the most central green lung in the city. Parc de la Ciutadella is perfect for winding down.

After the War of the Spanish Succession, Felipe V razed a swathe of La Ribera to build a huge fortress (La Ciutadella), designed to keep watch over Barcelona. It became a loathed symbol of everything Catalans hated about Madrid and the Bourbon kings, and was later used as a political prison. Only in 1869 did the central government allow its demolition, after which the site was turned into a park and used for the Universal Exhibition of 1888.

The monumental cascada (waterfall) near the Passeig de Pujades park entrance, created between 1875 and 1881 by Josep Fontserè with the help of an enthusiastic young Gaudí, is a dramatic combination of statuary, rugged rocks, greenery and thundering water. All of it perfectly artificial! Nearby, hire a rowing boat to paddle about the small lake.

To the southeast, in what might be seen as an exercise in black humour, the fort's former arsenal now houses the Parlament de Catalunya (☎ 93 304 66 45; www.parlament.cat; admission free; ☾ 10am-7pm Sat, 10am-2pm Sun & holidays). A symbol of Catalan identity, the regional parliament opens to the public on 11 and 12 September. You may follow a circuit alone or join an hourly guided tour (usually in Catalan). Head up the sweeping Escala d'Honor (Stairway of Honour) and through several solemn halls to the Saló de Sessions, the semicircular auditorium where parliament sits. At the centre of the garden in front of the Parlament is a statue of a seemingly heartbroken woman, Desconsol (Distress; 1907), by Josep Llimona.

The Passeig de Picasso side of the park is lined by several buildings constructed for, or just before, the Universal Exhibition. The medieval-looking caprice at the top end is the most engaging. Known as the Castell dels Tres Dragons (Castle of the Three Dragons), it long housed the Museu de Zoologia, which is now closed. Montaner put the 'castle's' trimmings on a pioneering steel frame. The coats of arms are all invented and the whole building exudes a teasing, playful air. It was used as a cafe-restaurant during the Universal Exhibition of 1888.

To the south is L'Hivernacle, an arboretum or miniature botanic garden. Next come the former Museu de Geologia and L'Umbracle, another arboretum. On Passeig de Picasso itself is Antoni Tàpies' typically impenetrable Homenatge a Picasso. Water runs down the panes of a glass box full of bits of old furniture and steel girders.

Northwest of the park, Passeig de Lluís Companys is capped by the Modernista Arc de Triomf, designed by Josep Vilaseca as the principal exhibition entrance, with unusual, Islamic-style brickwork.

MUSEU DE LA XOCOLATA

☎ 93 268 78 78; http://pastisseria.com; Plaça de Pons i Clerch; adult/under 7yr/senior & student €4.30/free/3.65; ☾ 10am-7pm Mon-Sat, 10am-3pm Sun & holidays; Ⓜ Jaume I

Chocoholics have a hard time containing themselves in this museum dedicated to the fundamental foodstuff. How not to launch yourself at the extraordinary scale models made out of chocolate? A little salivation for sweet tooths is inevitable as you trawl around the displays (in part of the former Convent de Sant Agustí), which trace the origins of chocolate, its arrival in Europe and the many myths and images associated with it. Among the informative stuff (with panels in various languages) and machinery used in the production of chocolate are choc models of buildings such as La Sagrada Família, along with various characters, local and international. That part of the display changes every year or so. It's all enough to have you making for the nearest sweet shop, but you don't have to – plenty of chocolate is sold right here! Kids and grown-ups can join guided tours or take part in chocolate-making and tasting sessions, especially on weekends.

MUSEU DEL REI DE LA MAGIA

☎ 93 319 73 93; www.elreydelamagia.com, in Catalan & Spanish; Carrer de l'Oli 6; admission with/without show €8/3; ⊙ 6-8pm Thu, with show 6pm Sat & noon Sun; Ⓜ Jaume I

This museum is a timeless curio. Run by the same people who have the nearby magic shop (p128) on Carrer de la Princesa, it is the scene of magic shows, home (upstairs) to collections of material that hark back to the 19th-century origins of the shop (everything from old posters and books for learning tricks to magic wands and trick cards) and the place for budding magicians of all ages to enrol in courses. Seeing is believing.

ESGLÉSIA DE SANT PERE DE LES PUELLES

Plaça de Sant Pere; admission free; Ⓜ Arc de Triomf

Not a great deal remains of the original church or convent that stood here since early medieval times. The church's pre-Romanesque Greek-cross floor plan survives, as do some Corinthian columns beneath the 12th-century dome and a much-damaged Renaissance vault leading into a side chapel. It was around this church that settlement began in La Ribera. In 985, a Muslim raiding force

GEOFF STRINGER

Cascada, Parc de la Ciutadella

under Al-Mansur attacked Barcelona and largely destroyed the convent, killing or capturing the nuns.

MERCAT DEL BORN

Plaça Comercial; Ⓜ Barceloneta

Excavation in 2001 at the former Mercat del Born, a late-19th-century produce market built of iron and glass, unearthed great chunks of one of the districts flattened to make way for the much-hated Ciutadella (see p118). Historians found intact streets and the remains of houses, dating as far back as the 15th century. Excitement was such that plans to locate a new city library in the long-disused market were dropped. Instead, the site will become a museum and cultural centre.

CASA LLOTJA DE MAR

La Llotja; ☎ 902 448448; www.casallotja.com; Carrer del Consolat de Mar; Ⓜ Jaume I

The centrepiece of the city's medieval stock exchange (more affectionately known as La Llotja) is the fine Gothic Saló de Contractacions (Transaction Hall), built in the 14th century. Pablo Picasso and Joan Miró attended the art school that from 1849 was housed in the Saló dels Cònsols. These and five other halls were encased in a neoclassical shell in the 18th century. The stock exchange was in action until well into the 20th century and the building remains in the hands of the city's chamber of commerce. Occasionally it opens its doors to the public but the rooms are more generally hired out for events.

SLEEPING

Several fine hotels are located on the fringes of the busy Born area and a growing number of the sometimes bombastic buildings on thundering Via Laietana

have been or are in the process of being converted into top-end hotels.

GRAND HOTEL CENTRAL
Design Hotel €€

☎ 93 295 79 00; www.grandhotelcentral.com; Via Laietana 30; d €224; Ⓜ Jaume I; ⚒ ▣ ⚟

With supersoundproofed rooms not smaller than 21 sq metres, this design hotel, complete with rooftop pool, is one of the standout hotel offerings along Via Laietana. Rooms are decorated in style, with high ceilings, muted colours (beiges, browns and creams), dark timber floors and subtle lighting. Some of the bigger rooms are the size of studio apartments.

CHIC & BASIC
Hotel €€

☎ 93 295 46 52; www.chicandbasic.com; Carrer de la Princesa 50; s €96, d €132-171; Ⓜ Jaume I; ⚒ ▣

In a completely renovated building with high vaults in the facade are 31 spotlessly white rooms. There are high ceilings, enormous beds (room types are classed as M, L and XL!) and lots of detailed touches such as LED lighting, TFT TV screens and the retention of many beautiful old features of the original building, such as the marble staircase. Have a drink in the ground-floor White Bar.

HOTEL BANYS ORIENTALS
Boutique Hotel €€

☎ 93 268 84 60; www.hotelbanysorientals.com; Carrer de l'Argenteria 37; s/d €93/107; Ⓜ Jaume I; ⚒ ▣ ⚟

Book well ahead to get into this magnetically popular designer haunt. Cool blues and aquamarines combine with dark-hued floors to lend this clean-lined, boutique hotel a quiet charm. All rooms, on the small side, look onto the street or back lanes. There are more spacious suites (€139) in two other nearby buildings.

PENSIÓ 2000 Pensión €

☎ 93 310 74 66; www.pensio2000.com; Carrer de Sant Pere més Alt 6; s/d €52/65, without bathroom €35/45; Ⓜ Urquinaona; 💻

This 1st-floor, family-run place is opposite the anything-but-simple Palau de la Música Catalana. Seven reasonably spacious doubles (which can be taken as singles) all have mosaic-tiled floors. Two have ensuite bathroom. Eat brekkie in the little courtyard.

EATING

If you'd mentioned El Born (El Borne in Spanish) in the early 1990s, you wouldn't have raised much interest. Now the area is peppered with bars, dance dives, groovy designer stores and restaurants. El Born is where Barcelona is truly cooking – avant-garde chefs and fusion masters have zeroed in on this southern corner of La Ribera to conduct their culinary experiments. If you don't want to play such wild games, there's plenty of the traditional stuff to choose from, too.

EL PASSADÍS DEL PEP Seafood €€€

☎ 93 310 10 21; www.passadis.com; Pla del Palau 2; meals €70-80; 🕑 lunch & dinner Tue-Sat, dinner Mon Sep-Jul; Ⓜ Barceloneta; ✗

There's no sign, but locals know where to head for a seafood feast. They say the restaurant's raw materials are delivered daily from fishing ports along the Catalan coast. There is no menu – what's on offer depends on what the sea has surrendered on the day. Just head down the long, ill-lit corridor and entrust yourself to their care.

CAL PEP Tapas €€

☎ 93 310 79 61; www.calpep.com; Plaça de les Olles 8; meals €45-50; 🕑 lunch Tue-Sat, dinner Mon-Fri Sep-Jul; Ⓜ Barceloneta; ✗

It's getting a foot in the door here that's the problem. And if you want one of the five tables out the back, you'll need to call ahead. Most people are happy elbowing their way to the bar for some of the tastiest gourmet seafood tapas in town. Pep recommends *cloïsses amb pernil* (clams and ham – seriously!) or the *trifàsic* (combo of calamari, whitebait and prawns).

LA RIBERA

EATING

IZZET KERIBAR

Tapas

TANTARANTANA
Mediterranean €€

☎ 93 268 24 10; Carrer d'en Tantarantana 24; meals €30; ⏲ dinner Mon-Sat; Ⓜ Jaume I

Surrounded as it is by the furiously fashionable, front-line nuclei of *nueva cocina española,* this spot is a refreshing contrast. There is something comforting about the old-style marble-top tables, upon which you can sample simple but well-prepared dishes such as risotto or grilled tuna served with vegetables and ginger. It attracts a 30-something crowd who enjoy the outdoor seating in summer.

WUSHU
Asian €€

☎ 93 310 73 13; www.wushu-restaurant.com; Avinguda del Marquès de l'Argentera 1; meals €25-30; ⏲ lunch & dinner Tue-Sat, lunch Sun; Ⓜ Barceloneta; ✂

This Australian-run wok restaurant serves up an assortment of tasty pan-Asian dishes, including *pad thai,* curries and more. What about kangaroo *yakisoba* ? It also offers various BBQ dishes and you can take away. Pull up a pew at the nut-brown tables or sit at the bar. Wash down your meal with Tiger beer or one of a handful of wines.

CUINES DE SANTA CATERINA
Mediterranean & Asian €€

☎ 93 268 99 18; www.cuinessantacaterina.com; Mercat de Santa Caterina; meals €25-30; ⏲ daily; Ⓜ Jaume I; ✂

With a contemporary feel and open kitchens, this multifaceted eatery inside the Mercat de Santa Caterina offers all sorts of food. Peck at the sushi bar, tuck into classic rice dishes or go vegetarian. They do some things better than others, so skip the hummus and *tarte tatin.* A drawback is the speed with which barely finished plates are whisked away from you, but the range of dishes and bustling atmosphere

are fun. Reservations aren't taken, so it's first come first served.

IKIBANA
Japanese Fusion €€

☎ 93 295 67 32; www.ikibana.es; Passeig de Picasso 32; meals €25-30; ⏲ daily; Ⓜ Barceloneta

It feels like you are walking on water as you enter this Japanese-fusion lounge affair. A broad selection of *makis,* tempuras, sushi and more are served at high tables with leather-backed stools. The wide-screen TV switches from chilled music clips to live shots of the kitchen your wasabi wandered from. The set lunch is €12.

PLA DE LA GARSA
Catalan €€

☎ 93 315 24 13; Carrer dels Assaonadors 13; meals €25; ⏲ dinner; Ⓜ Jaume I; ✂

This 17th-century house is the ideal location for a romantic candle-lit dinner. Timber beams, anarchically scattered tables and soft ambient music combine to make an enchanting setting over two floors for traditional, hearty Catalan cooking, with dishes such as *timbal de botifarra negra* (a black pudding dish with mushrooms).

BUBÓ
Patisserie-Restaurant €€

☎ 93 268 72 24; www.bubo.ws; Carrer de les Caputxes 6 & 10; ⏲ 4pm-midnight Mon, 10am-midnight Tue-Thu & Sun, 10am-2am Fri & Sat; Ⓜ Barceloneta; ✂

Carles Mampel is a sweet artist, literally. It is difficult to walk by his bar and pastry shop without taking a seat outside to try one of his fantasy-laden creations. They are limitless in style and number. Try saying no to a mousse of *gianduia* (a dark hazelnut cream) with mango cream, caramelised hazelnuts with spices and hazelnut biscuit. To balance things, it offers a series of savoury snacks at €2 to €4 and little sandwiches at €3 to €4.

DAMIEN SIMONIS

Spanish delicacies

HABANA VIEJA
Cuban €€

☎ 93 268 25 04; Carrer dels Banys Vells 2; meals €20-25; ⏰ Mon-Sat; Ⓜ Jaume I

Since the early 1990s this Cuban hideaway, the first of its kind in Barcelona and still one of the best, has offered old island faves such as the stringy meat dish *ropa vieja* (literally 'old clothes') and rice concoctions. With its antique light fittings and predilection for timber furnishings, this Ribera house could easily be an Old Havana eatery.

LA LLAVOR DELS ORÍGENS
Catalan €

☎ 93 310 75 31; www.lallavordelsorigens.com; Carrer de la Vidrieria 6-8; meals €15-20; ⏰ 12.30pm-12.30am; Ⓜ Jaume I; ✗

In this treasure chest of Catalan regional products, the shop shelves groan under the weight of bottles and packets of goodies. It also has a long menu of smallish dishes, such as *sopa de carbassa i castanyes* (pumpkin and chestnut soup) or *mandonguilles amb alberginies* (rissoles with aubergine), that you can mix and match over wine by the glass. At the

L'Eixample branch (☎ 93 453 11 20; Carrer d'Enric Granados 9; ⏰ 1pm-1am; Ⓜ Universitat), one of three others around town, you can dine outside.

CASA DELFIN
Spanish €

☎ 93 319 50 88; Passeig del Born 36; meals €15-20; ⏰ noon-1am; Ⓜ Barceloneta

While surrounding restaurants may serve exquisitely designed Sino-Moroccan-Venezuelan creations, the bustling waiters at the 'Dolphin House' content themselves with serving bountiful Spanish classics. And they are right to do so. Finding a free lunchtime table at the sprawling terrace requires a modest portion of luck. Choose from more than 30 tried-and-true dishes.

EL XAMPANYET
Tapas €

☎ 93 319 70 03; Carrer de Montcada 22; meals €15-20; ⏰ lunch & dinner Tue-Sat, lunch Sun; Ⓜ Jaume I

Nothing has changed for decades in this, one of the city's best-known *cava* (Catalan champagne) bars. Sit at the bar or seek out a table against the decoratively tiled

LA RIBERA

DRINKING

walls for a glass or three of *cava* and an assortment of tapas, such as the tangy *boquerons en vinagre* (white anchovies in vinegar). It's the timeless atmosphere that makes this place.

BAR JOAN Catalan €

☎ 93 310 61 50; Mercat de Santa Caterina; menú del día €11; ⏰ lunch Mon-Sat; M Jaume I

Along with the popular Cuines de Santa Caterina (p122), there are a couple of bar-eateries in the Mercat de Santa Caterina. Bar Joan is known especially to locals for its *arròs negre* (squid-ink rice) on Tuesdays at lunchtime. It's a simple spot, but always fills with hungry passers-by, black rice or no black rice.

DRINKING

Where the townsfolk once enjoyed a good public execution or rousing medieval joust along Passeig del Born, they now reach a heightened state of animation in a countless array of bars along this elongated square and in the web of streets winding off it and around the Església de Santa Maria del Mar. Much gentrified since the mid-1990s, the area around Passeig del Born has an ebullient, party feel. North of Carrer de la Princesa, things quieten down quite a bit, but there's a scattering of bars about, some barely glanced at by foreign visitors.

GIMLET Bar

☎ 93 310 10 27; Carrer del Rec 24; ⏰ 10pm-3am; M Jaume I

Transport yourself to a Humphrey Bogart movie. White-jacketed bar staff with all the appropriate aplomb will whip you up a gimlet or any other classic cocktail (around €10) your heart desires. Barcelona cocktail guru Javier Muelas is behind this and several other cocktail bars around the

city, so you can be sure of excellent drinks, some with a creative twist.

LA FIANNA Bar

☎ 93 315 18 10; www.lafianna.com; Carrer dels Banys Vells 15; ⏰ 6pm-1.30am Sun-Wed, 6pm-2.30am Thu-Sat; M Jaume I

There is something medieval about this bar, with its bare stone walls, forged iron candelabra and cushion-covered lounges. But don't think chill out. This place heaves and, as the night wears on, it's elbow room only. Earlier in the evening you can indulge in a little snack food, too.

LA VINYA DEL SENYOR Bar

☎ 93 310 33 79; Plaça de Santa Maria 5; ⏰ noon-1am Tue-Sun; M Jaume I

Relax on the *terrassa*, which lies in the shadow of Església de Santa Maria del Mar, or crowd inside at the tiny bar. The wine list is as long as *War and Peace* and there's a table upstairs for those who opt to sample by the bottle rather than the glass.

MIRAMELINDO Bar

☎ 93 319 53 76; Passeig del Born 15; ⏰ 8pm-2.30am; M Jaume I

A spacious tavern in a Gothic building, this remains a classic on Passeig del Born for mixed drinks, while soft jazz and soul sounds float overhead. Try for a comfy seat at a table towards the back before it fills to bursting. Several similarly barn-sized places line this side of the *passeig*.

MUDANZAS Bar

☎ 93 319 11 37; Carrer de la Vidrieria 15; ⏰ 10am-2.30am; M Jaume I

This was one of the first bars to get things into gear in El Born and it still attracts a faithful crowd. It's a straightforward place for a beer, a chat and perhaps a sandwich. Oh, and it does a nice line in Italian grappas.

Palau de la Música Catalana
KARL BLACKWELL

ENTERTAINMENT & ACTIVITIES

PALAU DE LA MÚSICA CATALANA
Classical Music & Opera

☎ 902 442882; www.palaumusica.org; Carrer de Sant Francesc de Paula 2; ☼ box office 10am-9pm Mon-Sat; Ⓜ Urquinaona

A feast for the eyes, this Modernista pudding is also the city's traditional venue for classical and choral music. Just being here for a performance is an experience. Sip a preconcert tipple in the foyer, its tiled pillars all a-glitter. Head up the grand stairway to the main auditorium, a whirlpool of Modernista whimsy that is seen at its best before lights are dimmed for the show. The Palau has a wide-ranging program. You could pay €10 or less for a cheap seat in a middling concert and €150 or more for prestigious international performances.

UPIAYWASI
Club

☎ 93 268 01 54; Carrer d'Allada Vermell 11; ☼ 5pm-2am Mon-Thu, 5pm-3am Fri & Sat, 4pm-1am Sun; Ⓜ Barceloneta

Slide into this dimly lit cocktail bar, which crosses a chilled ambience with Latin American music. A mix of lounges and intimate table settings, chandeliers and muted decorative tones lends the place a pleasingly conspiratorial feel.

AIRE DE BARCELONA
Spas & Massage

☎ 902 555789; www.airedebarcelona.com; Passeig de Picasso 22; thermal baths & aromatherapy €25; ☼ 10am-2am; Ⓜ Arc de Triomf

With low lighting and relaxing perfumes wafting around you, this hammam could be the perfect way to end a day. Hot, warm and cold baths, steam baths and options for various massages, including on a slab of hot marble, make for a delicious hour or so. Book ahead and bring a swimming costume.

SHOPPING

The former commercial heart of medieval Barcelona is today still home to a cornucopia of old-style specialist food and drink shops, a veritable feast of aroma and atmosphere. They have been joined, since the late 1990s, by a raft of hip little fashion stores.

OLD CURIOSITY SHOP
Antiques & Bric-A-Brac

☎ 93 310 45 89; Volta dels Tamborets 4;
Ⓜ Jaume I

For anything from handmade soaps to French calendar diaries of the 1930s or antique tea sets, this is a fun hole-in-the-wall shop to rummage about in, hidden in a side lane near the Església de Santa Maria del Mar.

GALERIA MAEGHT
Art

☎ 93 310 42 45; www.maeght.com; Carrer de Montcada 25; ⏲ 11am-2pm & 3-7pm Tue-Fri, 11am-2pm Sat; Ⓜ Jaume I

This high-end gallery, housed in one of the fine medieval mansions for which this street is known, specialises in 20th-century masters. It is as enticing for the building as the art.

CAFÉ DE LA PRINCESA
Boutique

☎ 93 268 15 18; www.cafeprincesa.com; Carrer dels Flassaders 21; Ⓜ Jaume I

In a dark lane named after the blanket makers that once worked here is this odd combination of cooperative store, art gallery and restaurant (entry to the latter is from Carrer de Sabateret). Its members make many of the oddities on sale, but others are objects imported from such disparate locations as Prague and Denmark. Leather bags, toys and clothes make up just part of the offerings.

EL MAGNÍFICO
Coffee

☎ 93 319 60 81; www.cafeselmagnifico.com, in Catalan & Spanish; Carrer de l'Argenteria 64; Ⓜ Jaume I

All sorts of coffee has been roasted here since the early 20th century. The variety of coffee (and tea) available is remarkable – and the aromas hit you as you walk in. Across the road, the same people run the exquisite and much newer tea shop, Sans i Sans (☎ 93 319 60 81; Carrer de l'Argenteria 59).

VILA VINITECA
Wine

☎ 902 327777; www.vilaviniteca.es, in Spanish; Carrer dels Agullers 7; ⏲ 8.30am-8.30pm Mon-Sat; Ⓜ Jaume I

One of the best wine stores in Barcelona (and Lord knows, there are a few), this place has been searching out the best in local and imported wines since 1932. On a couple of November evenings it organises what has by now become an almost riotous wine-tasting event in Carrer dels Agullers and surrounding lanes, at which cellars from around Spain present their young new wines. At No 9 it has another store devoted to gourmet food products.

COQUETTE
Fashion

☎ 93 295 42 85; www.coquettebcn.com; Carrer del Rec 65; Ⓜ Barceloneta

With its spare, cut back and designer look, this fashion is automatically attractive in its own right. Women will love to browse casual, feminine wear by such designers as Tsunoda, Vanessa Bruno, Chloé Baño and Hoss Intropia. To complement the clothes there are bags, footwear and costume jewellery. The store is a leading light on a street replete with fashion outlets.

CUSTO BARCELONA
Fashion

☎ 93 268 78 93; www.custo-barcelona.com; Plaça de les Olles 7; Ⓜ Jaume I

The psychedelic decor and casual atmosphere lend this avant-garde Barcelona fashion store a youthful edge. Custo presents daring new women's and men's collections each year on the New York catwalks. The dazzling colours and cut of anything from dinner jackets to hot pants are for the uninhibited. It has five other stores around town.

GAMAYA
Fashion

☎ 93 310 67 07; www.gamaya.es; Carrer dels Flassaders 36; Ⓜ Jaume I

A breath of fresh laid-back Ibiza air runs through this new women's wear store tucked away on a street that has gone from near abandonment in the 1990s to become a delightful shopping lane today. The woman who runs this shop designs the breezy summer dresses, pants-and-tops combinations and prints herself.

HOFMANN PASTISSERIA
Food

☎ 93 268 82 21; www.hofmann-bcn.com; Carrer dels Flassaders 44; Ⓜ Jaume I

With old timber cabinets, this bite-sized gourmet patisserie has an air of timelessness, although it is quite new. Choose between jars of delicious chocolates, the day's croissants and more dangerous pastries, or an array of cakes and other sweets.

CASA GISPERT
Food

☎ 93 319 75 35; www.casagispert.com; Carrer dels Sombrerers 23; Ⓜ Jaume I

Nuts to you at the wood-fronted Casa Gispert, where they've been toasting nuts and selling all manner of dried fruit since 1851. Pots and jars piled high on the shelves contain an unending variety of crunchy titbits: some roasted, some honeyed, all of them moreish.

LA BOTIFARRERIA
Food

☎ 93 319 91 23; www.labotifarreria.com; Carrer de Santa Maria 4; Ⓜ Jaume I

As they say, 'sausages with imagination'! Although this delightful deli sells all sorts of cheeses, hams, fresh hamburger patties, snacks and other goodies, the mainstay is an astounding variety of handcrafted sausages. Not just the pork variety, but stuffed with anything from green pepper and whisky to apple curry!

LA RIBERA

SHOPPING

DIEGO LEZAMA

Shoe shop, El Born district

OLISOLIVA   Food
☎ 93 268 14 72; www.olisoliva.com, in Spanish;
Avinguda de Francesc Cambó; Ⓜ Jaume I

Inside the Mercat de Santa Caterina (p117), this simple, glassed-in store is stacked with olive oils and vinegars from all over Spain. Taste some of the products before deciding. Some of the best olive oils come from southern Spain. The range of vinegars is astounding too.

EL REY DE LA MAGIA   Magic
☎ 93 319 39 20; www.elreydelamagia.com,
in Catalan & Spanish; Carrer de la Princesa 11;
☉ 11am-2pm & 5-8pm Mon-Fri, 10am-2pm Sat;
Ⓜ Jaume I

For more than 100 years, the people behind this box of tricks have been keeping locals both astounded and amused. Should you decide to stay in Barcelona and make a living as a magician, this is the place to buy levitation brooms, glasses of disappearing milk and decks of magic cards.

NU SABATES   Shoes & Accessories
☎ 93 268 03 83; www.nusabates.com; Carrer
dels Cotoners 14; Ⓜ Jaume I

A couple of modern-day Catalan cobblers have put together some original handmade leather shoes (and a handful of bags and other leather items) in their stylishly renovated locale.

↘ LA BARCELONETA & THE BEACHES

LA BARCELONETA & THE BEACHES

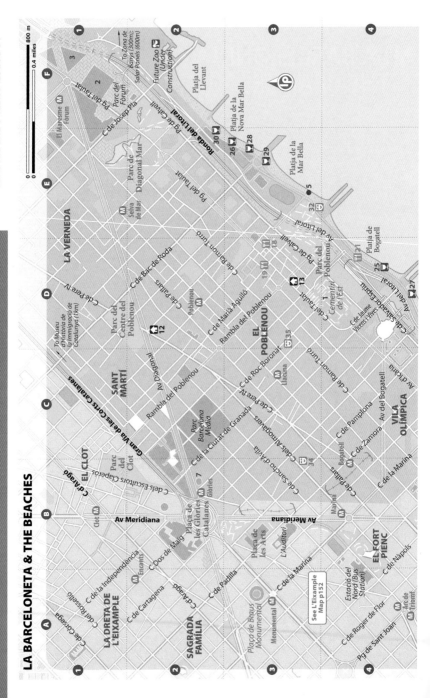

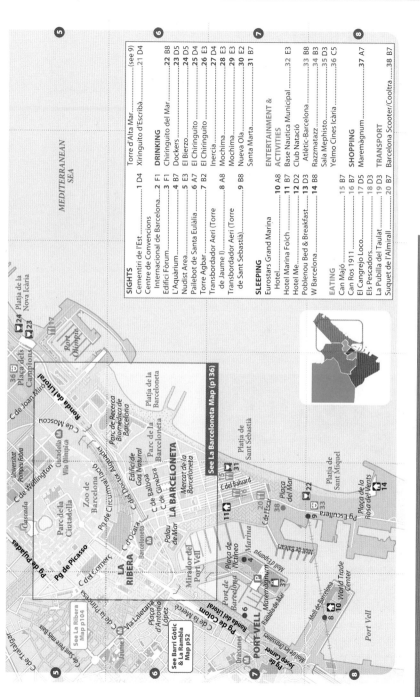

SIGHTS

Cementiri de l'Est	.1 D4
Centre de Convencions Internacional de Barcelona	.2 F1
Edifici Fòrum	.3 F1
L'Aquàrium	.4 B7
Nudist Area	.5 E3
Pailebot de Santa Eulàlia	.6 A7
Torre Agbar	.7 B2
Transbordador Aeri (Torre de Jaume I)	.8 A8
Transbordador Aeri (Torre de Sant Sebastià)	.9 B8
Torre d'Alta Mar	(see 9)
Xiringuito d'Escribà	.21 D4

DRINKING

Chiringuito del Mar	.22 B8
Dockers	.23 D5
El Bierzo	.24 D5
El Chiringuito	.25 D4
El Chiringuito	.26 E3
Inercia	.27 D4
Mochima	.28 E3
Mochima	.29 E3
Nueva Ola	.30 E2
Santa Marta	.31 B7

SLEEPING

Eurostars Grand Marina Hotel	.10 A8
Hotel Marina Folch	.11 B7
Hotel Me	.12 D2
Poblenou Bed & Breakfast	.13 D3
W Barcelona	.14 B8

ENTERTAINMENT & ACTIVITIES

Base Nautica Municipal	.32 E3
Club Natació Atlètic-Barcelona	.33 B8
Razzmatazz	.34 B3
Sala Mephisto	.35 D3
Yelmo Cines Icària	.36 C5

EATING

Can Majó	.15 B7
Can Ros 1911	.16 B7
El Cangrejo Loco	.17 D5
Els Pescadors	.18 D3
La Pubilla del Taulat	.19 D3
Suquet de l'Almirall	.20 B7

SHOPPING

Maremàgnum	.37 A7

TRANSPORT

Barcelona Scooter/Cooltra	.38 B7

HIGHLIGHTS

⚓ BEACHES

Other cities may have their diamond dust beaches; but how often are they juxtaposed with 2000 rollercoaster years of history? In 2010 *National Geographic* nominated Barcelona as the world's best 'beach city'. The reason: seven broad scimitars of sand within soccer ball–lobbing distance of the Ciutat Vella and a slew of other heavyweight sights. The action starts at busy, modern **Port Olímpic marina** (p138).

⚓ SEAFOOD

In Barcelona cooking is a form of alchemy, with the city exhibiting some of Spain's most daring and avant-garde cuisine. But down in the salty 18th-century grid of **La Barceloneta** (p143), fresh seafood is served with less pretension. Roam the streets between tightly packed, family-run restaurants and look for local specialities such as *arròs negre* (squid-ink rice) and scallops in *cava* (Catalan 'champagne').

⬏ L'AQUÀRIUM

There are approximately 450 species of aquatic animals in this water-side aquarium (p135), but it's the sharks that leave the biggest impression. An 80m-long underwater tunnel keeps the beasts at bay behind worryingly thin plexiglass. After you've scared the wits out of the kids, calm them down in the museum's Mediterranean-themed interactive section.

⬏ MUSEU D'HISTÒRIA DE CATALUNYA

Regional identity runs deep in Barcelona, a fiercely Catalan city with a history that often has more in common with Sardinia than Seville. To understand the complexities, head first to this multifarious museum (p135), where you can immerse yourself in various snapshots of Catalonia history, from cavepeople to the space age.

⬏ EL FÒRUM

Barcelona has confirmed its arrival in the 21st century with El Fòrum (p140), an ultra-modern water-side complex that was constructed between 1992 and 2004. The main attractions are boldly ambitious and still in development. There's the Tiananmen square–sized Parc Diagonal Mar, a giant futuristic solar panel, and a raft of water-orientated outdoor activities.

1 PASCALE BEROUJON; 2 VOX/IMAGEBROKER; 3 INGOLF POMPE 52/ALAMY; 4 KRZYSZTOF DYDYNSKI; 5 KRZYSZTOF DYDYNSKI

1 A scuplture by artist Rebecca Horn on a La Barceloneta beach (p138); 2 *Arròs negre* with seafood; 3 L'Aquàrium (p135); 4 Museu D'Història de Catalunya (p135); 5 El Fòrum (p140)

BEST...

◥ SEASIDE ACTIVITIES

- **Platja de Bogatell** (p138) Popular skateboarding area.
- **Port Fórum** (p141) Biking along the esplanade.
- **Base Nautica Municipal** (p150) Kayaking and windsurfing.
- **Poliesportiu Marítim** (p149) Spas, waterfalls and sea-water therapy.
- **L'Aquárium** (p135) Dive with sharks.

◥ REJUVENATION PROJECTS

- **Torre Agbar** (p139) Sleek new cucumber-shaped skyscraper.
- **Parc del Centre del Poblenou** (p139) Caustic collection of cement, metal and 1000 trees.
- **Parc de Diagonal Mar** (p141) Modern sculptures and eclectic trees.
- **Zona de Banys** (p140) Enormous water-side solar panel.
- **Edifici Fòrum** (p140) Huge controversial triangular auditorium/ exhibition hall.

◥ SEAFOOD

- **El Cangrejo Loco** (p146) Insanely popular Port Olímpic crab house.
- **Els Pescadors** (p145) Family-run Poblenou classic.
- **Can Ros 1911** (p144) Unfancy and simple – but that's the point.
- **Can Majó** (p144) Seafood at quintessential seaside setting.
- **Xiringuito d'Escribà** (p146) At last! Single-portion seafood paella.

◥ BEACH HEDONISM

- **Platja de Nova Icària** (p138) Municipal skin-roasting among the beach crowds.
- **Liquid** (p148) Megaclub on islet surrounded by moat.
- **Chiringuito del Mar** (p146) Chilled beachside bar in Barceloneta.
- **Platja de la Mar Bella** (p138) Legal nudity on a city beach.
- **Razzmatazz** (p150) Ibiza-style clubbing is alive in Poblenou.

KRZYSZTOF DYDYNSKI

Torre Agbar (p139)

DISCOVER LA BARCELONETA & THE BEACHES

Where La Rambla meets the Med, Port Vell (Old Port) stands as pretty testimony to the city's post-1980s transformation. Just beyond stretches the 18th-century waterfront district of La Barceloneta. What had become an industrial slum by the end of the 19th century is today in the grip of gradual gentrification. But La Barceloneta's narrow lanes still have an earthy feel, and countless seafood eateries lurk in this labyrinth.

Strolling, skating or cycling northeast from the beaches will take you to Port Olímpic, a crammed marina that was created for the 1992 Olympics. Inland, the southwest end of El Poblenou, a one-time industrial workers' district, was converted into the Vila Olímpica, apartments that housed athletes and were sold after the Olympics. Now, the rest of El Poblenou is being transformed in an ambitious urban regeneration scheme and its waterfront is lined by the city's better beaches, which spread northeast towards Barcelona's other major development project, El Forùm.

SIGHTS

PORT VELL & LA BARCELONETA

L'AQUÀRIUM Map p130

☎ 93 221 74 74; www.aquariumbcn.com; Moll d'Espanya; adult/under 4yr/4-12yr/senior over 60yr €17.50/free/12.50/14.50; ☼ 9.30am-11pm Jul & Aug, 9.30am-9.30pm Jun & Sep, 9.30am-9pm Mon-Fri & 9.30am-9.30pm Sat & Sun Oct-May; Ⓜ Drassanes

It is hard to help a slight shudder at the sight of a shark gliding above you, displaying its full munching apparatus. But this, the 80m shark tunnel, is the highlight of one of Europe's largest aquariums. It has the world's best Mediterranean collection and plenty of gaudy fish from as far off as the Red Sea, the Caribbean and the Great Barrier Reef. All up, some 11,000 fish (including a dozen sharks) of 450 species reside here.

Back in the shark tunnel, which you reach after passing a series of themed fish tanks with everything from bream to sea horses, various species of shark (white tip, sand tiger, bonnethead, black tip, nurse and sandbar) flit around you, along with a host of other critters, from flapping rays to bloated sunfish. An interactive zone, Planeta Agua, is host to a family of Antarctic penguins and a tank of rays that you watch close up.

Divers with a valid dive certificate may dive (€300; ☼ 9.30am-2pm Wed, Sat & Sun) in the main tank with the sharks.

MUSEU D'HISTÒRIA DE CATALUNYA Map p136

Museum of Catalonian History; ☎ 93 225 47 00; www.mhcat.net; Plaça de Pau Vila 3; adult/senior & under 7yr/student permanent exhibition only €4/free/3, permanent & temporary exhibitions €5/free/4, free 1st Sun of month; ☼ 10am-7pm Tue & Thu-Sat, 10am-8pm Wed, 10am-2.30pm Sun & holidays; Ⓜ Barceloneta

The Palau de Mar building facing the harbour once served as warehouses (Els

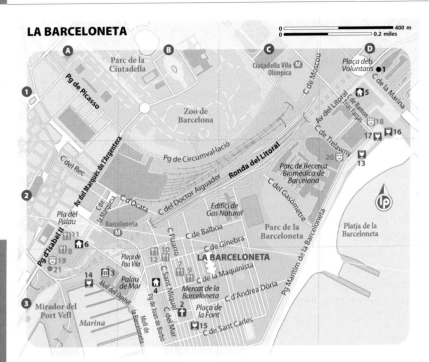

LA BARCELONETA

Magatzems Generals de Comerç), but was transformed in the 1990s. Below the seaward arcades is a string of good restaurants. Inside is the Museu d'Història de Catalunya, something of a local patriotic statement, but interesting nonetheless.

The permanent display covers the 2nd and 3rd floors, taking you, as the bumf says, on a 'voyage through history' from the Stone Age through to the early 1980s. It is a busy hodgepodge of dioramas, artefacts, videos, models, documents and interactive bits: all up, an entertaining exploration of 2000 years of Catalan history. See how the Romans lived, listen to Arab poetry from the time of the Muslim occupation of the city, peer into the dwelling of a Dark Ages family in the Pyrenees, try to mount a knight's horse or lift a suit of armour.

When you have had enough of all this, descend into a civil-war air-raid shelter, watch a video in Catalan on post-Franco

IMW/IMAGEBROKER

Pailebot de Santa Eulàlia

⮥ IF YOU LIKE...

If you like the **Museu d'Història de Catalunya** (p135), you might also appreciate the following two historical curiosities:

- **Pailebot de Santa Eulàlia** (Map p130; Moll de la Fusta; adult/under 7yr/senior & student incl Museu Marítim €2.50/free/1.25; ☽ noon-7.30pm Tue-Fri, 10am-7pm Sat & Sun & holidays May-Oct, noon-5.30pm Tue-Fri, 10am-5.30pm Sat & Sun & holidays Nov-Apr; Ⓜ Drassanes) A three-masted schooner of 1918 vintage restored by the Museu Marítim and moored alongside the palm-lined promenade Moll de la Fusta. The ship, on occasion, sails on demonstration trips up and down the coast.

- **Museu d'Història de la Immigració de Catalunya** (off Map p130; ☎ 93 381 26 06; www.mhic.net; Carretera de Mataró 124, Sant Adriàde Besòs; admission free; ☽ 10am-2pm & 5-8pm Tue & Thu, 10am-2pm Wed, Fri & Sat mid-Apr–Sep, 10am-2pm & 4-7pm Tue & Thu, 10am-2pm Wed, Fri & Sat Oct–mid-Apr; Ⓜ Verneda) A museum on the outskirts of town dedicated to the history of immigration in Catalonia whose pièce de resistance is a wagon of the train known as *El Sevillano*, which brought migrants from Andalucía to Barcelona in the 1950s.

Catalonia or head upstairs to the rooftop restaurant and cafe.

The temporary exhibitions are frequently as interesting as the permanent display.

TRANSBORDADOR AERI Map p130
Passeig Escullera; 1-way/return €9/12.50; ☽ 11am-8pm mid-Jun–mid-Sep, 10.45am-7pm Mar–mid-Jun & mid-Sep–late Oct, 10.30am-5.45pm late Oct-Feb; Ⓜ Barceloneta, ➥ 17, 39 or 64

This cable car, which is strung across the harbour to Montjuïc, provides a bubble-eye view of the city. The aerial cabins float between Miramar (in Montjuïc) and the Torre de Sant Sebastià (in La Barceloneta), with a stop about midway at the Torre de Jaume I, located in front of the World Trade Center. At the top of the Torre de Sant Sebastià you'll find the spectacularly located restaurant, Torre d'Alta Mar (p143).

GUY MOBERLY

La Barceloneta beach

⤵ BEACHES

A series of pleasant beaches stretches northeast from the Port Olímpic marina. They are largely artificial, but this doesn't stop an estimated seven million bathers from piling in every year.

The southernmost beach, **Platja de la Nova Icària**, is the busiest. Behind it, across the Avinguda del Litoral highway, is the Plaça dels Campions, site of the rusting three-tiered platform used to honour medallists in the sailing events of the 1992 games. Much of the athletes' housing-turned-apartments are in the blocks immediately behind Carrer de Salvador Espriu.

The next beach is **Platja de Bogatell**. There's a good skateboard area with half-pipes at the beach's northern end.

Just in from the beach is the **Cementiri de l'Est** (Eastern Cemetery), created in 1773. It was positioned outside the then city limits for health reasons. Its central monument commemorates the victims of a yellow-fever epidemic that swept across Barcelona in 1821. The cemetery is full of bombastic family memorials, but an altogether disquieting touch is the sculpture *El Petó de la Mort* (The Kiss of Death), in which a winged skeleton kisses a young, kneeling but lifeless body. There's a good skateboard area with half-pipes at the north end of the beach.

Platja de la Mar Bella (with its brief nudist strip and sailing school) and **Platja de la Nova Mar Bella** follow, leading into the new residential and commercial waterfront strip, the Front Marítim, part of the Diagonal Mar project in the Fòrum district. It is fronted by the last of these artificial beaches to be created, **Platja del Llevant**.

Things you need to know: beaches (Map p130; Ⓜ Ciutadella Vila Olímpic, Bogatell, Llacuna or Selva de Mar, 🚍 36 or 41); Cementiri de l'Est (☎ 902 079799; Carrer del Taulat 2; ⊗ 8am-6pm)

BURYING THE PAST

Buried beneath the concrete congress centre, bathing zone and marina created in El Fòrum lies the memory of more than 2000 people executed in the fields of Camp de la Bota between 1936 and 1952, most of them under Franco from 1939 onward. *Fraternitat* (Brotherhood), a sculpture by Miquel Navarro, stands to their memory, on Rambla de Prim.

ESGLÉSIA DE SANT MIQUEL DEL PORT Map p136

☎ 93 221 65 50; Plaça de la Barceloneta; admission free; ⏰ 7am-1.30pm Mon-Fri, 8am-1.30pm Sat; Ⓜ Barceloneta

Finished in 1755, this sober baroque church was the first building completed in La Barceloneta. Built low so that the cannon in the then Ciutadella fort could fire over it if necessary, it bears images of St Michael (Miquel) and two other saints considered protectors of the Catalan fishing fleet: Sant Elm and Santa Maria de Cervelló.

Just behind the church is the bustling marketplace, worth an early morning browse. Ferdinand Lesseps, the French engineer who designed the Suez Canal, did a stint as France's consul-general in Barcelona and lived in the house to the right of the church.

PORT OLÍMPIC, EL POBLENOU & EL FÒRUM

TORRE AGBAR Map p130

☎ 93 342 21 29; www.torreagbar.com; Avinguda Diagonal 225; Ⓜ Glòries

Barcelona's very own cucumber-shaped tower, Jean Nouvel's luminous Torre Agbar (which houses the city water company's headquarters), is the most daring addition to Barcelona's skyline since the first towers of La Sagrada Família went up. Completed in 2005, it shimmers at night in shades of midnight blue and lipstick red. Unfortunately, you can only enter the foyer on the ground floor, frequently used to host temporary exhibitions on water-related topics.

Nouvel was also behind the **Parc del Centre del Poblenou** (Avinguda Diagonal;

Facade of Torre Agbar

ALFREDO MAIQUEZ

Edifici Fòrum

KRZYSZTOF DYDYNSKI

10am-sunset), about halfway between the tower and El Fòrum. It is an odd park, with stylised metal seats and items of statuary. Barcelona is sprinkled with parks whose principal element is cement – the Gaudíesque cement walls here are increasingly covered by sprawling bougainvillea. Inside, some 1000 trees of mostly Mediterranean species are complemented by thousands of smaller bushes and plants.

EL FÒRUM Map p130
☎ 93 356 10 50; Ⓜ El Maresme Fòrum
Where before there was wasteland, half-abandoned factories and a huge sewage-treatment plant in the city's northeast corner, there are now high-rise apartment blocks, luxury hotels, a marina (Port Fòrum), a shopping mall and a conference centre.

The most striking element is the eerily blue, triangular *2001: A Space Odyssey*–style **Edifici Fòrum** building by Swiss architects Herzog & de Meuron. The navy-blue raised facades look like sheer cliff faces, with angular crags cut into them as if by divine laser. Grand strips of mirror create fragmented reflections of the sky. Now empty, it is being transformed into the **Espai Blau** (Blue Space), a modern showcase for the **Museu de Ciències Naturals** (www.bcn.es/museuciencies), a combination of the old Museu de Zoologia and Museu de Geologia that used to occupy buildings in the **Parc de la Ciutadella** (p118) and will be installed here in 2011.

Next door, Josep Lluís Mateo's **Centre de Convencions Internacional de Barcelona** (CCIB) has capacity for 15,000 delegates. The huge space around the two buildings is used for major outdoor events, such as concerts (eg during the Festes de la Mercè) and the **Feria de Abril** (p47).

A 300m stroll east from the Edifici Fòrum is the **Zona de Banys** (11am-8pm in summer), with kayaks and bikes available for rent, the option to learn diving, and other activities. This tranquil seawater swimming area was won from the sea by the creation of massive cement-block dykes. At its northern end, like a great rectangular sunflower, an enormous photovoltaic panel turns its face up to the sun to power the area with solar energy. Along with another set of **solar panels** in the form of porticoes, it generates enough electricity for 1000 households. Just behind it spreads **Port Fòrum**, Barcelona's third marina. The area is unified by an undulating esplanade and walkways that are perfect for walking, wheelchair access, bikes and skateboards.

In summer, a weekend **amusement park** (11am-2.30pm & 5-9pm Sat & Sun Jun-Sep) sets up with all the usual suspects: rides, shooting galleries, snack stands, inflatable castles and dodgem cars.

The **Parc de Diagonal Mar**, designed by Enric Miralles, contains pools, fountains, a didactic botanical walk (with more than 30 species of trees and other plants) and modern sculptures.

SLEEPING

PORT VELL & LA BARCELONETA

The handful of seaside options around Port Vell and La Barceloneta ranges from a rowdy youth hostel to a couple of grand five-stars, one of which is destined to become an iconic, waterfront landmark.

W BARCELONA Map p130 Hotel €€€

93 295 28 00; www.w-barcelona.com; Plaça de la Rosa del Vents 1; r €283-385; M Barceloneta; 17, 39, 57 or 64; P

The spinnaker-shaped tower of glass contains 473 rooms and suites that are the last word in contemporary hotel chic. In an admirable location at the end of a beach, it has rooms in a variety of shapes, orientations and sizes. Self-indulgence is a byword and guests can flit between the gym, infinity pool (with bar) and Bliss@spa. There's avant-garde dining on the 2nd floor in Carles Abellán's Bravo restaurant and hip cocktail sipping in the top-floor Eclipse bar.

EUROSTARS GRAND MARINA HOTEL Map p130 Hotel €€

93 295 99 08; www.grandmarinahotel.com; Moll de Barcelona; r €150-255; M Drassanes; P

Housed in the World Trade Center, the Grand Marina has a maritime flavour that

GUY MOBERLY

Port Fòrum marina

LA BARCELONETA & THE BEACHES

SLEEPING

continues into the rooms, with lots of polished timber touches and hydro-massage bathtubs. Some rooms on either side of the building offer splendid views of the city, port and open sea. The rooftop gym and outdoor pool have equally enticing views.

HOTEL DEL MAR Map p136　Hotel €€
☎ 93 319 33 02; www.gargallohotels.es; Pla del Palau 19; s/d €139/171; Ⓜ Barceloneta; ✖ ▯

The nicely modernised Sea Hotel is strategically placed between Port Vell and El Born. Some of the rooms in this classified building have balconies with waterfront views. You're in a fairly peaceful spot but no more than 10 minutes' walk from the beaches and seafood of La Barceloneta, and the bars and mayhem of El Born.

HOTEL 54 Map p136　Hotel €€
☎ 93 225 00 54; www.hotel54barceloneta.com; Passeig de Joan de Borbó 54; s/d €130/140; Ⓜ Barceloneta; ✖ ▯ 🛜

This place is all about location. Modern rooms, with dark tile floors, designer bathrooms and LCD TVs are sought after for the marina and sunset views. Other (cheaper) rooms look out over the lanes of La Barceloneta. You can also sit on the roof terrace and enjoy the harbour views.

HOTEL MARINA FOLCH
Map p130　Hotel €€
☎ 93 310 37 09; www.hotelmarinafolchbcn.com; Carrer del Mar 16; s/d €40/75; Ⓜ Barceloneta; ✖

A simple dig above a busy seafood restaurant, this hotel has just one teeny single and 10 doubles of varying sizes and quality. The most attractive are those looking out towards the marina. The rooms are basic enough but kept spick and span, and

the location is unbeatable, just a couple of minutes from the beach.

PORT OLÍMPIC, EL POBLENOU & EL FÒRUM
For years the breathtakingly located Hotel Arts Barcelona has been *the* place to stay in Barcelona. It gets some tower-hotel competition in the Fòrum area, mostly aimed at a business crowd and generally considerably cheaper.

HOTEL ARTS BARCELONA
Map p130　Hotel €€€
☎ 93 221 10 00; www.hotelartsbarcelona.com; Carrer de la Marina 19-21; r from €485; Ⓜ Ciutadella Vila Olímpica; Ⓟ ✖ ▯ 🛜 ⚲

In one of the two sky-high towers that dominate Port Olímpic, this is Barcelona's most fashionable hotel, frequented by VIPs from all over the planet. It has more than 450 rooms with unbeatable views, and prices vary greatly according to size, position and time of year. Luxury suites shoot into five-figure sums. Services range from enticing spa facilities on the 42nd and 43rd floors, to fine dining in Arola, run by the Michelin-starred Sergi Arola.

HOTEL ME Map p130　Hotel €€
☎ 902 144440; www.me-barcelona.com; Carrer de Pere IV 272-286; r from €155; Ⓜ Poblenou; Ⓟ ✖ ▯ 🛜 ⚲

Designed by Dominique Perrault, this daring, slim tower consisting of two filigree slabs of glass caked one vertically on the other, overlooks Jean Nouvel's Parc del Centre del Poblenou and offers designer digs in which whites, creams and reds dominate much of the decor. Rooms come in an array of sizes and comfort levels. You may get views of the city or the sea. The 6th-floor Angels & Kings Club, with its terrace and swimming pool, can get quite lively.

Seafood paella at Xiringuito D'Escribà (p146)

DIEGO LEZAMA

POBLENOU BED & BREAKFAST

Map p130   Hotel €€

☎ 93 221 26 01; www.hostalpoblenou.com;
Carrer del Taulat 30; s €60, d €80-90, tr €100;
Ⓜ Llacuna; 🔀 🖥 🛜

Experience life in this colourful working-class neighbourhood, just back from the beach and increasingly home to a diverse population of loft-inhabiting gentrifiers. The 1930s house, with its high ceilings and beautiful tiled floors, offers 10 rooms, each a little different and all with a fresh feel, light colours, comfortable beds and, occasionally, a balcony. You can have breakfast in the rear terrace or parade the infectiously busy Rambla del Poblenou.

EATING
PORT VELL & LA BARCELONETA

In the Maremàgnum complex (p150) on the Moll d'Espanya you can eat close to the water's edge at a handful of fun, if fairly slapdash, joints. For good food and atmosphere, head around to La Barceloneta, whose lanes bristle with everything from good-natured, noisy tapas bars to upmarket seafood restaurants. Almost everything shuts on Sunday and Monday evenings.

EL LOBITO Map p136   Seafood €€€

☎ 93 319 91 64; Carrer de Ginebra 9; meals
€70-80; 🕑 lunch & dinner Tue-Sat, lunch Sun;
Ⓜ Barceloneta

A coquettish corner spot with pleasingly cluttered decor, dark timber tables and lime-green linen, the 'Little Wolf' is a seafood-lover's paradise. The usual procedure is a set menu, with a procession of sea critters (preceded by a few landlubberly amuse-gueules). Avoid the seriously busy Friday and Saturday nights.

TORRE D'ALTA MAR

Map p130   Seafood €€€

☎ 93 221 00 07; www.torredealtamar.com;
Torre de Sant Sebastià, Passeig de Joan de Borbó
88; meals €70-80; 🕑 lunch & dinner Tue-Sat,
dinner Sun-Mon; Ⓜ Barceloneta, 🚌 17, 39, 57
or 64; 🔀

Head up to the top of the Torre de Sant Sebastià and, instead of taking the

Transbordador Aeri, take a ringside seat for the best city dining views and fine seafood, such as a *Gall de Sant Pere amb salsa de garotes* (John Dory with sea-urchin sauce). The setting alone, high up above the city and port, makes this perfect for a romantic couple.

SUQUET DE L'ALMIRALL

Map p130   Seafood €€

☎ 93 221 62 33; Passeig de Joan de Borbó 65; meals €45-50; 🕙 lunch & dinner Tue-Sat, lunch Sun; Ⓜ Barceloneta, 🚌 17, 39, 57 or 64; ⊠

A family business run by an alumnus of Ferran Adrià's El Bulli, the order of the day is top-class seafood with the occasional unexpected twist. The house specialty is *suquet*. A good option is the *pica pica marinera* (a seafood mix, €38) or you could opt for the tasting menu (€44). Grab one of the few outdoor tables.

CAN MAJÓ Map p130   Seafood €€

☎ 93 221 58 18; Carrer del Almirall Aixada 23; meals €30-40; 🕙 lunch & dinner Tue-Sat, lunch Sun; Ⓜ Barceloneta, 🚌 45, 57, 59, 64 or 157

Virtually on the beach (with tables outside in summer), Can Majó has a long and steady reputation for fine seafood, particularly its rice dishes (€15 to €22) and cornucopian *suquets* (fish stews). The *bollabessa de peix i marisc* (fish and seafood bouillabaisse) is succulent. Or try a big *graellada* (mixed seafood grill). Sit outside and admire the beach goers.

CAN ROS 1911 Map p130   Seafood €€

☎ 93 221 45 79; Carrer del Almirall Aixada 7; meals €30-35; 🕙 Thu-Tue; Ⓜ Barceloneta, 🚌 45, 57, 59, 64 or 157; ⊠

The fifth generation is now at the controls in this immutable seafood favourite. In a restaurant where the decor is a reminder of simpler times, there's a straightforward guiding principle: give the punters juicy

fresh fish cooked with a light touch. They also do a rich *arròs a la marinera* (seafood rice), a generous *suquet* and a mixed seafood platter for two.

RESTAURANT 7 PORTES

Map p136   Seafood €€

☎ 93 319 30 33; www.7portes.com; Passeig d'Isabel II 14; meals €30-35; 🕙 1pm-1am Ⓜ Barceloneta; ⊠

Founded in 1836 as a cafe and converted into a restaurant in 1929, this is a classic. In the hands of the Parellada clan, which runs several quality restaurants in and beyond Barcelona, it exudes an old-world atmosphere with its wood panelling, tiles, mirrors and plaques naming some of the famous – such as Orson Welles – who have passed through. Paella is the speciality, or go for the surfeit of seafood in the *gran plat de marisc* (literally 'big plate of seafood'). We dare you to finish it!

CAN RAMONET Map p136   Seafood €€

☎ 93 319 30 64; Carrer de la Maquinista 17; meals €30; Ⓜ Barceloneta; ⊠

Perching at one of the little tables across the lane is the perfect way to pass a warm summer evening, perhaps over some *vieires al cava* (scallops in Catalan 'champagne'). Or step inside and enjoy your tapas around a barrel-cum-table. Rice dishes cost around €20 for two and the catch of the day is around €20 to €25. It claims to have been in business since 1763.

VASO DE ORO Map p136   Tapas €€

☎ 93 319 30 98; Carrer de Balboa 6; meals €20-25; Ⓜ Barceloneta; ⊠

This must be one of the world's narrowest bars. At either end, the space balloons a little to allow for a handful of tables. Squeeze in and enjoy the show. Fast-talking, white-jacketed waiters will serve up a few quick quips with your tapas of grilled

DIEGO LEZAMA

Xiringuito D'Escribà (p146)

gambes (prawns) or *solomillo* (sirloin) chunks. Want something a little different to drink? Ask for a *flauta cincuenta* – half lager and half dark beer.

CAN MAÑO Map p136 Spanish €
☎ 93 319 30 82; Carrer del Baluard 12; meals €20; ☽ Mon-Sat; Ⓜ Barceloneta
The owners have been dealing with an on-slaught of punters for decades and swear they are going to retire soon (but never do). You'll need to be prepared to wait before being squeezed in at a packed table for a raucous dinner (or lunch) of *raciones* (listed on a board at the back) over a bottle of *turbio*, a pleasing cloudy white plonk.

CAN PAIXANO Map p136 Tapas €
☎ 93 310 08 39; Carrer de la Reina Cristina 7; meals €15-20; ☽ 9am-10.30pm; Ⓜ Barceloneta; ✂
Tucked away amid the bright tacky lights of cheap electronics stores in what could almost be a backstreet in Southeast Asia, this lofty old champagne bar has long run on a winning formula. The standard poi-

son is bubbly rosé in elegant little glasses, combined with bite-sized *bocadillos* (filled rolls). This place is jammed to the rafters, and elbowing your way to the bar to ask harried staff for menu items can be a titanic struggle.

PORT OLÍMPIC, EL POBLENOU & EL FÒRUM
The Port Olímpic marina is lined on two sides by dozens of restaurants and tapas bars, popular in spring and summer but mostly underwhelming. A more upmarket series of places huddles at the northeast end of Platja de la Barceloneta – it's hard to beat the sand, sea and palm tree back-drop. Otherwise, the search for culinary curios will take you behind the scenes in El Poblenou, where a few nuggets glitter.

ELS PESCADORS Map p130 Seafood €€
☎ 93 225 20 18; www.elspescadors.com; Plaça de Prim 1; meals €50; ☽ daily, closed Easter week; Ⓜ Poblenou
Set on a cute square lined with low houses and *bella ombre* trees long ago

CHILLIN' ON THE BEACH

Summer lounging on the beach is not just about towels on the sand. Scattered along Barcelona's strands is a series of hip little beach bars bringing chilled club sounds to the seaside. Sip on your favourite cocktail as you take in the day's last rays. There's no need to head straight home at sundown either, as these places keep humming from about 10am until as late as 2am (Easter to October), depending on the forces of law and order and how good business is. Along the beaches of La Barceloneta (from Platja de Sant Miquel up to Port Olímpic), there are several spots. A good one is Chiringuito del Mar (Map p130).

Better are those northeast of Port Olímpic. There are three on Platja de Nova Icària: Dockers (Map p130; http://dockers bcn.com, in Spanish), El Bierzo (Map p130) and Inercia (Map p130; www.inerciabeach.com). The Pachá club people have one each on Platja de Bogatell and Platja de la Nova Mar Bella, both called El Chiringuito (Map p130; www.elchiringuitogroup.com). Mochima (Map p130; www.mochimabar.com, in Spanish), popular with a mixed crowd, has a bar on Platja de la Mar Bella and another a little further up on Platja de la Nova Mar Bella. Nueva Ola (Map p130) is the last of these bars, at the northern end of Platja de la Nova Mar Bella.

By far the best beach booty experience takes place outside Barcelona, a train ride to the northeast in Mataró. Lasal (www.lasal.com; ☉ May-Sep), on Platja Sant Simó (northeast of the marina), offers top local DJs, food and a great party atmosphere.

imported from South America, this bustling family restaurant continues to serve some of the city's great seafood-and-rice dishes. There are three dining areas inside: two quite modern, while the main one preserves its old tavern flavour. A better option is sitting outside. All the products – fish, meat and vegetables – are trucked in fresh from various parts of Catalonia.

EL CANGREJO LOCO

Map p130   Seafood €€

☎ 93 221 05 33; www.elcangrejoloco.com; Moll de Gregal 29-30; meals €45-60, menú del día €23; ☉ daily; Ⓜ Ciutadella Vila Olímpica; ✗

Of the hive of eating activity along the docks of Port Olímpic, the 'Mad Crab' is the best. It inevitably has a thoroughfare feel, attracting swarms of tourists, but the difference is that the food is

generally of a reasonable quality. Fish standards, such as *bacallà* (salted cod) and *rap* (monkfish), are served in various guises and melt in the mouth. The rich *mariscada* (seafood platter) for two includes half a lobster.

XIRINGUITO D'ESCRIBÀ

Map p130   Seafood €€

☎ 93 221 07 29; www.escriba.es; Ronda del Litoral 42, Platja de Bogatell; meals €40-50; ☉ lunch daily; Ⓜ Llacuna

The clan that brought you Escribà sweets and pastries also operates one of the most popular waterfront seafood eateries in town. This is one of the few places where one person can order from a selection of paella and *fideuà* (normally reserved for a minimum of two people). Prices are higher than average, but quality matches. You can also choose from a selection of Escribà pastries for dessert – worth the trip alone.

LA PUBILLA DEL TAULAT

Map p130   Tapas €€

☎ 93 225 30 85; www.lapubilladeltaulat.com;
Carrer de Marià Aguiló 131; meals €20-30;
☾ Tue-Sun; Ⓜ Poblenou

Get inside the eatery in this late-19th-century building quickly, as you'll find the bar has been stripped of all its tapas delights if you arrive much after 10pm. Tucked away in backstreets still partly lined with low-slung houses of another era, this place is a popular stop. All the classics are present: *patatas bomba* (spicy meat stuffed potatoes), *mejillones al vapor* (steamed mussels), *chocos* (lightly fried cuttlefish slices) and more.

DRINKING

The northeastern end of the beach on the Barceloneta waterfront near Port Olímpic is a pleasant corner of evening chic that takes on a balmy, almost Caribbean air in the warmer months. A selection of restaurant-lounges and trendy bar-clubs vies for your attention. Several other at-tractive options are scattered away from this core of night-time entertainment.

Several options present themselves along the coast. The line-up of raucous bars along the marina at Port Olímpic is one. More chilled are the beach bars (see p146).

CDLC Map p136   Bar

☎ 93 224 04 70; www.cdlcbarcelona.com;
Passeig Marítim de la Barceloneta 32; ☾ noon-3am; Ⓜ Ciutadella Vila Olímpica

Seize the night by the scruff at the Carpe Diem Lounge Club, where you can lounge in Asian-inspired surrounds. Ideal for a slow warm-up before heading to the nearby clubs, if you can be bothered lifting yourself back up onto your feet, that is. You can come for the food or wait until about midnight, when they start to roll up the tables and the DJs and dancers take full control.

LUZ DE GAS PORTVELL Map p136   Bar

☎ 93 484 23 26; Moll del Dipòsit; ☾ noon-3am Mar-Nov; Ⓜ Barceloneta

Sit on the top deck of this boat and let go of the day's cares. Sip wine or beer, nibble

La Barceloneta beach

PSF/IMAGEBROKER

tapas and admire the yachts. On shore they play some good dance music at night.

OKE Map p136   Bar
Carrer del Baluard 54; ⏱ **11am-2am;**
Ⓜ **Barceloneta**
An eclectic and happy little crowd, with a slight predominance of Dutch, hangs about this hippie-ish little bar near La Barceloneta's market. Lounges, tables and chairs seem to have been extracted willy-nilly from garage sales. Juices, cocktails and snacks are the main fare, along with animated conversation wafting out over the street.

PEZ PLAYA Map p136   Bar
Carrer de Ramon Trias Fargas 2-4; ⏱ **8pm-3am Thu-Fri, 4pm-3am Sat-Sun;** Ⓜ **Ciutadella Vila Olímpica**
A mean mojito is served in this cheerful, makeshift beachside dance bar. It's a bare-bones structure, mostly open to the balmy night air, and attracts a mixed crowd with broad musical tastes, without the urban-Buddha chilling thing. Just a good fun place to sip and jive.

SANTA MARTA Map p130   Bar
Carrer de Guitert 60; ⏱ **10.30am-7pm Sun, Mon, Wed & Thu, 10.30am-10pm Fri & Sat;** Ⓜ **Barceloneta,** 🚌 **45, 57, 59 & 157**
Foreigners who have found seaside nirvana in Barcelona hang out in this chilled

bar back from the beach. A curious crowd of Rastas, beach bums and switched-on dudes chats over light meals and beer inside or relaxes outside over a late breakfast. It has some tempting food, too: a mix of local and Italian items, with a range of filled rolls *(bocatas)* for €5, or a dish of *mozzarella di bufala* (buffalo-milk cheese) for €8.

SHÔKO Map p136   Bar
☎ **93 225 92 00; www.shoko.biz; Passeig Marítim de la Barceloneta 36;** ⏱ **8pm-3am Tue-Sun;** Ⓜ **Ciutadella Vila Olímpica**
Too cool for anything really, let alone school, this chilled restaurant and bar is all far-out concepts. Wafting over your mixed Asian-Med food is an opiate blend of Shinto music and Japanese electro. As the food is cleared away, the place turns into a funky-beat kinda place, into which you may or may not enter without dinner, depending on the bouncer's mood.

ENTERTAINMENT & ACTIVITIES
PORT VELL & LA BARCELONETA

CATWALK Map p136   Club
☎ **93 224 07 40; www.clubcatwalk.net; Carrer de Ramon Trias Fargas 2-4; €15;** ⏱ **midnight-6am Thu-Sun;** Ⓜ **Ciutadella Vila Olímpica**

MAKING A SPLASH
Guys and gals board their metal steeds on hot summer nights to bear down on one of the top outdoor club scenes in town (or rather out of town, since it's in neighbouring L'Hospitalet de Llobregat). **Liquid** (☎ **670 221209; www.liquid bcn.com; Complex Esportiu Hospitalet Nord, Carrer de Manuel Azaña 21-23;** ⏱ **Jun-Sep)** says what it is. A palm-studded islet is surrounded by a bottom-lit azure moat that tempts surprisingly few folks to plunge in while dancing the night away in this megaclub. Local and foreign DJs keep the punters, a mixed crowd from all over town, in the groove in a series of different internal spaces, as well as poolside.

Maremàgnum mall (p150)

DAMIEN SIMONIS

A well-dressed crowd piles into this club for good house music, occasionally mellowed down with more body-hugging electro, R&B, hip hop and funk. Alternatively, you can sink into a fat lounge for a quiet tipple and whisper. Popular local DJ Jekey leads the way most nights.

MONASTERIO Map p136 Live Music

☎ 616 287197; www.salamonasterio.com, in Spanish; Passeig d'Isabel II 4; ⏱ 9pm-2.30am Sun-Thu, 9.30pm-3am Fri & Sat; Ⓜ Barceloneta
Wander downstairs to the brick vaults of this jamming basement music den. There's a little of everything, from jazz on Sunday nights, blues jams on Thursdays, rock and roll on Tuesdays and up-and-coming singer-songwriters on Mondays. It has Murphy's on tap, along with several other imported beers.

CLUB NATACIÓ ATLÈTIC-BARCELONA Map p130 Swimming

☎ 93 221 00 10; www.cnab.org; Plaça de Mar s/n; adult/under 10yr €10.55/6.13; ⏱ 6.30am-11pm

Mon-Fri, 7am-11pm Sat, 8am-5pm Sun & holidays Oct-mid-May, 8am-8pm Sun & holidays mid-May–Sep; Ⓜ Barceloneta, 🚌 17, 39, 57 or 64
This athletic club has one indoor and two outdoor pools. Of the latter, one is heated for lap swimming in winter. Admission includes use of the gym and private beach access. Membership costs €35.70 a month, plus €71 joining fee.

POLIESPORTIU MARÍTIM

Map p136 Swimming
☎ 93 224 04 40; www.claror.cat, in Catalan; Passeig Marítim de la Barceloneta 33-35; Mon-Fri €15, Sat-Sun & holidays €17.80; ⏱ 7am-midnight Mon-Fri, 8am-9pm Sat, 8am-4pm Sun & holidays Sep-Jul, 7am-10.30pm Mon-Fri, 8am-9pm Sat, 8am-3pm Sun Aug; Ⓜ Ciutadella Vila Olímpica
Water babies will squeal with delight in this thalassotherapeutic (simply meaning sea-water therapy) sports centre. In addition to the small pool for lap swimming, there is a labyrinth of spa pools that range from hot to warm to freezing, along with thundering waterfalls for massage relief.

PORT OLÍMPIC, EL POBLENOU & EL FÓRUM

YELMO CINES ICÀRIA

Map p130   Cinema

☎ 93 221 75 85; www.yelmocineplex.es, in Spanish; Carrer de Salvador Espriu 61;
Ⓜ Ciutadella Vila Olímpica

This vast cinema complex screens movies in their original language on a whopping 15 screens, making for plenty of choice. Aside from the screens, you'll find several cheerful eateries, bars and the like to keep you occupied before and after the movies.

RAZZMATAZZ

Map p130   Club & Live Music

☎ 93 272 09 10; www.salarazzmatazz.com; Carrer dels Almogàvers 122 & Carrer de Pamplona 88; admission €15-30; ⏱ live music Tue-Sat, clubs 1-6am Fri & Sat; Ⓜ Marina or Bogatell

Bands from far and wide occasionally create scenes of near hysteria in this, one of the city's classic live-music and clubbing venues. Bands generally appear Thursday to Saturday evenings (occasionally Tuesdays and Wednesdays). On weekends the live music then gives way to club sounds. Five different clubs in one huge postindustrial space attract people of all dance persuasions and ages. The main space, the Razz Club, is a haven for the latest international rock and indie acts. The Loft does house and electro, while the Pop Bar offers anything from garage to soul. The Lolita room is the land of techno pop and deep house, and upstairs in the Rex Room guys and girls sweat it out to high-rhythm electro-rock.

SALA MEPHISTO

Map p130   Live Music

☎ 659 163652; www.mephistobcn.com; Carrer de Roc Boronat 33; ⏱ 10pm-6am Fri & Sat;
Ⓜ Llacuna

Heavy metal, Gothic and hard-rock fans converge on this one-time workshop for concerts by groups from all over Europe. The music determines the crowd, so expect pale people in theatrically dark clothing. Long-haired lads with tats and leather mingle with pale wraiths in flowing black dresses and heavy make-up. It's all in the name of good fun. Heavy metal lovers should especially check the place out from 1am on Saturdays.

BASE NAUTICA MUNICIPAL

Map p130   Sailing

☎ 93 221 04 32; www.basenautica.org; Avinguda de Litoral s/n; Ⓜ Poblenou

Have you come to Barcelona to learn how to become a sea dog? If so, head to this place, which is located just back from Platja de la Mar Bella, and enrol yourself in a course in boat handling, kayaking (€125 for 10 hours' tuition), windsurfing (€185 for 10 hours' tuition) or catamaran (€216 for 12 hours' tuition).

SHOPPING

Aside from the shopping-mall fun of Maremàgnum, there are precious few outlets for maxing out your cards along the waterfront.

MAREMÀGNUM

Map p130   Shopping Centre

☎ 93 225 81 00; www.maremagnum.es; Moll d'Espanya; ⏱ 10am-10pm; Ⓜ Drassanes

Created out of largely abandoned docks, this chirpy shopping centre, with its bars, restaurants and cinemas, is pleasant enough for a stroll virtually in the middle of the old harbour. You'll find outlets for anything from Calvin Klein underwear to Brazilian flip-flops (Havaianas). Football fans will be drawn to the paraphernalia at FC Barcelona (☎ 93 225 80 45). The big news is that shops here open on Sundays, pretty much unheard of anywhere else in the city.

L'EIXAMPLE

L'EIXAMPLE

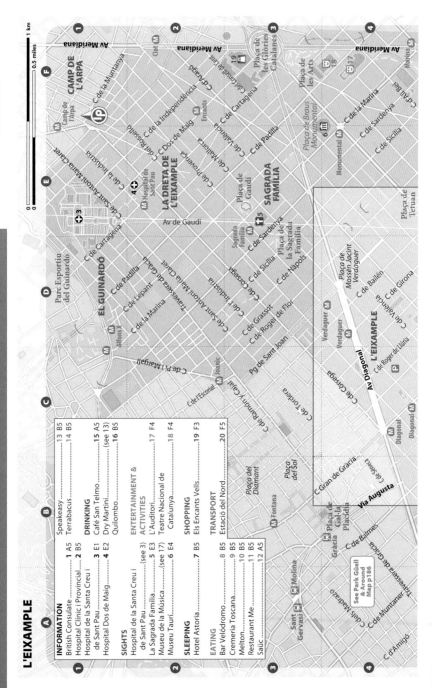

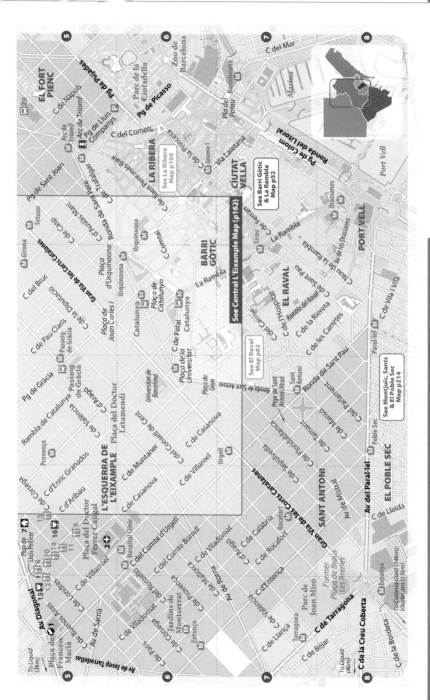

HIGHLIGHTS

1 LA SAGRADA FAMÍLIA

BY JORDI FAULÍ, DEPUTY ARCHITECTURAL DIRECTOR FOR LA SAGRADA FAMÍLIA

The Temple Expiatori de la Sagrada Família is Antoni Gaudí's masterpiece, on which he worked for 43 years. It's a slender structure where everything is devoted to geometric perfection and sacred symbolism. It has spanned generations but never lost Gaudí's breathtaking modernity, originality and architectural synthesis of natural forms.

↘ JORDI FAULÍ'S DON'T MISS LIST

❶ PASSION FACADE

Among the Fachada de la Pasión's stand-out features are the angled columns, dramatic scenes from Jesus' last hours, an extraordinary rendering of the Last Supper and a bronze door that reads like a sculptured book. But the most surprising view is from inside the door on the extreme right (especially in the afternoon with the sun in the west).

❷ MAIN NAVE

The majestic Nave Principal showcases Gaudí's use of tree motifs for columns

to support the domes. But it's the skylights that give the nave its luminous quality, with light flooding into the apse and main altar from the skylight 75m above the floor.

❸ SIDE NAVE AND NATIVITY TRANSEPT

Although beautiful in its own right, this is the perfect place to view the sculpted treelike columns and get an overall perspective of the main nave. Turn around and you're confronted with the inside of the Nativity Facade,

Clockwise from top: Bronze door detail, Passion Facade (p161), La Sagrada Família; Western facade; Detail of Nativity Facade (p163); Stained glass windows

L'EIXAMPLE

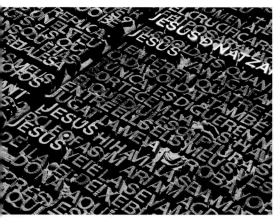

HIGHLIGHTS

an alternative view that most visitors miss; the stained-glass windows are superb.

❹ NATIVITY FACADE

The Fachada del Nacimiento is Gaudí's grand hymn to Creation. Begin by viewing it front-on, then draw close (but to one side) to make out the details of its sculpted figures. The complement to the finely wrought detail is the majesty of the four parabolic towers that are topped by Venetian stained glass.

❺ MODEL OF COLÒNIA GÜELL

The most interesting model in the Museu Gaudí is the church at Colònia Güell. It's upside down because that's how Gaudí worked to best study the building's form and structural balance.

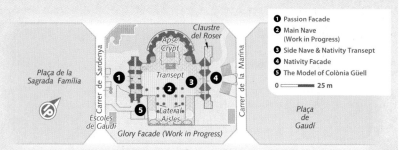

❶ Passion Facade
❷ Main Nave (Work in Progress)
❸ Side Nave & Nativity Transept
❹ Nativity Facade
❺ The Model of Colònia Güell

0 ⸺ 25 m

Claustre del Roser
Apse
Crypt
Plaça de la Sagrada Família
Carrer de Sardenya
Transept
Carrer de la Marina
Escoles de Gaudí
Lateral Aisles
Plaça de Gaudí
Glory Facade (Work in Progress)

⌲ THINGS YOU NEED TO KNOW

How it's done Gaudí spent the last 12 years of his life preparing plans for how the building was to be finished **Expected completion date** 2020 to 2040 **Best photo op** Take a lift (€2) up one of the towers **Admission** €8 **Guided tours** €3.50, up to four daily **See p161 for more information**

HIGHLIGHTS

L'EIXAMPLE

HIGHLIGHTS

2

☜ NIGHTLIFE

Although much of Barcelona's coolest nightlife has migrated to the Ribera and Raval districts, **L'Eixample** (p179 and p181) still retains pockets of resistance, most notably along lively Carrer d'Aribau. A highlight is the so-called 'Gaixample', an ebullient sprinkling of gay bars and clubs along Carrers Consell and de la Diputación that have catapulted Barcelona into being one of Europe's premier gay destinations.

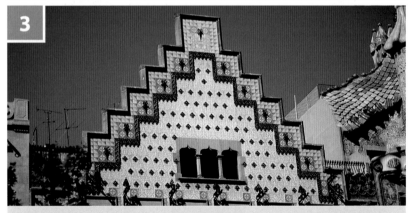

3

☜ MANZANA DE LA DISCORDIA

One block on Passeig de Gràcia is embellished with three starkly different **apartment buildings** (p165 and p166) renovated by the three *enfants terribles* of early 20th-century Modernisme. The houses highlight the discordant clash between the architects' styles: Puig i Cadafalch, gabled and faintly Dutch; Domènech i Montaner, whimsical with a strong regal quality; and Gaudí, downright other-worldly.

4

⬊ LA PEDRERA

Number 92 Passeig de Gràcia rarely goes by its normal street address. The building known as La Pedrera (p163) fairly kidnaps you as you walk, minding your own business, along Barcelona's finest urban thoroughfare. Anyone vaguely familiar with Gaudí will recognise all the hallmarks: swirling staircases, hallucinogenic curves and not a straight line in sight.

5

⬊ SHOPPING ON THE PASSEIG DE GRÀCIA

Once a lane that linked Barcelona to the village of Gràcia, the Passeig de Gràcia has metamorphosed into the city's fanciest street. Heaving with posh hotels and punctuated with architectural nods to Catalonia's Modernista movement, the Passeig is feted most for its shopping (p183). Luxury labels share space with the odd indie fashion guerrilla.

6

⬊ FUNDACIÓ ANTONI TÀPIES

Take a pioneering Modernista building and stuff it with works by one of Spain's greatest living painters. The result: art inside art or, to be more specific, Antoni Tàpies (the artist) inside Luís Domènech i Montaner (the architect). This exhaustive Tàpies collection (p167) helps confirm Barcelona's place as one of the world's great art cities.

2 DIEGO LEZAMA; 3 BETHUNE CARMICHAEL; 4 RACHEL LEWIS; 5 KRZYSZTOF DYDYNSKI; 6 KRZYSZTOF DYDYNSKI

2 Dry Martini bar (p180); 3 Casa Amatller, part of the Manzana de la Discordia (p165); 4 Roof of La Pedrera (p163); 5 Mannequins in Mango (p184); 6 Roof of Fundació Antoni Tàpies (p167)

MODERNISME WALK IN L'EIXAMPLE

Modernisme defines L'Eixample the way Gothic characterises the Barri Gòtic. Put aside an hour and a half for this 3.8km walk starting at the vaguely conformist Casa Calvet and finishing at the slightly more out-of-the-box Casa Macaya.

❶ CASA CALVET

Gaudí's most conventional contribution to L'Eixample is **Casa Calvet** (Carrer de Casp 48), built in 1900. Inspired by baroque, the noble ashlar facade is broken up by protruding wrought-iron balconies. Inside, the main attraction is the staircase, viewed from the swank **restaurant** (p175).

❷ CASA PIA BATLLÓ

Vilaseca's **Casa Pia Batlló** (Rambla de Catalunya 17), built between 1891 and 1896, is interesting in its use of ironwork, especially along the 1st- and top-floor galleries around the three facades. Stonework is pre-eminent, and pseudo-Gothic touches, such as the witch's hat towers, abound.

❸ CASA MULLERAS

In among the big three of the Manzana de la Discordia (p165), **Casa Mulleras** (Passeig de Gràcia 37), built in 1906 by Enric Sagnier (1858–1931), is a relatively demure contribution. The facade transmits a restrained classicism, but it has light floral decoration and a fine gallery.

❹ CASA ENRIC BATLLÓ

Another apartment building by Vilaseca is **Casa Enric Batlló** (Passeig de Gràcia 75), completed in 1896 and part of the Comtes de Barcelona hotel (p172). Lit up at night, the brickwork facade is especially graceful.

❺ CASA SERRA

Puig i Cadafalch let his imagination loose on **Casa Serra** (Rambla de Catalunya 126), a neo-Gothic whimsy that is home to government offices. With its central tower topped by a witch's hat, grandly decorated upper-floor windows and tiled roof, it must have been a strange house to live in!

❻ CASA COMALAT

Built in 1911 by Salvador Valeri (1873–1954), **Casa Comalat** (Avinguda Diagonal 442) is striking. The Gaudí influence on the main facade, with its wavy roof and bulging balconies, is obvious. Head around the back to Carrer de Còrsega to see a more playful facade, with its windows stacked like cards.

❼ CASA THOMAS

Completed in 1912, **Casa Thomas** (Carrer de Mallorca 291) was one of Domènech i Montaner's earlier efforts. The ceramic details are a

MODERNISME WALK IN L'EIXAMPLE

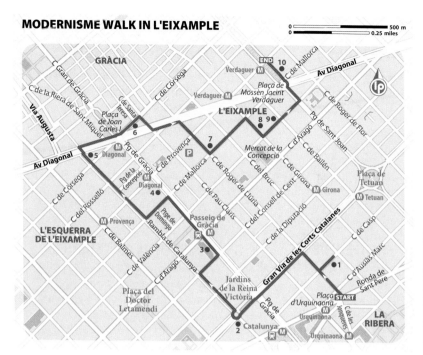

trademark and the massive ground-level wrought-iron decoration (and protection?) is magnificent. Wander inside to the **Cubiña design store** (p183) to admire his interior work.

❽ CASA GRANELL

The colourful **Casa Granell** (Carrer de Girona 122), built by Jeroni Granell (1867–1931), is a peculiar building, with its serpentine lines (check out the roof) and gently curving decorative facade framing the rectangular windows. If you get the chance, take a peek inside the entrance and stairwell, both richly decorated.

❾ CASA LLOPIS I BOFILL

Built in 1902, **Casa Llopis i Bofill** (Carrer de València 339) is an interesting block of flats designed by Antoni Gallissà (1861–1903). The graffiti-covered facade is particularly striking to the eye. The use of parabolic arches on the ground floor is a clear Modernista touch, as are the wrought-iron balconies.

❿ CASA MACAYA

Constructed in 1901, Puig i Cadafalch's **Casa Macaya** (Passeig de Sant Joan 108) has a wonderful courtyard and features the typical playful, pseudo-Gothic decoration that characterises many of the architect's projects. It is occasionally used for temporary exhibitions, when visitors may enter.

BEST...

GAIXAMPLE

- **Nosotraos** (p184) Specialist gay/lesbian shop.
- **Metro** (p182) Casual gay bar and dance club.
- **Dietrich Gay Teatro Club** (p181) Drag queens and Hollywood legends.
- **Museum** (p180) The best exhibits are the 'twinks'.
- **Carrer de Diputación** (p179) Main artery in Gaixample.

MODERNISTA ARCHITECTURE

- **La Pedrera** (p163) Madly swirling Gaudí apartment block.
- **Casa Batlló** (p165) Gaudí goes psychedelic 60 years too early.
- **Palau Montaner** (p169) Doménech i Montaner's interior design masterpiece.
- **Casa Lleó Morera** (p166) Doménech's contribution to the Manzana de la Discordia.
- **Casa Amatller** (p165) Puig i Cadafalch's fantastical answer to Casa Batlló.

ACTION STREETS

- **Carrer d'Aribau** (p179) Bar-strip that defies Eixample's shut-down image.
- **Passeig de Gràcia** (p183) Barcelona's finest urban artery.
- **Carrer del Consell** (p179) Gay bars and nightlife.
- **Quadrat d'Or** (p174) One block; countless restaurants.
- **La Rambla de Catalunya** (p183) The definitive shopping street.

ETHNIC EATERIES

- **Patagonia** (p175) Argentine-run, so there's beef – obviously.
- **Melton** (p175) Italian restaurant recommended by Italians.
- **Yamadory** (p175) Long-time tranquil Japanese dining haven.
- **Thai Gardens** (p176) Plenty of greenery to complement the food.
- **El Rincón Maya** (p178) Mexican without the tacky touches.

GUY MOBERLY

Passeig de Gràcia (p183)

DISCOVER L'EIXAMPLE

By far the most extensive of Barcelona's districts, this sprawling grid is full of subidentities. Almost all the city's Modernista buildings were raised in L'Eixample. The pick of them line Passeig de Gràcia, but hundreds adorn the area. Work on Gaudí's La Sagrada Família church continues.

As Barcelona's population exploded, the medieval walls were knocked down by 1856, and in 1869 work began on L'Eixample (the Extension) to fill the open country that then lay between Barcelona and Gràcia. Building continued until well into the 20th century. Well-to-do families snapped up prime plots and raised fanciful buildings in the eclectic style of the Modernistas.

Shoppers converge on Passeig de Gràcia and La Rambla de Catalunya. At night, mainly from Thursday to Saturday, Carrer d'Aribau and nearby streets pound with nightlife as local punters let their hair down. The 'Gaixample', around Carrer del Consell de Cent and Carrer de Muntaner, is a pole of gay nightlife.

SIGHTS

LA SAGRADA FAMÍLIA Map p152

☎ 93 207 30 31; www.sagradafamilia.org; Carrer de Mallorca 401; adult/under 10yr/senior & student €12/free/10, incl Casa-Museu Gaudí in Park Güell €14/free/12; ☻ 9am-8pm Apr-Sep, 9am-6pm Oct-Mar; Ⓜ Sagrada Família

La Sagrada Família inspires awe by its sheer verticality, and in the manner of the medieval cathedrals it emulates, it's still under construction after more than 100 years. When completed, the highest tower will be more than half as high again as those that stand today. Unfinished it may be, but it attracts around 2.8 million visitors a year and is the most visited monument in Spain.

Although a building site, the completed sections and museum may be explored at leisure. Fifty-minute guided tours (€4) are offered. Alternatively, pick up an audio tour (€4), for which you need ID. Enter from Carrer de Sardenya and Carrer de la Marina. Once inside, €2.50 will get you into lifts that rise inside towers in the

Nativity and Passion Facades. These two facades, each with four sky-scraping towers, are the sides of the church. The main Glory Facade, on which work is underway, closes off the southeast end on Carrer de Mallorca.

Gaudí devised a temple 95m long and 60m wide, able to seat 13,000 people, with a central tower 170m high above the transept (representing Christ) and another 17 of 100m or more. The 12 along the three facades represent the Apostles, while the remaining five represent the Virgin Mary and the four Evangelists. With his characteristic dislike for straight lines (there were none in nature, he said), Gaudí gave his towers swelling outlines inspired by the weird peaks of the holy mountain Montserrat outside Barcelona, and encrusted them with a tangle of sculpture that seems an outgrowth of the stone.

At Gaudí's death, only the crypt, the apse walls, one portal and one tower had been finished. Three more towers were

CENTRAL L'EIXAMPLE

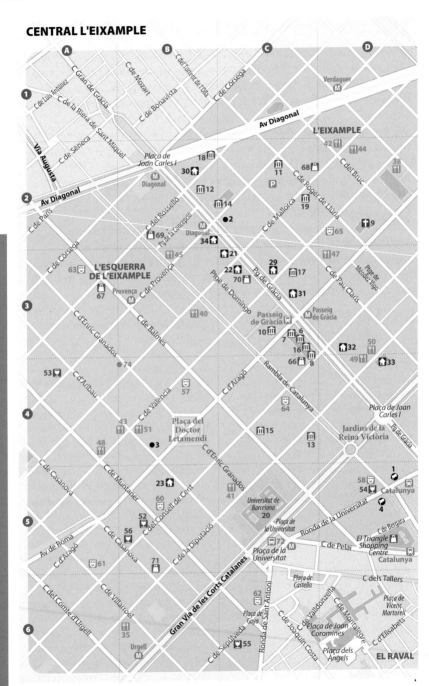

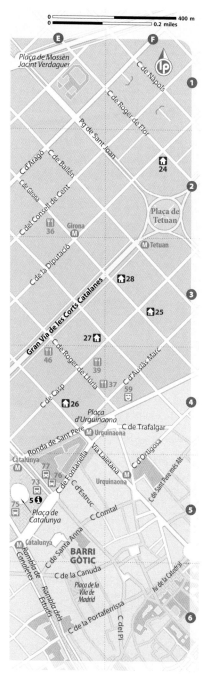

added by 1930, completing the northeast (Nativity) facade. In 1936, anarchists burned and smashed everything they could in the church, including workshops, plans and models. Work began again in 1952, but controversy has always clouded progress. Opponents of the continuation of the project claim that the computer models based on what little of Gaudí's plans survived the anarchists' ire have led to the creation of a monster that has little to do with Gaudí's plans and style. It is a debate that appears to have little hope of resolution. Like or hate what is being done, the fascination it awakens is undeniable.

Guesses on when construction might be complete range from the 2020s to the 2040s. Even before reaching that point, some of the oldest parts of the church, especially the apse, have required restoration work.

LA PEDRERA Map p162

Casa Milà; ☎ 902 400973; www.fundaciocaixa catalunya.es; Carrer de Provença 261-265; adult/under 13yr/student & EU senior €10/free/6; ⏰ 9am-8pm Mar-Oct, 9am-6.30pm Nov-Feb; Ⓜ Diagonal

This undulating beast is another madcap Gaudí masterpiece, built in 1905–10 as a combined apartment and office block. Formally called Casa Milà, after the businessperson who commissioned it, it is better known as La Pedrera (the Quarry) because of its uneven grey stone facade, which ripples around the corner of Carrer de Provença.

The Fundació Caixa Catalunya has opened the top-floor apartment, attic and roof, together called the **Espai Gaudí** (Gaudí Space), to visitors. The roof is the most extraordinary element, with its giant chimney pots looking like multicoloured medieval knights (they say

L'EIXAMPLE

SIGHTS

INFORMATION
- Barcelona Walking Tours (see 5)
- Canadian Consulate **1** D5
- Farmàcia Castells Soler **2** C2
- Farmàcia Torres **3** B4
- French Consulate **4** D5
- Oficina d'Informació de Turisme de Barcelona **5** E5

SIGHTS
- Casa Amatller **6** C3
- Casa Batlló **7** C3
- Casa Lleó Morera **8** C4
- Església de la Puríssima Concepció i Assumpció de Nostra Senyora **9** D2
- Fundació Antoni Tàpies **10** C3
- Fundació Joan Brossa **11** C2
- Fundació Suñol **12** B2
- Fundación Francisco Godia **13** C4
- La Pedrera **14** C2
- Museu del Modernisme Català **15** C4
- Museu del Perfum **16** C3
- Museu Egipci **17** C3
- Palau del Baró Quadras **18** B2
- Palau Montaner **19** C2
- Universitat de Barcelona **20** C5

SLEEPING
- Comtes de Barcelona **21** C3
- Comtes de Barcelona **22** C3
- Hostal Aribau **23** B5
- Hostal Central **24** F2
- Hostal Girona **25** F3
- Hostal Goya **26** E4
- Hotel Constanza **27** E3
- Hotel d'Uxelles **28** F3
- Hotel Majèstic **29** C3
- Hotel Omm **30** B2
- Hotel Sixtytwo **31** C3
- Mandarin Oriental **32** D3
- St Moritz Hotel **33** D4
- Suites Avenue **34** B2

EATING
- Amaltea **35** B6
- Cafè del Centre **36** E2
- Casa Alfonso **37** E4
- Casa Amalia **38** D2
- Casa Calvet **39** E4
- Cerveseria Catalana **40** B3
- Cosmo **41** C5
- De Tapa Madre **42** D2
- El Rincón Maya **43** B4
- Embat **44** D2
- Mauri **45** B3
- Patagonia **46** E4
- Relais de Venise **47** D3
- Taktika Berri **48** A4
- Tapaç 24 **49** D4
- Thai Gardens **50** D3
- Yamadory **51** B4

DRINKING
- Dacksy **52** B5
- La Fira **53** A4
- Milano **54** D5
- Museum **55** C6
- Plata Bar **56** B5

ENTERTAINMENT & ACTIVITIES
- Aire **57** B4
- Bankers' Bar (see 32)
- Bel-Luna Jazz Club **58** D5
- DBoy **59** F4
- Dietrich Gay Teatro Café **60** B5
- Méliès Cinemes **61** A5
- Metro **62** C6
- Palacio del Flamenco **63** A3
- Roxy Blue **64** C4
- Silom Spa **65** D2

SHOPPING
- Antonio Miró **66** C4
- Come In **67** A3
- Cubiña **68** C2
- Farrutx **69** B2
- Mango **70** C3
- Nosotraos **71** B5
- Regia (see 16)

TRANSPORT
- A1 Aerobús Stop (From Airport) **72** C5
- A1 Aerobús Stop (To/From Airport) **73** E5
- BEB **74** B4
- Bus Turístic (Blue Route Terminus) **75** E5
- Bus Turístic (Red Route Terminus) **76** E5
- Catalunya Bus Turìstic **77** E5

the evil imperial soldiers in the *Star Wars* movies were inspired by them). Gaudí wanted to put a tall statue of the Virgin up here too: when the Milà family said no, fearing it might make the building a target for anarchists, Gaudí resigned from the project in disgust. Mrs Milà was no fan of Gaudí and it is said that

TREMORS BELOW GROUND & ABOVE THE LAW

In 2010, a giant tunnel-making machine began to bore a 6km tunnel for the AVE high-speed train that one day will run from France to Madrid via Barcelona. The tunnel will link Estació Sants with the future second railway station in La Sagrera, crossing L'Eixample and passing under streets next to two of Gaudí's masterpieces: La Sagrada Família and La Pedrera.

Since the collapse of several blocks of flats in 2005 in the district of El Carmel because of tunnelling for a Metro line, locals have had little faith in the safety of such projects and neighbourhood groups have protested long and loud against the new tunnel, albeit in vain. Protesting louder than anyone, the administrators of La Sagrada Família tried, and failed, to block the work. In early 2010, work began on the placement of protective panels deep below the road surface in front of the church's Glory Facade to reduce the vibration effects of the passing borer on the foundations.

L'EIXAMPLE

SIGHTS

KRZYSZTOF DYDYNSKI

Interior detail, Casa Batlló

no sooner had the job been completed than she had all his personally designed furniture tossed out!

One floor below the roof, where you can appreciate Gaudí's taste for McDonald's-style parabolic arches, is a modest museum dedicated to his work.

The next floor down is the apartment (El Pis de la Pedrera). It is fascinating to wander around this elegantly furnished home, done up in the style a well-to-do family might have enjoyed in the early 20th century.

CASA BATLLÓ Map p162

☎ 93 216 03 06; www.casabatllo.es; Passeig de Gràcia 43; adult/under 7yr/student, 7-18yr & senior €17.80/free/14.25; ⏲ 9am-8pm; Ⓜ Passeig de Gràcia

One of the strangest residential buildings in Europe, this is Gaudí at his hallucinogenic best. The facade, sprinkled with bits of blue, mauve and green tiles and studded with wave-shaped window frames and balconies, rises to an uneven blue-tiled roof with a solitary tower.

It is one of the three houses on the block between Carrer del Consell de Cent and Carrer d'Aragó that gave it the playful name **Manzana de la Discordia**, meaning 'Apple (Block) of Discord'. The others are Puig i Cadafalch's Casa Amatller and Domènech i Montaner's Casa Lleó Morera. They were all renovated between 1898 and 1906 and show how eclectic a 'style' Modernisme was.

CASA AMATLLER Map p162

☎ 93 487 72 17; www.amatller.org; Passeig de Gràcia 41; admission free; ⏲ 10am-8pm Mon-Sat, 10am-3pm Sun; Ⓜ Passeig de Gràcia

One of Puig i Cadafalch's most striking bits of Modernista fantasy, Casa Amatller combines Gothic window frames with a stepped gable borrowed from Dutch urban architecture. But the busts and reliefs of dragons, knights and other characters dripping off the main facade are pure caprice. The pillared foyer and staircase lit by stained glass are like the inside of some romantic castle.

The building was renovated in 1900 for the chocolate baron and philanthropist Antoni Amatller (1851–1910) and will one day open partly to the public. Renovation due for completion in 2012 will see the 1st (main) floor converted into a museum with period pieces, while the 2nd floor will house the Institut Amatller d'Art Hispanic (Amatller Institute of Hispanic Art).

For now, you can wander into the foyer, admire the staircase and lift, and head through the shop to see the latest temporary exhibition out the back. Depending on the state of renovation, it is also possible to join a 1½-hour **guided tour** (€10; in English noon Fri, in Catalan & Spanish noon Wed) of the 1st floor, with its early-20th-century furniture and decor intact, and Amatller's photo studio. Groups can book guided visits for Monday to Friday.

CASA LLEÓ MORERA Map p162
Passeig de Gràcia 35; M Passeig de Gràcia
Domènech i Montaner's 1905 contribution to the Manzana de la Discordia, with Modernista carving outside and a bright, tiled lobby in which floral motifs predominate, is perhaps the least odd-looking of the three main buildings on the block. If only you could get inside – they are private apartments. The 1st floor is giddy with swirling sculptures, rich mosaics and whimsical decor.

HOSPITAL DE LA SANTA CREU I DE SANT PAU Map p152
☎ 93 317 76 52; www.rutadelmodernisme.com, www.santpau.es; Carrer de Cartagena 167; adult/senior & student €10/5; 10am, 11am, noon & 1pm in English, others in Catalan, French & Spanish; M Hospital de Sant Pau
Domènech i Montaner outdid himself as architect and philanthropist with this Modernista masterpiece, long considered one of the city's most important hospitals. He wanted to create a unique environment that would also cheer up patients. The complex, including 16 pavilions – together with the Palau de la Música Catalana (p115), a joint World Heritage Site – is lavishly decorated and each pavilion is unique.

KRZYSZTOF DYDYNSKI

Administrative Pavilion, Hospital de la Santa Creu i de Sant Pau

L'EIXAMPLE

SIGHTS

GEOFF STRINGER

Fundació Antoni Tàpies

FUNDACIÓ ANTONI TÀPIES

The Fundació Antoni Tàpies is both a pioneering Modernista building (completed in 1885) and the major collection of a leading 20th-century Catalan artist.

The building, designed by Domènech i Montaner for the publishing house Editorial Montaner i Simón (run by a cousin of the architect), combines a brick-covered iron frame with Islamic-inspired decoration. Tàpies saw fit to crown it with the meanderings of his own mind – to some it looks like a pile of coiled barbed wire, to others…well, it's difficult to say. He calls it *Núvol i Cadira* (Cloud and Chair). Renovation work on it finished in early 2010.

Antoni Tàpies, whose experimental art has often carried political messages (not always easily decipherable) – he opposed Francoism in the 1960s and '70s – launched the Fundació in 1984 to promote contemporary art, donating a large part of his own work. The collection spans the arc of Tàpies' creations (with more than 800 works) and contributions from other contemporary artists. In the main exhibition area (level 1, upstairs) you can see an ever-changing selection of around 20 of Tàpies' works, from early self-portraits of the 1940s to grand items like *Jersei Negre* (Black Jumper; 2008), in which the outline of a man with a hard-on is topped with a pasted-on black sweater. Level 2 hosts a small space for temporary exhibitions. Rotating exhibitions take place in the basement levels. At the time of writing, one held about 15 grand Tàpies works and a one-hour documentary on his life, while the other was dedicated to part of Tàpies' eclectic personal collections, anything from centuries-old medical treatises and Japanese calligraphy to lithographs on bullfighting by Francisco Goya.

Things you need to know: Map p162; ☎ 93 487 03 15; www.fundaciotapies.org; Carrer d'Aragó 255; adult/under 16yr €7/5.60; 🕙 10am-8pm Tue-Sun; Ⓜ Passeig de Gràcia

The hospital facilities have been transferred to a new complex on the premises, freeing up the century-old structures, which are now being restored to glory in a plan to convert the complex into an international centre on the Mediterranean. Whether or not the site will be open to visits was unclear at the time of writing. For the time being, **guided tours** allow the curious to get inside this unique site.

PALAU DEL BARÓ QUADRAS
Map p162

Casa Asia; ☎ 93 368 08 36; www.casaasia.es; Avinguda Diagonal 373; ⏱ 10am-8pm Tue-Sat, 10am-2pm Sun; Ⓜ Diagonal

Puig i Cadafalch designed Palau del Baró Quadras (built 1902–06) for the baron in question in an exuberant Gothic-inspired style. The main facade is its most intriguing, with a soaring, glassed-in gallery. Take a

DIEGO LEZAMA

Ceramic hall, Fundación Francisco Godia

⤵ IF YOU LIKE...

If you like the **Fundació Antoni Tàpies** (p167), you will relish these other exhibition spaces:

- **Fundació Joan Brossa** (Map p162; ☎ 93 467 69 52; www.fundaciojoanbrossa.cat; Carrer de Provença 318; admission free; ⏱ 10am-2pm & 3-7pm Mon-Fri; Ⓜ Diagonal) A peep into the life of Renaissance man Joan Brossa, a difficult-to-classify mix of poet, artist, theatre man, Catalan nationalist and all-round visionary.
- **Fundación Francisco Godia** (Map p162; ☎ 93 272 31 80; www.fundacionfgodia.org; Carrer de la Diputació 250; adult/under 5yr/student €5/free/3.50; ⏱ 10am-8pm Mon & Wed-Sun; Ⓜ Passeig de Gràcia) Francisco Godia's penchant was fast cars mixed with fine art. This carefully restored Modernista residence juxtaposes his own driving trophies (and goggles) with a varied collection of medieval art, ceramics and modern paintings.
- **Fundació Suñol** (Map p162; ☎ 93 496 10 32; www.fundaciosunol.org; Passeig de Gràcia 98; adult/concession €5/3; ⏱ 4-8pm Mon-Sat; Ⓜ Diagonal) This private collection of some 1200 works is showcased in rotating exhibitions. Most of it is modern; anything from Man Ray's photography to Picasso's painting.

L'EIXAMPLE

Palau del Baró Quadras

KRZYSZTOF DYDYNSKI

SIGHTS

closer look at the gargoyles and reliefs, among them a pair of toothy fish and a knight wielding a sword – clearly the same artistic signature as the architect behind Casa Amatller (p165).

ESGLÉSIA DE LA PURÍSSIMA CONCEPCIÓ I ASSUMPCIÓ DE NOSTRA SENYORA Map p162
Carrer de Roger de Llúria 70; 8am-1pm & 5-9pm; M Passeig de Gràcia
One hardly expects to run into a medieval church on the grid pattern streets of the late-19th-century city extension, yet that is just what this is. Transferred stone by stone from the old centre in 1871–88, this 14th-century church has a pretty 16th-century cloister with a peaceful garden. Behind is a Romanesque-Gothic bell tower (11th to 16th century), moved from another old town church that didn't survive, Església de Sant Miquel.

PALAU MONTANER Map p162
93 317 76 52; www.rutadelmodernisme.com; Carrer de Mallorca 278; adult/child & senior €6/3;

guided visit in English 10.30am & in Spanish 12.30pm Sat, in Catalan 10.30am, in Spanish 11.30am & in Catalan 12.30pm Sun; M Passeig de Gràcia
Interesting on the outside and made all the more enticing by its gardens, this creation by Domènech i Montaner is spectacular on the inside. Completed in 1896, its central feature is a grand staircase beneath a broad, ornamental skylight. The interior is laden with sculptures (some by Eusebi Arnau), mosaics and fine woodwork. Interior and exterior decoration depicts themes related to the printing industry. It is advisable to call ahead if you want to be sure to visit, as the building is sometimes closed to the public on weekends, too.

UNIVERSITAT DE BARCELONA Map p162
93 402 11 00; www.ub.edu; Gran Via de les Corts Catalanes 585; admission free; 9am-9pm Mon-Fri; M Universitat
Although a university was first set up on what is now La Rambla in the 16th century, the present, glorious mix of

(neo) Romanesque, Gothic, Islamic and Mudéjar architecture is a caprice of the 19th century (built 1863–82). Wander into the main hall, up the grand staircase and around the various leafy cloisters. On the 1st floor, the main hall for big occasions is the Mudéjar-style Paranimfo. Take a stroll in the rear gardens.

MUSEU DEL MODERNISME CATALÀ Map p162

☎ 93 272 28 96; www.mmcat.cat; Carrer de Balmes 48; adult/under 5yr/5-16yr/student €10/free/5/7; ⏲ 10am-8pm Mon-Sat, 10am-3pm Sun; Ⓜ Passeig de Gràcia

It's hard to believe that Modernisme, Catalonia's answer to art nouveau, was until not so long ago considered a wacky aberration of limited interest. Now everyone seems to be into this architectural and design period, so it was only a matter of time before a dedicated museum should open.

Housed in a Modernista building, the ground floor seems a like a big Modernista furniture showroom. Several items by Antoni Gaudí, including chairs from Casa Batlló and a mirror from Casa Calvet, are supplemented by a host of items by his lesser-known contemporaries, including some typically whimsical, mock medieval pieces by Josep Puig i Cadafalch.

The basement, showing off Modernista traits such as mosaic-coated pillars, bare brick vaults and metal columns, is lined with Modernista art, including paintings by Ramon Casas and Santiago Rusiñol, and statues by Josep Llimona and Eusebi Arnau.

SLEEPING

It comes as little surprise that this extensive bourgeois bastion should also be home to the greatest range of hotels in most classes. The grid avenues house some of the city's classic hotels and a long list of decent midrange places.

HOTEL MAJÈSTIC Map p162   Hotel €€€

☎ 93 488 17 17; www.hotelmajestic.es; Passeig de Gràcia 68; d from €399; Ⓜ Passeig de Gràcia; Ⓟ ✖ ⌘ ⌨ 🛜 🛋

This sprawling, central option has the charm of one of the great European hotels. The rooftop pool is great for views and relaxing, or you can pamper yourself in the spa after a workout in the gym. The standard rooms (no singles) are smallish but comfortable and with marble bathrooms. Various categories of larger rooms allow you to spread out more.

MANDARIN ORIENTAL

Map p162   Design Hotel €€€

☎ 93 151 88 88; www.mandarinoriental.com; Passeig de Gràcia 38; d from €355; Ⓜ Passeig de Gràcia; Ⓟ ✖ ⌨ 🛜 🛋

At this imposing former bank, 98 rooms combine contemporary designer style with subtle Eastern touches. Straight lines, lots of white and muted colours dominate the look. Many of the standard rooms (no smaller than 32 sq metres) have tempting tubs in the bathroom and all rooms overlook either Passeig de Gràcia or an interior sculpted garden. You can indulge in the spa and gym or linger over a cocktail in the stylish Banker's Bar (complete with safety deposit boxes).

HOTEL OMM Map p162   Design Hotel €€€

☎ 93 445 40 00; www.hotelomm.es; Carrer de Rosselló 265; d from €345; Ⓜ Diagonal; Ⓟ ✖ ⌨ 🛋

Design meets plain zany here, where the balconies look like strips of skin peeled back from the shiny hotel surface. The idea would no doubt have appealed to Dalí. In the foyer, a sprawling, minimalist and popular bar opens before you. Light,

AA WORLD TRAVEL LIBRARY/ALAMY

Museu Egipci

L'EIXAMPLE

SLEEPING

⬎ IF YOU LIKE...

If you like the **Museu del Modernisme Català**, you should also enjoy these other L'Eixample museums:

- **Museu Egipci** (Map p162; ☎ 93 488 01 88; www.museuegipci.com; Carrer de València 284; adult/senior & student €11/8; ☷ 10am-8pm Mon-Sat, 10am-2pm Sun; Ⓜ Passeig de Gràcia) A collection of ancient Egyptian artifacts including funereal implements, jewellery and ceramics horded by hotel magnate Jordi Clos.

- **Museu del Perfum** (Map p162; ☎ 93 216 01 21; www.museudelperfum.com; Passeig de Gràcia 39; adult/student & senior €5/3; ☷ 10.30am-1.30pm & 4.30-8pm Mon-Fri, 11am-2pm Sat; Ⓜ Passeig de Gràcia) A weighty collection of mainly bottle-shaped paraphernalia related to perfume, from Egyptian scent receptacles to ancient bronze Etruscan tweezers. Who knew?

- **Museu Taurí** (Map p152; ☎ 93 245 58 03; Gran Via de les Corts Catalanes 749; adult/child €6/5; ☷ 11am-2pm & 4-8pm Mon-Sat, 10am-1pm Sun Apr-Sep; Ⓜ Monumental) Housed in the Plaça de Braus Monumental bullring, this bullfighting museum displays stuffed bulls' heads, old posters and other memorabilia. You also get to wander around the ring and corrals.

- **Museu de la Música** (Map p152; ☎ 93 256 36 50; www.museumusica.bcn.cat; Carrer de Lepant 150; adult/senior & student €4/3, free 3-8pm Sun; ☷ 10am-6pm Mon, Wed-Sat, 10am-8pm Sun; Ⓜ Monumental) Some 500 instruments (less than a third of those held) are on show in this museum housed on the 2nd floor of the administration building in L'Auditori (p181), the city's main classical-music concert hall.

clear tones dominate in the ultramodern rooms, of which there are several categories. After a hard time tramping the city, chill in the Spaciomm spa, which offers everything from a water circuit (including underwater massage) to oxygen treatment for the skin, and rocking gravitational beds.

L'EIXAMPLE

SLEEPING

COMTES DE BARCELONA

Map p162　　　　　　　　　　　　　　　Hotel €€

☎ 93 445 00 00; www.condesdebarcelona.com; Passeig de Gràcia 73-75; s/d €177/230; Ⓜ Passeig de Gràcia; Ⓟ 🔀 🖳 🛜 🔊

Also known by its Spanish name, the most attractive half of the Comtes (Condes) de Barcelona occupies the 1890s Modernista Casa Enric Batlló. Across the road stands a more modern extension. Inside both, clean, designer lines dominate, with hardwood floors, architectural touches reminiscent of the Modernista exterior, and luxurious rooms. The standard rooms are, at 25 sq metres, the smallest. The pool on the roof is a great place to relax after a hard day's sightseeing. There's also a gym, sauna and a pair of prestige restaurants to choose from onsite.

HOTEL SIXTYTWO

Map p162　　　　　　　　　　　　Design Hotel €€

☎ 93 272 41 80; www.sixtytwohotel.com/en; Passeig de Gràcia 62; d €140-245; Ⓜ Passeig de Gràcia; Ⓟ 🔀 🖳 🛜

Under new ownership, this 21st-century designer setting (housed in a well-preserved 1930s edifice) boasts rooms with Bang & Olufsen TVs and soft backlighting above expansive beds. Inside the block is a pretty garden to chill in, or you could opt for a massage in your room. All rooms enjoy the same designer features (and Etro bath products) but the more tempting (and dearer ones) have balconies or little private terraces.

ST MORITZ HOTEL Map p162　　Hotel €€

☎ 93 481 73 50; www.hcchotels.com; Carrer de la Diputació 262bis; s/d €171/193; Ⓜ Passeig de Gràcia; Ⓟ 🔀 🔀 🖳 🛜

This upmarket hotel, set in a late-19th-century building, has 91 fully equipped rooms and boasts an elegant restaurant, terrace bar and small gym. Some of the bigger rooms, with marble bathrooms, even have their own exercise bikes. The place was refurbished in 2009, lending it a fresh new feel. You can dine in the modest terrace garden.

MARTIN HUGHES

Door handle detail, Comtes de Barcelona

SUITES AVENUE Map p162   Hotel €€

☎ 93 487 41 59; www.derbyhotels.es; Passeig de Gràcia 83; apt from €192; Ⓜ Diagonal; P ⊠ ▢ 🛜 ▣

Fancy apartment-style living is the name of the game in this apart-hotel. Self-contained little apartments with own kitchen and access to a terrace, gym and pool (not to mention the minimuseum of Hindu and Buddhist art) lie behind the daring facade by Japanese architect Toyo Ito.

HOTEL ASTORIA Map p152   Hotel €€

☎ 93 209 83 11; www.derbyhotels.es; Carrer de Paris 203; s/d from €120/130; Ⓜ Diagonal; P ⊠ ▢ 🛜 ▣

Nicely situated a short walk from Passeig de Gràcia, this three-star is equally well placed for long nights out in the restaurants, bars and clubs of adjacent Carrer d'Aribau. Room decor and types vary wildly – you might have black-and-white floor tiles or dark parquet. The hotel has its own minigym and a display of art by Catalan painter Ricard Opisso.

HOTEL CONSTANZA
Map p162   Boutique Hotel €€

☎ 93 270 19 10; www.hotelconstanza.com; Carrer del Bruc 33; s/d €110/130; Ⓜ Girona or Urquinaona; ⊠ ▢

This boutique beauty has stolen the hearts of many a visitor to Barcelona. Even smaller single rooms are made to feel special with broad mirrors and strong colours. Design touches abound, and little details like flowers in the bathroom add charm. Suites and studios are further options. The terrace is a nice spot to relax for a while, looking over the rooftops of L'Eixample.

HOTEL D'UXELLES Map p162   Hotel €€

☎ 93 265 25 60; www.hotelduxelles.com; Gran Via de les Corts Catalanes 688; s/d €90/109; Ⓜ Tetuan; ⊠ ▢

A charming simplicity pervades the rooms here. Wrought-iron bedsteads are overshadowed by flowing drapes. Room decor varies (from blues and whites to beige-and-cream combos), with a vaguely Andalucian flavour in the bathrooms. Some rooms have little terraces (€16 extra). Get a back room if you can, as Gran Via is noisy. Hotel d'Uxelles has similar rooms in another building across the road.

HOSTAL GOYA Map p162   Hostal €€

☎ 93 302 25 65; www.hostalgoya.com; Carrer de Pau Claris 74; s €70, d €96-113; Ⓜ Passeig de Gràcia; ⊠

The Goya is a modestly priced gem on the chichi side of L'Eixample. Rooms have a light colour scheme that varies from room to room. In the bathrooms, the original mosaic floors have largely been retained, combined with contemporary design features. The more expensive doubles have a balcony.

HOSTAL CENTRAL Map p162   Hostal €€

☎ 93 245 19 81; www.hostalcentralbarcelona .com; Carrer de la Diputació 346; s/d/tr €50/85/106; Ⓜ Tetuan; ✂ ⊠ 🛜

In a pretty early-20th-century apartment building you'll find 13 renovated rooms (all nonsmoking and most with own bathroom). They are not excessively big but are pleasant and clean.

HOSTAL GIRONA Map p162   Hostal €€

☎ 93 265 02 59; www.hostalgirona.com; Carrer de Girona 24; s/d €70/85; Ⓜ Girona

This 2nd-floor family-run *hostal* is a simple but clean and friendly spot of the old world. Some of the rooms have been freshened with bright colour schemes and all have modern bathrooms. Rooms range from rather small, if cute, singles with communal bathroom to airy doubles

BRENT WINEBRENNER

Waiter, La Rambla

with balcony (but beware of traffic noise in summer, when you'll have to keep the windows open).

HOSTAL ARIBAU Map p162   Hostal €

☎ 93 453 11 06; www.hostalaribau.com; Carrer de Aribau 37; s/d/tr €60/65/80, s/d without bathroom €45/55; Ⓜ Universitat; ✂

Handily located within brisk walking distance of Ciutat Vella and in a busy part of L'Eixample, this is a straightforward family-run *hostal* with 11 rooms. Some rooms have a balcony (but this also means a fair degree of traffic noise, so they're not for light sleepers).

EATING

This huge grid area can seem daunting, but remember that most of the many varied and enticing restaurants are concentrated in the Quadrat d'Or between Carrer de Pau Claris and Carrer de Muntaner, Avinguda Diagonal and Gran Via de les Corts Catalanes. There is no shortage of perfectly acceptable bar-restaurants

(often with street-side tables) that offer reasonable *menús del día* and standard dishes *a la carta*.

SAÜC Map p152   Catalan €€€

☎ 93 321 01 89; www.saucrestaurant.com; Passatge de Lluís Pellicer 12; meals €70-80, menú del día €27; ✲ Tue-Sat; Ⓜ Hospital Clínic; ✖

Pop into this basement place down a little Eixample laneway and you enter a soothing sanctuary. Sober designer decor, dominated by ochres, creams and buttercup yellows, allows you to concentrate on what emerges from the kitchen, such as *tàrtar de anguila fumada, poma verda i caviar d'arengada* (smoked eel tartare with green apples and salted sardine caviar). You can request half-size portions at 60% of the price. The tasting menu comprises an appetiser, four courses, then a cheese selection and two desserts (€78).

SPEAKEASY Map p152   International €€

☎ 93 217 50 80; Carrer d'Aribau 162-166; meals €70; ✲ lunch & dinner Mon-Fri, dinner Sat Sep-Jul; Ⓜ Diagonal

This clandestine restaurant lurks behind the Dry Martini (p180). You will be shown a door through the open kitchen area to the 'storeroom', lined with hundreds of bottles of backlit, quality tipples. Dark decorative tones, a few works of art, low lighting, light jazz music and smooth service complete the setting. What's on the menu depends on the markets and the cook's whim. A tempting option is the creamy *burrata di Puglia con yemas de espárragos blancos y jamón Joselito* (a huge hunk of mozzarella from southern Italy with white asparagus hearts and strips of high-quality cured ham).

CASA CALVET Map p162   Catalan €€

☎ 93 412 40 12; www.casacalvet.es; Carrer de Casp 48; meals €55-70; ⏰ Mon-Sat; Ⓜ Urquinaona; ✗

An early Gaudí masterpiece loaded with his trademark curvy features now houses a swish restaurant (just to the right of the building's main entrance). Dress up and ask for an intimate *taula cabina* (wooden booth). You could opt for *vieires a la planxa amb tagliatelle i tomàquet confitat* (grilled scallops with ribbon pasta and tomato confit). It has various tasting menus for up to €69, and a child's menu for €16.

RESTAURANT ME Map p152 Pan-Asian €€

☎ 93 419 49 33; www.catarsiscuisine.com; Carrer de París 162; meals €45-50; ⏰ lunch & dinner Thu-Sat, dinner Tue-Wed; Ⓜ Hospital Clínic; ✗

The chef whips up wonders in the kitchen at this surprise fusion establishment. At a time when fusion is often synonymous with nothing in particular, it manages to create superb Asian dishes with the occasional New Orleans or other international intrusion. Some vegetarian options, like the *banh xeo* (Vietnamese pancake filled with bamboo, seitan and mushrooms), accompany such self-indulgent choices as stuffed New Orleans prawns with tartare sauce.

MELTON Map p152   Italian €€

☎ 93 363 27 76; Carrer de Muntaner 189; meals €45; ⏰ Tue-Sat; Ⓜ Hospital Clínic

You know you're onto something when Italians recommend an Italian restaurant. This slick place offers well-prepared pasta and risotto dishes (the latter, for example, with foie gras) and a tempting array of meat and fish mains. For an unusual pasta option, try the *lasagnetta de tòfona negra i múrgules* (little lasagna with black truffle and morel mushrooms).

PATAGONIA Map p162   Argentine €€

☎ 93 304 37 35; Gran Via de les Corts Catalanes 660; meals €40-45; ⏰ daily; Ⓜ Passeig de Gràcia; ✗

An elegant Argentinean beef-fest awaits in this stylish restaurant. Start with *empanadas* (tiny meat-crammed pies). You might want to skip the *achuras* (offal) and head for a hearty meat main, such as a juicy beef *medallón con salsa de colmenillas* (a medallion in a morel sauce) or such classics as *bife de chorizo* (sirloin) or Brazilian *picanha* (rump). You can choose from one of five side dishes to accompany your pound of flesh.

YAMADORY Map p162   Japanese €€

☎ 93 453 92 64; Carrer d'Aribau 68; meals €35-40; ⏰ Mon-Sat; 🚃 FGC Provença

Yamadory, one of the city's first Japanese restaurants, still attracts visiting Japanese business people today. As the door slips closed behind you, the first thing you notice is the hushed atmosphere. Divided into several dining areas with a contemporary Japanese decor, it is notable for its gliding efficiency. Head upstairs to sit on a floor-level tatami. The sushi, sashimi, udon and tempura are all good.

L'EIXAMPLE

EATING

L'EIXAMPLE

EATING

THAI GARDENS Map p162   Thai €€

☎ 93 487 98 98; www.thaigardensgroup.com; Carrer de la Diputació 273; meals €35, menú del día €15; ☉ daily; Ⓜ Passeig de Gràcia; ⊠

One of the first and still one of the best for Thai food in Barcelona. Tables for two set in quiet corners contrast with great round-party sittings amid a veritable forest of tropical greenery. The set menu (€31) allows you to try a broad range of dishes and can be a good idea for larger groups.

DE TAPA MADRE Map p162   Catalan €€

☎ 93 459 31 34; www.detapamadre.com; Carrer de Mallorca 301; meals €35; ☉ 8am-1am; Ⓜ Verdaguer; ⊠

A chatty atmosphere greets you from the bar the moment you swing open the door. Head upstairs for more space in the gallery, which hovers above the array of tapas on the bar below, or go deeper inside past the bench with the ham legs. Choose from a range of tapas or opt for a full meal. The *arròs caldós amb llagostins* (a hearty rice dish with king prawns) is delicious. The kitchen is open all day long so you can pop by any time hunger strikes.

RELAIS DE VENISE Map p162   French €€

☎ 93 467 21 62; Carrer de Pau Claris 142; meals €35; ☉ daily Sep-Jul; Ⓜ Passeig de Gràcia; ⊠

You can eat anything you want here, so long as it's meat. Indeed, there's just one dish, a succulent beef entrecôte with a secret 'sauce Porte-Maillot' (named after the location of the original restaurant in Paris), chips and salad (€22), to which you can add a little wine and dessert. It is served in slices and in two waves so that it doesn't go cold.

TERRABACUS Map p152   Tapas & Wine €€

☎ 93 410 86 33; www.terrabacus.com; Carrer de Muntaner 185; meals €30-35, menú del día €18; ☉ lunch & dinner Tue-Fri, dinner Mon & Sat; Ⓜ Hospital Clínic

Food exists to accompany wine, or so one could be led to believe here. In this 'Land of Bacchus', one of the joys is sampling from the extensive wine list and choosing bites to go down with the nectar. You might try the various cheese platters or select a dish of high-grade Joselito cured ham. More substantial dishes range from risotto to steak tartare.

PASCALE BEROUJON

Tapas selection

EMBAT Map p162 — Mediterranean €€

☎ 93 458 08 55; www.restaurantembat.es; Carrer de Mallorca 304; meals €30-35; ☾ lunch Tue & Wed, lunch & dinner Thu-Sat; Ⓜ Girona

Enthusiastic young chefs turn out beautifully presented dishes in this basement eatery, whose brown and cream decor might not enchant all comers. You can eat three courses for around €20 to €25 at lunch, indulging perhaps in *raviolis de pollo amb bacon i calabassó* (chicken ravioli bathed in a sauce of finely chopped bacon, zucchini and other vegetables) followed by melt-in-the-mouth *lluç amb pa amb tomàquet, carxofes i maionesa de peres* (a thick cut of hake on a tomato-drenched clump of bread dressed with artichoke slices and a pear mayonnaise).

TAPAÇ 24 Map p162 — Tapas €€

☎ 93 488 09 77; www.carlesabellan.com; Carrer de la Diputació 269; meals €30-35; ☾ 9am-midnight Mon-Sat; Ⓜ Passeig de Gràcia

Carles Abellán, master of Comerç 24 in La Ribera, runs this basement tapas haven known for its gourmet versions of old faves. Specials include the *bikini* (toasted ham and cheese sandwich – here the ham is cured and the truffle makes all the difference), a thick black *arròs negre de sípia* (squid-ink black rice), the McFoie-Burguer and, for dessert, *xocolata amb pa, sal i oli* (delicious balls of chocolate in olive oil with a touch of salt and wafer). You can't book.

TAKTIKA BERRI Map p162 — Basque €€

☎ 93 453 47 59; Carrer de València 169; meals €45-50, tapas €20-30; ☾ lunch & dinner Mon-Fri, lunch Sat; Ⓜ Hospital Clínic

Get in early as the bar teems with punters from far and wide, anxious to wrap their mouths around some of the best Basque tapas in town. The hot morsels are all snapped up as soon as they arrive from the kitchen, so keep your eyes peeled.

The seated dining area out the back is also good. In the evening, it's all over by about 10.30pm.

BAR VELÓDROMO Map p152 — Tapas €€

☎ 93 430 60 22; Carrer de Muntaner 213; meals €25; ☾ daily; Ⓜ Hospital Clínic

The reopening of this once-classic tavern in 2009 brings back a fine-looking establishment in which to take breakfast, stop for an aperitif or sit for a meal. The low, corner building retains much of its original look, with timber omnipresent. Food largely consists of tapas and smallish renderings of fairly typical Catalan and Spanish dishes. More than anything, this place is about its history and atmosphere.

CERVESERIA CATALANA
Map p162 — Tapas €€

☎ 93 216 03 68; Carrer de Mallorca 236; meals €25; ☾ daily; Ⓜ Passeig de Gràcia; ✗

The 'Catalan Brewery' is good for breakfast, lunch and dinner. Come in for your morning coffee and croissant, or wait until lunch to enjoy choosing from the abundance of tapas and *montaditos* (canapés). You can sit at the bar, on the pavement terrace or in the restaurant at the back. The variety of hot tapas, salads and other snacks draws a well-dressed crowd of locals and outsiders. It has expanded the premises to deal with demand.

CASA AMALIA Map p162 — Catalan €€

☎ 93 458 94 58; Passatge del Mercat 4-6; meals €20-25; ☾ lunch & dinner Tue-Sat, lunch Sun Sep-Jul; Ⓜ Girona

This restaurant is popular for its hearty Catalan cooking using fresh produce, mainly sourced from the busy market next door. The orange and white decorated joint has split-level dining that makes the most of its space. On Thursdays during winter it offers the Catalan mountain

L'EIXAMPLE

EATING

Dry Martini bar (p180)
DIEGO LEZAMA

classic, *escudella*. Otherwise, you might try light variations on local cuisine, such as the *bacallà al allioli de poma* (cod in an apple-based aioli sauce). The four-course *menú del día* is exceptional lunchtime value at €12.

CASA ALFONSO Map p162   Spanish €
☎ 93 301 97 83; www.casaalfonso.com; Carrer de Roger de Llúria 6; meals €20; ⏰ 9am-1am Mon-Sat; Ⓜ Urquinaona

In business since 1934, Casa Alfonso is perfect for a morning coffee or a tapas stop at the long marble bar. Timber panelled and festooned with old photos, posters and swinging hams, it attracts a faithful local clientele at all hours for its *flautas* (thin custom-made baguettes with your choice of filling), hams, cheeses, hot dishes and homemade desserts. Consider rounding off with an *alfonsito* (a miniature Irish coffee).

EL RINCÓN MAYA Map p162   Mexican €
☎ 93 451 39 46; Carrer de València 183; meals €20; ⏰ lunch & dinner Tue-Sat, dinner Mon; Ⓜ Passeig de Gràcia

Getting a seat in this Mexican eatery can be a trial. The setting is warm, modest and, thankfully, devoid of the excesses of pseudo-Mexican decor. The pocket-sized serves of nachos, guacamole and fajitas all burst with flavour. You'll also discover lesser-known items like *tacos de pibil* (pork tacos) and *tinga,* little pasta pockets of chicken. There are also more-substantial dishes for €9.50. The owner-chef spent much of his life in the restaurant business in Mexico City.

AMALTEA Map p162   Vegetarian €
☎ 93 454 86 13; www.amalteaygovinda.com; Carrer de la Diputació 164; meals €10-15; ⏰ Mon-Sat; Ⓜ Urgell; ⌧

The ceiling fresco of blue sky sets the scene in this popular vegetarian eatery. The weekday set lunch (€10.50) offers a series of dishes that change frequently with the seasons. At night, the set two-course dinner (€15) offers good value. The homemade desserts are tempting. The place is something of an alternative lifestyle centre, with yoga, t'ai chi and belly-dancing classes.

CAFÈ DEL CENTRE Map p162   Cafe €
☎ 93 488 11 01; Carrer de Girona 69;
⏲ 8.30am-midnight Mon-Fri; Ⓜ Girona
Step back a century in this cafe, in business since 1873. The timber-top bar extends down the right side as you enter, fronted by a slew of marble-topped tables and dark timber chairs. It exudes an almost melancholy air by day but gets busy at night.

COSMO Map p162   Cafe €
☎ 93 453 70 07; www.galeriacosmo.com; Carrer d'Enric Granados 3; ⏲ 10am-10pm Mon-Thu, noon-2am Fri & Sat, noon-10pm Sun;
Ⓜ Universitat; 📶
This groovy space with psychedelic colouring in the tables and bar stools, high white walls out back for exhibitions and events, a nice selection of teas, pastries and snacks, all set on a pleasant pedestrian strip just behind the university is perfect for a morning session on your laptop or a civilised evening tipple while admiring the art.

MAURI Map p162   Pastries €
☎ 93 215 10 20; Rambla de Catalunya 102;
⏲ 8am-9pm Mon-Sat, 8am-3pm Sun;
Ⓜ Diagonal; ✗
Since it opened in 1929, this grand old pastry shop has had its regular customers salivating over the endless range of sweets, chocolate croissants and gourmet delicatessen items.

CREMERIA TOSCANA Map p152   Gelato €
☎ 93 539 38 25; Carrer de Muntaner 161;
⏲ 1-9pm Tue-Sun Oct-Easter, 1pm-midnight Tue-Sun Easter-Sep; Ⓜ Hospital Clínic; ✗
Yes, you can stumble across quite reasonable ice cream in Barcelona, but close your eyes and imagine yourself across the Mediterranean with the real ice-cream wizards. Creamy *stracciatella* and wavy

nocciola…and myriad other flavours await at the most authentic gelato outlet in town. Buy a cone or a tub! There's another branch with similar hours in **El Born** (☎ 93 268 07 29; Carrer dels Canvis Vells 2; Ⓜ Barceloneta).

DRINKING
Much of middle-class L'Eixample is dead at night, but several streets are exceptions. Noisy Carrer de Balmes is lined with a rowdy adolescent set. Much more interesting is the cluster of locales lining Carrer d'Aribau between Avinguda Diagonal and Carrer de Mallorca. Lower down, on and around Carrer del Consell de Cent and Carrer de la Diputació, is the heart of Gaixample, with several gay bars and clubs.

CAFÉ SAN TELMO Map p152   Bar
☎ 93 439 73 09; Carrer de Buenos Aires 60;
⏲ Mon-Sat; Ⓜ Diagonal
This narrow bar has an appealingly busy feel, with big windows along Carrer de Casanova revealing the crowds and traffic of nearby Avinguda Diagonal. Perch at the bar for a couple of low-key drinks early in your night out (some of the area's key bars and clubs are just over the other side of Avinguda Diagonal).

DACKSY Map p162   Bar
☎ 93 217 50 72; Carrer del Consell de Cent 247; ⏲ 1pm-2am Sun-Thu, 1pm-3am Fri & Sat;
Ⓜ Universitat
Eye-candy bartenders know their stuff when it comes to mixing, shaking and/or stirring their way to your heart with a fine selection of cocktails in this chilled lounge in the heart of the Gaixample action. It makes a perfect start to the evening, or a nice way to finish off if clubbing is not on the night's agenda.

DRY MARTINI Map p152   Bar

☎ 93 217 50 72; www.drymartinibcn.com; Carrer d'Aribau 162-166; ⏲ 5pm-3am; ⊠ FGC Provença

Waiters with a discreetly knowing smile will attend to your cocktail needs here. The house drink, taken at the bar or in one of the plush green leather lounges, is a safe bet. The gin and tonic comes in an enormous mug-sized glass – a couple of these and you're well on the way! There's also a restaurant out the back, Speakeasy (p174).

LA FIRA Map p162   Bar

www.lafiraclub.com, in Spanish; Carrer de Provença 171; admission €8-12; ⏲ 10.30pm-3am Wed-Sat; ⊠ FGC Provença

A designer bar with a difference. Wander in past distorting mirrors and ancient fairground attractions from Germany – put in coins and listen to hens squawk. Speaking of squawking, the music swings wildly from whiffs of house through '90s hits to Spanish pop classics. You can spend the earlier part of the night trying some of the bar's shots – it claims to have 500 varieties (but we haven't counted them).

MILANO Map p162   Bar

☎ 93 481 38 27; www.camparimilano.com; Rond de la Universitat 35; ⏲ noon-2.30am; Ⓜ Catalunya

You don't quite know what to expect as you head downstairs into this cocktail den. Then you are confronted by its vastness and the happily imbibing crowds ensconced at tables or perched at the broad, curving bar to the right.

MUSEUM Map p162   Bar

Carrer de Sepúlveda 178; ⏲ 6.30pm-3am; Ⓜ Universitat

'Kitsch gone mad' is the artistic theme here, where chandeliers meet mock Renaissance sculpture and light pop. Drinks are served behind a stage-lit bar and can be hard to come by from 1.30am on. Twinks and muscle builders mix happily in this gay starter bar perfectly located for a hop over to Metro (see p182) later on.

OLIVER STREWE

L'Eixample shopfront

PLATA BAR Map p162   Bar

☎ 93 452 46 36; Carrer del Consell de Cent 235; ⏰ 8pm-3am; Ⓜ Universitat

A summer seat on the corner terrace of this wide-open bar attracts a lot of lads in the course of an evening hopping the area's gay bars. Inside, metallic horse-saddle stools are lined up at the bar and high tables, the music drifts through modes of dance and trance, and waiters whip up drinks from behind a couple of candelabra on the bar.

QUILOMBO Map p152   Bar

☎ 93 439 54 06; Carrer d'Aribau 149; ⏰ 7pm-2.30am daily Jun-Sep, Wed-Sun Oct-May; ® FGC Provença

Some formulas just work, and this place has been working since the 1970s. Set up a few guitars in the back room, which you pack with tables and chairs, add some cheapish pre-prepared mojitos and plastic tubs of nuts, and let the punters do the rest. They pour in, creating plenty of *quilombo* (fuss).

ENTERTAINMENT & ACTIVITIES

L'AUDITORI

Map p152   Classical Music & Opera

☎ 93 247 93 00; www.auditori.org; Carrer de Lepant 150; admission €10-60; ⏰ box office 3-9pm Mon-Sat; Ⓜ Monumental

Barcelona's modern home for serious music lovers, L'Auditori (designed by Rafael Moneo) puts on plenty of orchestral, chamber, religious and other music. L'Auditori is perhaps ugly on the outside (to the less kind-hearted it looks like a pile of rusting scrap metal) but beautifully tuned on the inside. It is home to the Orquestra Simfònica de Barcelona i Nacional de Catalunya.

AIRE Map p162   Club

☎ 93 487 83 42; www.arenadisco.com, in Spanish; Carrer de València 236; ⏰ 11pm-3am Thu-Sat; Ⓜ Passeig de Gràcia

A popular locale for lesbians, the dance floor is spacious and there is usually a DJ in command of the tunes, which range from hits of the '80s and '90s to techno. As a rule, only male friends of the girls are allowed entry, although in practice the crowd tends to be fairly mixed. Things can heat up on Thursday nights with live music.

DBOY Map p162   Club

☎ 93 453 05 10; www.dboyclub.com; Ronda de Sant Pere 19-21; ⏰ midnight-6am Sat; Ⓜ Urquinaona

With bright pink laser lights and a dense crowds of fit young lads, this is one of Barcelona's big dance-club locations on a Saturday night. Electronic music dominates the dance nights here and, in spite of the 6am finish, for many clubbers this is only the start of the 'evening'. From 5am, buses line up to ferry punters to the suburb of Viladecans, where the party continues at **Souvenir** (http://09 .matinee group.com; Carrer del Noi de Sucre 75) until 3.30pm on Sunday afternoon, which just leaves time for a snooze at the beach afterwards.

DIETRICH GAY TEATRO CAFÉ

Map p162   Club

☎ 93 451 77 07; Carrer del Consell de Cent 255; ⏰ 10.30pm-3am; Ⓜ Universitat

It's show time at 1am, with at least one drag-queen gala each night in this cabaret-style locale dedicated to Marlene Dietrich. Soft house is the main musical motif and the place has an interior garden. In between performances, gogo boys heat up the ambience.

L'EIXAMPLE

ENTERTAINMENT & ACTIVITIES

STEFANO PATERNA/ALAMY

Els Encants Vells (p184)

METRO Map p162   Club
☎ 93 323 52 27; www.metrodiscobcn.com;
Carrer de Sepúlveda 185; ⏲ 1am-5am Mon,
midnight-5am Sun & Tue-Thu, midnight-6am Fri
& Sat; Ⓜ Universitat

Metro attracts a casual gay crowd with
its two dance floors, three bars and very
dark room. Keep an eye out for shows and
parties, which can range from parades of
models to bingo nights (on Thursday
nights, with sometimes-interesting
prizes). On Wednesday nights there's a
live sex show.

ROXY BLUE Map p162   Club
☎ 93 272 66 97; www.roxyblue.es; Carrer del
Consell de Cent 294; ⏲ midnight-5am Wed
& Thu, midnight-6am Fri & Sat; Ⓜ Passeig de
Gràcia

Blue is indeed the predominant colour in
this split-level miniclub. Tastes in music
swing from New York beats to Brazil night
on Sunday. On weekends you are likely to
find queues of 20-somethings waiting to
pile in. Sit out the music on long leather

lounges or investigate the couple of
different bars.

BEL-LUNA JAZZ CLUB
Map p162   Live Music
☎ 93 302 22 21; www.bel-luna.com, in Spanish; Rambla de Catalunya 5; admission €5-15;
⏲ 9pm-2am Sun-Thu, 9pm-3am Fri & Sat;
Ⓜ Catalunya

This basement restaurant-cum-bar-cum-
club is not the prettiest location but attracts a full jazz program, seven nights
a week, with local and visiting acts. You
can join in for dinner, but frankly you're
better off dining elsewhere. When the last
act finishes, the place turns into a kind of
preclub-club with tunes from the 1980s
and '90s.

PALACIO DEL FLAMENCO
Map p162   Flamenco
☎ 93 218 72 37; www.palaciodelflamenco.com;
Carrer de Balmes 139; show €32, with dinner
€65-75; ⏲ shows 7.45pm & 10.45pm Mon-Sat;
Ⓜ Diagonal

A relative newcomer on the Barcelona *tablao* circuit, the Palace of Flamenco is basically the same arrangement as its older confrères, with two sessions an evening. No attempt is made at creating a folkloric atmosphere. Rather, a series of long dinner tables spreads away from the busy stage.

TEATRE NACIONAL DE CATALUNYA Map p152 Theatre
☎ 93 306 57 00; www.tnc.cat; Plaça de les Arts 1; admission €12-32; Plaça de les Arts 1; ☺ box office 3-7pm Wed-Fri, 3-8.30pm Sat, 3-5pm Sun & 1hr before show; Ⓜ Glòries or Monumental
Ricard Bofill's ultra-neoclassical theatre, with the bright, airy foyer, hosts a wide range of performances, principally drama (anything from King Lear in Catalan to La Fura dels Baus) but occasionally dance and other performances.

MÉLIÈS CINEMES Map p162 Cinema
☎ 93 451 00 51; www.cinesmelies.net; Carrer de Villarroel 102; admission €3-5; Ⓜ Urgell
A cosy cinema with two screens, the Méliès specialises in old classics from Hollywood and European cinema.

SILOM SPA Map p162 Spa
☎ 93 272 66 62; www.silomspa.com, in Spanish; Carrer de València 304; massages €35-100; ☺ 11am-9.30pm Mon-Sat; Ⓜ Girona
A touch of the Orient is the promise in this city spa, where you can combine a series of Thai, aromatic and other massages with aroma baths. Options for couples abound and you can get a facial while you're at it. The masseurs are all Thai.

SHOPPING
Most of the city's classy shopping spreads across the heart of L'Eixample, in particular along Passeig de Gràcia, Rambla de Catalunya and adjacent streets. All about are dotted a surprising array of speciality stores, selling anything from gloves to glues.

CUBIÑA Map p162 Design
☎ 93 476 57 21; www.cubinya.es; Carrer de Mallorca 291; Ⓜ Verdaguer
Even if interior design doesn't ring your bell, a visit to this extensive temple to furniture, lamps and just about any home accessory your heart might desire is worth it just to see this Domènech i Montaner building. Admire the enormous and whimsical wrought iron decoration at street level before heading inside to marvel at the ceiling, timber work, brick columns and windows. Oh, and don't forget the furniture.

COME IN Map p162 Books
☎ 93 453 12 04; www.libreriainglesa.com; Carrer de Balmes 129bis; Ⓜ Diagonal
English-teachers, those thirsting for the latest thrillers in English and learners of Shakespeare's tongue will all find something to awaken their curiosity in this, one of the city's main English-language bookshops. There are even a few odds and ends in other languages.

ANTONIO MIRÓ Map p162 Fashion
☎ 93 487 06 70; www.antoniomiro.es, in Spanish; Carrer del Consell de Cent 349; ☺ 10am-8pm Mon-Sat; Ⓜ Passeig de Gràcia
Antonio Miró is one of Barcelona's *haute couture* kings. The entrance to the airy store, with dark hardwood floor, seems more like a hip hotel reception. Miró concentrates on light, natural fibres to produce smart, unpretentious men's and women's fashion. High-end evening dresses and shimmering, smart suits lead the way. Or you could just settle for an Antonio Miró T-shirt.

L'EIXAMPLE

SHOPPING

MANGO Map p162   Fashion & Accessories
☎ 93 215 75 30; www.mango.com; Passeig de Gràcia 65; ⏰ 10am-9pm Mon-Sat; Ⓜ Passeig de Gràcia

At home in the basement of a modest Modernista town house (check out the white, cast-iron columns inside) and a dozen other locations around town, Mango offers locally produced, affordable and mostly casual fashion for women and men. Smart but easy evening wear, skirts, jackets, high heels and leather bags for her contrast with collarless shirts, jeans, khakis and T-shirts for him.

ELS ENCANTS VELLS
Map p152   Flea Market
Fira de Bellcaire; ☎ 93 246 30 30; www.encants bcn.com, in Catalan; Plaça de les Glòries Catalanes; ⏰ 7am-6pm Mon, Wed, Fri & Sat; Ⓜ Glòries

Also known as the Fira de Bellcaire, the 'Old Charms' flea market is the biggest of its kind in Barcelona. The markets moved here in 1928 from Avinguda de Mistral, near Plaça d'Espanya. It's all here, from antique furniture through to secondhand clothes. A lot of it is junk, but occasionally you'll stumble across a *ganga* (bargain). The most interesting time to be here is from 7am to 9am on Monday, Wednesday and Friday, when the public auctions take place. Debate on a future location for the market has ebbed and flowed for years but at the time of writing it was still firmly anchored to its spot on the north flank of the Plaça de les Glòries Catalanes.

NOSOTRAOS Map p162   Gay & Lesbian
☎ 93 451 51 34; http://nosotras.cat; Carrer de Casanova 56; Ⓜ Urgell

Everything from gay girl calendars to bear T-shirts and books appear in this multi-faceted gay and lesbian store in the heart of 'Gaixample'.

REGIA Map p162   Perfume
☎ 93 216 01 21; www.regia.es, in Catalan & Spanish; Passeig de Gràcia 39; ⏰ 9.30am-8.30pm Mon-Fri, 10.30am-8.30pm Sat; Ⓜ Passeig de Gràcia

Reputed to be one of the best perfume stores in the city and in business since 1928, Regia stocks all the name brands and also has a private perfume museum (p171) out the back. Aside from the range of perfumes, Regia sells all sorts of creams, lotions and colognes. It also has its own line of bath products.

FARRUTX Map p162   Shoes
☎ 93 215 06 85; www.farrutx.es; Carrer de Rosselló 218; Ⓜ Diagonal

Another Mallorcan shoemaker, Farrutx specialises in exclusive upmarket footwear for uptown gals. You might fall for high-heeled summer sandals or elegant winter boots. There are matching bags and leather jackets, and even a limited line in men's footwear.

PARK GÜELL & AROUND

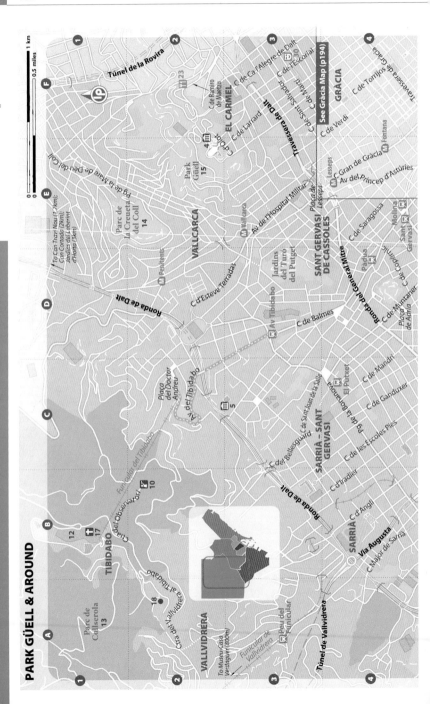

See Gràcia Map (p194)

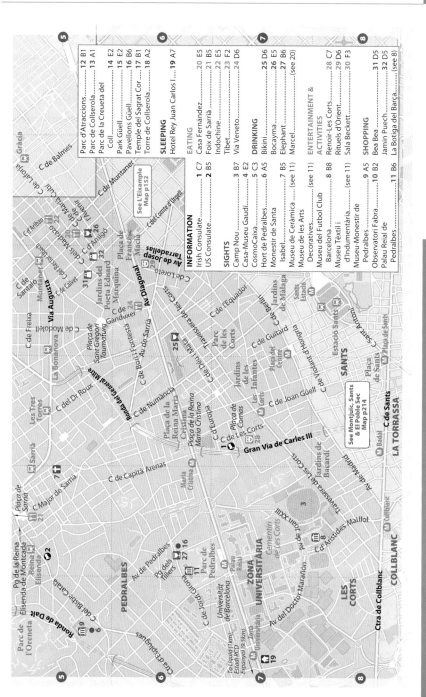

INFORMATION
Irish Consulate.................................. **1** C7
US Consulate.................................... **2** B5

SIGHTS
Camp Nou... **3** B7
Casa-Museu Gaudí........................... **4** E2
CosmoCaixa..................................... **5** C3
Hort de Pedralbes.......................... **6** A5
Monestir de Santa
  Isabel...(see 11)
Museu de Ceràmica.....................(see 11)
Museu de les Arts
  Decoratives.............................(see 11)
Museu del Futbol Club
  Barcelona..................................... **8** B8
Museu Tèxtil i
  d'Indumentària.......................(see 11)
Museu-Monestir de
  Pedralbes...................................... **9** A5
Observatori Fabra.......................... **10** B2
Palau Reial de
  Pedralbes.................................... **11** B6
Parc d'Atraccions........................... **12** B1
Parc de Collserola.......................... **13** A1
Parc de la Creueta del
  Coll.. **14** E2
Park Güell....................................... **15** E2
Pavellons Güell............................... **16** B6
Temple del Sagrat Cor................... **17** B1
Torre de Collserola........................ **18** A2

SLEEPING
Hotel Rey Juan Carlos I................ **19** A7

EATING
Casa Fernández.............................. **20** E5
Foix de Sarrià................................ **21** B5
Indochine.. **22** E5
Tibet... **23** F2
Via Veneto...................................... **24** D6

DRINKING
Bikini.. **25** D6
Bocayma... **26** E5
Elephant... **27** B6
Marcel...(see 20)

ENTERTAINMENT &
ACTIVITIES
Renoir-Les Corts............................ **28** C7
Rituels d'Orient.............................. **29** D6
Sala Beckett................................... **30** F3

SHOPPING
Bea Bea.. **31** D5
Jamin Puech................................... **32** D5
La Botiga del Barça......................(see 8)

HIGHLIGHTS

1   PARK GÜELL

Imagine a Disney fairytale, scripted by Tolkien and filmed by Fellini, and you've conjured a picture of Park Güell. The park's construction was initiated in 1900 when Count Eusebi Güell bought a scrubby hillside and hired Antoni Gaudí to create a miniature city of posh houses in landscaped grounds. The project was a commercial flop, but the abandoned site was saved in the 1920s and soon garnered a dedicated following.

↘ OUR DON'T MISS LIST

❶ THE GATEHOUSES

'Fairy tale' is an overused term when describing whimsical Modernista architecture, but in these two curvaceous gatehouses, the cliche couldn't be more apt. The wonderfully weird buildings were inspired by the story of Hansel and Gretel and provide a harbinger for the psychedelia to come.

❷ SALA HIPÓSTILA

Visitors from Andalucía could get flashbacks of Córdoba's Mezquita in the so-called Hall of 100 Columns (there are actually only 88) designed originally as a marketplace. There's a palpable Hellenic atmosphere in the pillared interior until you look up at the ceiling mosaics and realise that Gaudí is, as ever, bending the rules to his own liking.

❸ MAIN TERRACE

Above the Sala Hipóstila is the park's main nexus, an open, view-embellished terrace designed for relaxation and

Clockwise from top: Detail of entrance to Park Güell; Park entrance; Walkways in the park; Park bench; Sala Hipóstila

CLOCKWISE FROM TOP: ALFREDO MAIQUEZ; GREG ELMS; DONALD C. & PRISCILLA ALEXANDER EASTMAN; DONALD C. & PRISCILLA ALEXANDER EASTMAN; CHRISTOPHER GROENHOUT

lazy lingering. The most striking feature is a serpent-shaped bench that hugs the terrace's perimeter, intricately decorated with broken pieces of coloured ceramic known as *trencadís*. Its alternating waves are supposed to create nooks for peace-seeking wanderers to enjoy comfort and privacy.

❹ CASA-MUSEU GAUDÍ

Married to his all-consuming project, Gaudí lived onsite, in this distinctive structure known as the Torre Rosa (red tower), while Park Güell was being built. The striking terracotta building with its churchlike spire was designed, not by Gaudí, but by one of his protégés, Francesc Berenguer, in 1904. It served as the park's original 'show home'.

❺ THE TRAILS

Yes, bring your walking shoes. The park covers over 15 hectares, spread over a steep hillside and, surreally, there's peace to be found among all the people. Wander at will after you've seen the main sights and enjoy some of the best views over Barcelona. Even better, bring a picnic.

↘ THINGS YOU NEED TO KNOW

Entry Park entry is free, but you must pay €5.50 to see the Casa-Museu Gaudí **Recycling project** Gaudí's mosaics (known as *trencadís*) were made of old broken pieces of glass and tiles often scavenged from rubbish dumps **See p195 for more information**

PARK GÜELL & AROUND

HIGHLIGHTS

HIGHLIGHTS

⇘ VIEWPOINTS

Barcelona is surrounded by the Serra de Collserola, a mini–mountain range that culminates in the peak of Tibidabo, reachable by funicular and home to the **Temple del Sagrat Cor** (p201). The sweeping panoramas of the city and Mediterranean are magnificent and can be further amplified by ascending the temple's lift or zipping to level 10 of the space-age **Torre de Collserola** (p201) – views stretch for 70km.

⇘ PARC DE LA COLLSEROLA

When Barcelona feels like it's closing in on you, find elbow room in a **park** (p201) that makes all other parks look like miniatures. Comprising 8000 hectares (22 times the size of New York's Central Park), Collserola is the largest municipal park in the world. Its view-laced ridges provide enough terrain to run multiple marathons, cycle a mini–Tour de España and spot everything from wild boars to eagles.

⬊ CAMP NOU

Spanish soccer is a sometimes bitter tale of two teams, Real Madrid and Barcelona, with the latter currently enjoying a spell as one of the best in the world, courtesy of such living legends as Lionel Messi and Xavi Hernández. The team's home **stadium** (p196) is the largest in Europe and its on-site museum is a manifestation of fervour, football and intense Catalan pride.

⬊ COSMOCAIXA

Barcelona's **science museum** (p193) was refurbished in 2004, and its humungous footprint renders it an all-day attraction. Making even seemingly boring exhibits interesting, the museum has interactive displays guaranteed to impress kids and adults alike. You can wander from a mocked-up Amazonian rainforest to the outer limits of the solar system within minutes.

⬊ MUSEU-MONESTIR DE PEDRALBES

The city's periphery still hides occasional oases of peace, including this monastic **museum** (p197) set in an impressive 14th-century Catalan-Gothic monastery crammed with art, atmosphere and a mural-bedizened chapel. Enjoy the *silentium* (silence) and pray that the urban hullabaloo never reaches as far as this tranquil quarter.

2 PASCALE BEROUJON; 3 PIXTAL IMAGES/PHOTOLIBRARY; 4 MARK AVELLINO; 5 DIEGO LEZAMA; 6 JEAN-PIERRE LESCOURRET

2 Temple del Sagrat Cor (p201), on Tibidabo hill; 3 The edge of the Parc de la Collserola (p201); 4 Camp Nou (p196); 5 CosmoCaixa (p193); 6 Museu-Monestir de Pedralbes (p197)

BEST...

⬏ VIEWPOINTS

- **Parc de la Collserola** (p201)
  An 8000-hectare park in the hills.
- **Temple del Sagrat Cor** (p201)
  Giant Christ statue with lift to top.
- **Torre de Collserola** (p201)
- A 288m tower with glass elevator
  to an observation deck.
- **Restaurant Evo** (p208) Fine dining
  105m above ground.
- **Observatori Fabra** (p202)
  Telescopic views of outer space.

⬏ RELAXATION

- **Sarriá Walk** (p202) Pedestrianised
  pocket of tranquillity.
- **Parc de la Creuta del Coll** (p196)
  Relaxing family park.
- **Parc de la Collserola** (p201) Find
  a quiet spot in Barcelona's green
  lungs.
- **Bilbao** (p205) Quiet inviting
  Spanish-food restaurant.
- **Park Güell** (p195) Bodyswerve the
  crowds with a path into the woods.

⬏ ENTERTAINMENT

- **Sala Beckett** (p211) Challenging
  alternative theatre.
- **Camp Nou** (p196) Soccer as ballet
  at FC Barcelona stadium.
- **Parc d'Atraccions** (p200) Lofty
  funfair in Tibidabo.
- **Bikini** (p211) Old stalwart on club
  and live-music circuit.
- **Verdi** (p211) Original-language
  movie house.

⬏ MUSEUMS

- **Casa-Museu Gaudí** (p195) Gaudí
  residence-turned-museum.
- **Cosmocaixa** (p193) Subterranean
  science museum.
- **Museu del Futbol Club Barcelona**
  (p196) Soccer legends, from Cruyff
  to Messi.
- **Museu-Monestir de Pedralbes**
  (p197) Monk museum.
- **Museu-Casa Verdaguer** (p201)
  Memorabilia of Catalan writer
  Jacint Verdaguer.

GUY MOBERLY

Torre de Collserola (p201)

DISCOVER PARK GÜELL & AROUND

The undulating terrain north of L'Eixample is dominated by Park Güell, one of Gaudí's most extraordinary creations, which inhabits a hillside offering stellar views over Barcelona's city centre and port.

South of here is Gràcia, a separate village until 1897, when it was definitively annexed to an expanding Barcelona. Fashionable among bohemians in the 1960s and '70s, it has since been somewhat gentrified. Immediately to the west lies La Zona Alta, 'The High Zone', where most *barcelonins* with healthy bank accounts aspire to live, if possible in gated complexes or mansions with gardens.

Further north is Tibidabo, the district's (and city's) high point, great for fresh air and views – on a good day you can see inland as far as Montserrat. The mountain, with its amusement park and rather bombastic church, is at the heart of the much wider Parc de la Collserola, one of the city's few green lungs. Closer to the urban hub lies the CosmoCaixa science museum and the monuments of Pedralbes.

SIGHTS

GRÀCIA & PARK GÜELL

MERCAT DE LA LLIBERTAT Map p194

☎ 93 217 09 95; Plaça de la Llibertat; admission free; ☉ 8am-8.30pm Mon-Fri, 8am-3pm Sat; ⓡ FGC Gràcia

Built in the 1870s, the 'Liberty Market' was covered in 1893 in typically fizzy Modernista style, employing generous whirls of wrought iron. It got a considerable facelift in 2009 and has lost some of its aged charm, but the market remains emblematic of the Gràcia district, full of life and all kinds of fresh produce. The man behind the 1893 remake was Francesc Berenguer i Mestres (1866–1914), Gaudí's long-time assistant.

LA ZONA ALTA

COSMOCAIXA Map p186

Museu de la Ciència; ☎ 93 212 60 50; www .fundacio.lacaixa.es, in Catalan & Spanish; Carrer de Teodor Roviralta 47-51; adult/senior & under 7yr/student €3/free/2; ☉ 10am-8pm Tue-Sun & holidays; ⓐ 60, ⓡ FGC Avinguda Tibidabo

This bright science museum is housed in a Modernista building (completed in 1909). Kids (and kids at heart) are fascinated by displays here and the museum has become one of the city's most popular attractions. The single greatest highlight is the recreation over 1 sq km of a chunk of flooded Amazon rainforest (Bosc Inundat). More than 100 species of Amazon flora and fauna (including anacondas, colourful poisonous frogs and caymans) prosper in this unique, living diorama in which you can even experience a tropical downpour. In another original section, the Mur Geològic, seven great chunks of rock (90 tonnes in all) have been assembled to create a 'geological wall'.

These and other displays on the lower 5th floor (the bulk of the museum is underground) cover many fascinating areas of science, from fossils to physics, and from the alphabet to outer space. To gain access to other special sections, such as the Planetari (planetarium), check for guided visits. Most of these activities are

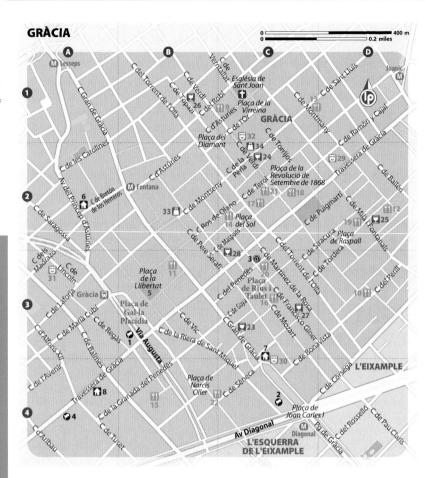

GRÀCIA

INFORMATION		
Australian Consulate	1	B3
German Consulate	2	C4
Internet MSN	3	C3
New Zealand Consulate	4	A4

SIGHTS		
Mercat de la Llibertat	5	B3

SLEEPING		
Aparthotel Silver	6	A2
Hotel Casa Fuster	7	C3
Hotel Medium Confort	8	A4

EATING		
A Casa Portuguesa	9	C1

Bilbao	10	D3
Botafumeiro	11	B3
Cal Boter	12	D2
El Glop	13	C1
Envalira	14	C2
Hofmann		B4
Ipar-Txoko	16	C3
La Llar de Foc	17	C2
La Nena	18	C2
Lac Majùr	19	D2
Nou Candanchú	20	C3
O'Gràcia!	21	C2
Restaurant Roig Robí	22	B4

DRINKING		
Alfa	23	C3

La Baignoire	24	C2
La Cigale	25	D2
Noise i Art	26	B1
Sabor A Cuba	27	C3
Taverna La Violeta	28	C3

ENTERTAINMENT &		
ACTIVITIES		
Heliogàbal	29	D2
Martin's	30	C4
Otto Zutz	31	A3
Verdi	32	C1

SHOPPING		
Hibernian	33	B2
Red Market	34	C2

CHRISTOPHER GROENHOUT

Decorative tile work at Park Güell

PARK GÜELL

North of Gràcia and about 4km from Plaça de Catalunya, Park Güell is where Gaudí turned his hand to landscape gardening. It's a strange, enchanting place where his passion for natural forms really took flight – to the point where the artificial almost seems more natural than the natural.

Just inside the main entrance on Carrer d'Olot, immediately recognisable by the two Hansel-and-Gretel gatehouses, is the park's Centre d'Interpretac (closed for restoration at the time of writing) in the Pavelló de Consergeria, which is a typically curvaceous former porter's home that hosts a display on Gaudí's building methods and the history of the park.

The steps up from the entrance, guarded by a mosaic dragon/lizard (a copy of which you can buy in many downtown souvenir shops), lead to the Sala Hipóstila (aka the Doric Temple), a forest of 88 stone columns (some of them leaning like mighty trees bent by the weight of time), intended as a market. On top of the Sala Hipóstila is a broad open space whose centrepiece is the Banc de Trencadís, a tiled bench curving sinuously around its perimeter and designed by one of Gaudí's closest colleagues, architect Josep Maria Jujol (1879–1949).

The spired house to the right is the Casa-Museu Gaudí, where Gaudí lived for most of his last 20 years (1906–26). It contains furniture by him (including items that were once at home in La Pedrera, Casa Batlló and Casa Calvet) and other memorabilia.

Much of the park is still wooded, but it's laced with pathways.

Things you need to know: Park Güell (Map p186; ☎ 93 413 24 00; Carrer d'Olot 7; admission free; ◷ 10am-9pm Jun-Sep, 10am-8pm Apr, May & Oct, 10am-7pm Mar & Nov, 10am-6pm Dec-Feb; Ⓜ Lesseps or Vallcarca, ◻ 24); Casa-Museu Gaudí (Map p186; ☎ 93 219 38 11; www .casamuseugaudi.org; adult/under 10yr/senior & student €5.50/free/4.50; ◷ 10am-8pm Apr-Sep, 10am-6pm Oct-Mar)

PARK GÜELL & AROUND

SIGHTS

XAVIER FLORENSA/PHOTOLIBRARY

Elogio del Agua sculpture in the Parc de la Creueta del Coll

◥ IF YOU LIKE...

If you like Park Güell (p195), you may want to savour these other slightly less bodacious green spaces:

- **Jardins del Laberint d'Horta** (☎ 010; Carrer dels Germans Desvalls; adult/student €2.20/1.40, free Wed & Sun; ◷ 10am-sunset daily; Ⓜ Mundet) Anchored by a maze in its centre (hence the name) this museum-garden near the Mundet Metro station was laid out in the twilight years of the 18th century by romantic Antoni Desvalls, Marquès d'Alfarras i de Llupià.

- **Parc de la Creueta del Coll** (Map p186; ☎ 010, 93 413 24 00; www.bcn.cat/parcsi jardins, in Catalan & Spanish; Passeig de la Mare de Déu del Coll 77; admission free; ◷ 10am-sunset; Ⓜ Penitents) Not far from Park Güell, this relaxing family park (with pool, swings and snack bar) showcases an enormous cement sculpture, *Elogio del Agua* (Eulogy to Water), and trails leading to views of the city and Tibidabo. From the Penitents Metro station, it's a 15-minute walk.

interactive and directed at children, and cost €2/1.50 per adult/child. The planetarium has been adapted so that the vision- and hearing-impaired may also enjoy it.

CAMP NOU Map p186

☎ 93 496 36 00; www.fcbarcelona.com; Carrer d'Aristides Maillol; adult/senior & child €17/14; ◷ 10am-8pm Mon-Sat, 10am-2.30pm Sun & holidays early Apr-early Oct, 10am-6.30pm Mon-Sat, 10am-2.30pm Sun & holidays early Oct-early Apr; Ⓜ Palau Reial or Collblanc

Among Barcelona's most-visited museums is the Museu del Futbol Club Barcelona, near the club's giant Camp Nou (aka Nou Camp) stadium. Barça is one of Europe's top football clubs, and its museum is a hit with football fans the world over.

Camp Nou, built in 1957 and enlarged for the 1982 World Cup, is one of the world's biggest stadiums, holding 99,000 people. The football club has a world-record membership of 173,000.

Football fans who can't get to a game may find a visit to the museum, with guided tour of the stadium, worthwhile. The best bits of the museum itself are the photo section, the goal videos and the views out over the stadium. Among the quirkier paraphernalia are old sports board games, the life-sized diorama of old-time dressing rooms, posters and magazines from way back and the *futbolín* (table soccer) collection. You can admire the (in at least one case literally) golden boots of great goalscorers of the past and stacks of trophies. Hi-tech multimedia displays project great moments in Barça history. Sound installations include the club's anthem and match-day sounds from the stadium.

The **guided tour** of the stadium takes in the team's dressing rooms, heads out through the tunnel, onto the pitch and winds up in the presidential box.

Set aside about 2½ hours for the whole visit.

MUSEU-MONESTIR DE PEDRALBES Map p186

☎ 93 256 34 34; www.museuhistoria.bcn.cat; Baixada del Monestir 9; adult/under 7yr/senior & student €7/free/5; ◷ 10am-5pm Tue-Sat, 10am-8pm Sun, 10am-3pm holidays Apr-Sep, 10am-2pm Tue-Sat, 10am-8pm Sun, 10am-3pm holidays Oct-Mar; ◉ FGC Reina Elisenda, ◻ 22, 63, 64 or 75 This peaceful old convent was first opened to the public in 1983 and is now a museum of monastic life (the few remaining nuns have moved into more modern neighbouring buildings). It stands at the top of Avinguda de Pedralbes in a residential area that was countryside until the 20th century, but which remains a divinely quiet corner of Barcelona.

The architectural highlight is the large, elegant, three-storey cloister, a jewel of Catalan Gothic, built in the early 14th century. Following its course to the right, stop at the first chapel, the **Capella de Sant Miquel**, whose murals were done in 1346 by Ferrer Bassá, one of Catalonia's earliest documented painters. A few steps on is the ornamental grave of Queen Elisenda, who founded the convent. It is curious, as it is divided in two: the side in the cloister shows her dressed as a penitent widow, while the other part, an alabaster

PARK GÜELL & AROUND

SIGHTS

DAMIEN SIMONIS

Museu-Monestir de Pedralbes

masterpiece inside the adjacent church, shows her dressed as queen.

As you head around the ground floor of the cloister, you can peer into the restored refectory, kitchen, stables, stores and a reconstruction of the infirmary – all giving a good idea of convent life. Eating in the refectory must not have been a whole lot of fun, judging by the exhortations to *Silentium* (Silence) and *Audi Tacens* (Listen and Keep Quiet) written around the walls. Harder still must have been spending one's days in the cells on the ground and 1st floors in a state of near-perpetual prayer and devotional reading.

Upstairs is a grand hall that was once the **Dormidor** (sleeping quarters). It was lined by tiny night cells but they were long ago removed. Today a modest collection of the monastery's art, especially Gothic devotional works, and furniture grace this space. Most is by largely unknown Catalan artists, with some 16th-century Flemish works, and was acquired thanks to the considerable wealth of the convent's mostly high-class nuns.

Next to the convent, the sober church is an excellent example of Catalan Gothic. Just west of the convent, where Carretera d'Esplugues meets Carrer del Bisbe Català, is a peaceful park, the **Hort de Pedralbes**.

PALAU REIAL DE PEDRALBES
Map p186

☎ 93 256 34 65; Avinguda Diagonal 686; all collections adult/student & senior €5/3, free 1st Sun of the month & 3-6pm Sun; ☺ museums 10am-6pm Tue-Sun, 10am-3pm holidays, park 10am-6pm daily; Ⓜ Palau Reial

Across Avinguda Diagonal from the main campus of the Universitat de Barcelona is the entrance to **Parc del Palau Reial**. In the park is the Palau Reial de Pedralbes, an early-20th-century building that belonged to the family of Eusebi Güell (Gaudí's patron) until they handed it over to the city in 1926 to serve as a royal residence. Among its guests have been King Alfonso XIII, the president of Catalonia and General Franco.

The palace houses three museums, two of them rolled into one and temporarily housed here.

DAMIEN SIMONIS

Palau Reial de Pedralbes

The **Museu de Ceràmica** (www.museu ceramica.bcn.es) has a good collection of Spanish ceramics from the 10th to 19th centuries, including work by Picasso and Miró. Spain inherited from the Muslims, and then further refined, a strong tradition in ceramics – here you can compare some exquisite work (tiles, porcelain tableware and the like) from some of the greatest centres of pottery production across Spain, including Talavera de la Reina in Castilla–La Mancha, Manises and Paterna in Valencia, and Teruel in Aragón. There are also some fanciful ceramics from the 20th century – here they have ceased to be a tool with aesthetic value and are purely decorative. The museum also has a collection of ceramics created elsewhere in the world, from 14th century Iranian tiles to Italian Renaissance pieces. Much of this, unfortunately, is not on view at the moment.

The **Disseny Hub** (Design Hub; www.dhub -bcn.cat) is the fusion of two collections, along with a space for temporary exhibitions in La Ribera (see p115).

The **Museu de les Arts Decoratives**, across the hall from the Museu de Ceràmica on the 1st floor, brings together an eclectic assortment of furnishings,

---

TRANSPORT: LA ZONA ALTA

Transport options vary wildly depending on where you want to go. Metro Línia 3 will get you to the Jardins del Laberint d'Horta (Ⓜ Mundet) and Palau Reial de Pedralbes (Ⓜ Palau Reial). From the latter you could walk to the Museu-Monestir de Pedralbes. Otherwise, take an FGC train to the monastery. FGC trains are generally the easiest way of getting close to most of the sights in and around Tibidabo and the Parc de la Collserola.

Take an FGC train to Avinguda Tibidabo from Catalunya station on Plaça de Catalunya (€1.40, 10 minutes). Outside Avinguda de Tibidabo station, hop on the *tramvia blau*, Barcelona's last surviving tram, which runs between fancy Modernista mansions (particularly Casa Roviralta at 31 Avinguda de Tibidabo) to Plaça del Doctor Andreu (one-way/return €2.80/4.30, 15 minutes, every 15 or 30 minutes 10am to 8pm daily late June to early September, 10am to 6pm Saturdays, Sundays and holidays early September to late June) – it has been doing so since 1901. On days and at times when the tram does not operate, a bus serves the route (€1.40).

From Plaça del Doctor Andreu, the Tibidabo funicular railway climbs through the woods to Plaça de Tibidabo at the top of the hill (one-way/return €2.50/4, five minutes). Departures start at 10.45am and continue until shortly after the Parc d'Atraccions closing time.

An alternative is bus T2, the 'Tibibús', from Plaça de Catalunya to Plaça de Tibidabo (€2.60, 30 minutes, every 30 to 50 minutes on Saturdays, Sundays and holidays year-round and hourly from 10.30am Monday to Friday late June to early September). Purchase tickets on the bus, which operates only when Parc d'Atraccions is open. The last bus down leaves Tibidabo 30 minutes after the park closes. You can also buy a combined ticket that includes the bus and entry to the Parc d'Atraccions (€25).

ornaments and knick-knacks dating as far back as the Romanesque period. The plush and somewhat stuffy elegance of Empire- and Isabelline-style divans can be neatly compared with some of the more tasteless ideas to emerge on the subject of seating in the 1970s.

The **Museu Tèxtil i d'Indumentària** (www.museu textil.bcn.es), on the 2nd floor, contains some 4000 items that range from 4th-century Coptic textiles to 20th-century local embroidery. The heart of the collection is the assortment of clothing from the 16th century to the 1930s.

These two collections will form the bedrock of the new Disseny Hub museum being built at Plaça de les Glòries Catalanes and due to open in 2011.

Over by Avinguda de Pedralbes are the stables and porter's lodge designed by Gaudí for the Finca Güell, as the Güell estate here was called. Known also as the **Pavellons Güell** (☎ 93 317 76 52; www .rutadelmodernisme.com; guided tour adult/senior & under 18yr €6/3; ☺ in English 10.15am & 12.15pm, in Catalan 11.15am, in Spanish 1.15pm Fri-Mon), they

were built in the mid-1880s, when Gaudí was strongly impressed by Islamic architecture. Outside visiting hours, there is nothing to stop you admiring Gaudí's wrought-iron dragon gate from the exterior.

PARC D'ATRACCIONS off Map p186

☎ 93 211 79 42; www.tibidabo.es; Plaça de Tibidabo 3-4; adult/child shorter than 0.9m/child shorter than 1.2m & senior €25/free/9; ☺ closed Jan-Feb

The reason most *barcelonins* come up to Tibidabo is for some thrills (but hopefully no spills) in this funfair, close to the top funicular station. Among the main attractions are El Pndol, La Muntanya Russa and Hurakan. El Pndol is a giant arm holding four passengers, which drops them at a speed that reaches 100km/h in a period of less than three seconds (a force of four times gravity) before swinging outward – not for the squeamish. La Muntanya Russa is a massive new big dipper, which at its high point affords wonderful views before plunging you at 80km/h through woods. Hurakan tosses its passengers about

Parc d'Atraccions Ferris wheel, in front of the Temple del Sagrat Cor

GUY MOBERLY

with sudden drops and stomach-turning 360-degree turns.

With your feet more firmly planted on the ground, you can visit the Dididado 4-D cinema (basically 3-D with the appropriate glasses and some sound and movement effects thrown in), which puts on 10-minute films that seem to pop out at you. A curious sideline is the Museu d'Autòmats, around 50 automated puppets going as far back as 1880 and part of the original amusement park.

PARC DE LA COLLSEROLA Map p186

☎ 93 280 35 52; www.parccollserola.net; Carretera de l'Església 92; ⓔ FGC Peu del Funicular, then funicular to Baixador de Vallvidrera

Barcelonins needing an escape from the city without heading too far into the countryside seek this extensive, 8000-hectare park in the hills. It is a great place to hike and bike and bristles with eateries and snack bars. Pick up a map from the Centre d'Informació (ⓒ 9.30am-3pm).

Aside from nature, the principal point of interest is the sprawling Museu-Casa Verdaguer (off Map p186; ☎ 93 204 78 05; www .museuhistoria.bcn.cat; Vil·la Joana, Carretera de l'Església 104; admission free; ⓒ 10am-2pm Sat, Sun & holidays Sep-Jul), 100m from the information centre and a short walk from the train station. Catalonia's revered writer Jacint Verdaguer lived in this late-18th-century country house before his death on 10 July 1902. On the ground floor is a typical 19th-century country kitchen, with coal-fired stove and hobs in the middle. Upstairs you can see a raft of Verdaguer memorabilia (from original published works through to photos and documents) as you wander through the rooms. The bed in which he died remains exactly where it was in 1902. Labels are in Catalan only.

Beyond, the park has various other minor highlights, including a smattering

of country chapels (some Romanesque), the ragged ruins of the 14th-century Castellciuro castle in the west, various lookout points and, to the north, the 15th-century Can Coll (ⓒ 9.30am-3pm Sun & holidays, closed Jul & Aug), a grand farmhouse. It's used as an environmental education centre where you can see how richer farmers lived around the 17th to 19th centuries.

Bus 111 runs between Tibidabo and Vallvidrera (passing in front of the Torre de Collserola).

TEMPLE DEL SAGRAT COR

off Map p186

☎ 93 417 56 86; Plaça de Tibidabo; admission free; ⓒ 8am-7pm

The Church of the Sacred Heart, looming above the top funicular station, is meant to be Barcelona's answer to Paris' Sacré-Cœur. The church, built from 1902 to 1961 in a mix of styles with some Modernista influence, is certainly as visible as its Parisian namesake, and even more vilified by aesthetes. It's actually two churches, one on top of the other. The top one is surmounted by a giant statue of Christ and has a lift (€2; ⓒ 10am-7pm) to take you to the roof for the panoramic (and often windchilled) views.

TORRE DE COLLSEROLA Map p186

☎ 93 211 79 42; www.torredecollserola.com; Carretera de Vallvidrera al Tibidabo; adult/child & senior/student €5/3/3.50; ⓒ 11am-2pm & 3.30-8pm daily Jul & Aug, 11am-2pm & 3.30-8pm Sat, Sun & holidays Sep-Jun; Funicular de Vallvidrera, then ⓑ 111

Sir Norman Foster designed the 288m-high Torre de Collserola telecommunications tower, which was built between 1990 and 1992. The external glass lift to the visitors' observation area, 115m up, is as hair-raising as anything at the nearby Parc d'Atraccions. People say you can see for 70km from the top on a clear day. If ever anyone wanted to knock out Barcelona's TV and radio sets, this would be the place to do it: all transmissions are sent from here, and repeater stations across Catalonia are also controlled from this tower. Closing hours shorten in the cooler months.

OBSERVATORI FABRA Map p186
☎ 902 222191; www.observatorifabra.com; Carretera del Observatori; admission €9
Inaugurated in 1904, this Modernista observatory is still a functioning scientific foundation. It can be visited on certain evenings to allow people to observe the stars through its grand old telescope. Visits (generally in Catalan or Spanish) have to be booked. From mid-June to mid-September an option is to join in for the nightly Sopars amb Estrelles (Dinner under the Stars). You dine outside, tour the building, peer into the telescope and get a lecture (in Catalan) on the heavens. The evening starts at 8.30pm and costs €65 per person. The easiest way here is by taxi.

SLEEPING

GRÀCIA & PARK GÜELL
Staying up in Gràcia takes you out of the mainstream tourist areas and gives you a more authentic feel for the town. All the touristy bits are never far away by Metro and the restaurant and bar life in Gràcia is great on its own.

HOTEL CASA FUSTER
Map p194   Hotel €€€
☎ 93 255 30 00, 902 202345; www.hotelcasafuster.com; Passeig de Gràcia 132; s/d from €294/321; Ⓜ Diagonal; Ⓟ ✗ ✗ ▢ 🛜 ✗
This sumptuous Modernista mansion (built in 1908–11) at the top end of the city's showcase boulevard has been transformed into one of Barcelona's most luxurious hotels. Standard rooms are plush, if smallish. Period features have been restored at considerable cost and complemented with hydro-massage tubs, plasma TVs and king-size beds. The rooftop terrace (with pool) offers great views and relaxation. The Café Vienés, once a meeting place for Barcelona intellectuals in the

---

A WANDER THROUGH OLD SARRIÀ
Hugging the left flank of thundering Via Augusta, the old centre of Sarrià is a largely pedestrianised haven of peace. Probably founded in the 13th century and only incorporated into Barcelona in 1921, ancient Sarrià is formed around sinuous Carrer Major de Sarrià (Map p186), today a mix of old and new, with a sprinkling of shops and restaurants. At its top end is pretty Plaça de Sarrià (from where Passeig de la Reina Elisenda de Montcada leads west to the medieval Museu-Monestir de Pedralbes), where you'll want to check out Foix de Sarrià, an exclusive pastry shop. As you wander downhill, duck off into Plaça del Consell de la Vila, Plaça de Sant Vicenç de Sarrià and Carrer de Rocaberti, at the end of which is the Monestir de Santa Isabel, with its neo-Gothic cloister. Built in 1886 to house Clarissan nuns, whose order had first set up in El Raval in the 16th century, it was abandoned during the civil war and used as an air-raid shelter.

Detail, Temple del Sagrat Cor (p201)

NEIL SETCHFIELD

building's heyday, is the perfect spot for an aperitif before heading out at night.

APARTHOTEL SILVER Map p194 Hotel €€
☎ 93 218 91 00; www.hotelsilver.com; Carrer de Bretón de los Herreros 26; s €79-120, d €85-145; Ⓜ Fontana; ✻ 🖳 📶
There are no fewer than five types of rooms here, from chintzy, tiny basic rooms to the very spacious 'superior rooms'. Aim for the better rooms. All come with a kitchenette and some have a terrace or balcony. There is a little garden too.

LA ZONA ALTA
Except for a certain business clientele, this mostly residential area is a little too far from the action for most people. Several exceptional places are well worth considering if being in the centre of things is not a priority.

HOTEL REY JUAN CARLOS I
Map p186   Hotel €€€
☎ 93 364 40 40; www.hrjuancarlos.com; Avinguda Diagonal 661-671; d from €299; Ⓜ Zona Universitària; 🅿 ✖ ✻ 🖳 ♨

Like an ultramodern lighthouse at this southwest gateway to the city, the glass towers of this luxury mega-hotel hold more than 430 spacious rooms, most with spectacular views. The hotel has pools and a gym, along with extensive gardens belonging to the farmhouse that stood here until well into the 20th century. Room prices can sink surprisingly low in slow periods. With the Metro close by, you can be in central Barcelona in about 20 minutes.

HOTEL MEDIUM CONFORT
Map p194   Hotel €€
☎ 93 238 68 28; www.mediumhoteles.com; Travessera de Gràcia 72; s/d €90/95; 🚆 FGC Gràcia; 🅿 ✻ 🖳 📶
This strangely named two-star lodging is a comfortable business-oriented hotel in an area handy for some uptown bars and restaurants, and is only a short stroll from Gràcia. It sometimes offers tempting deals on price (€50 for a double is not unheard of), and while rooms do not bubble over with character, they're neat, modern and spacious. You can sit out on the terrace for a coffee.

EATING

GRÀCIA & PARK GÜELL

Spread across this busy *barri* (neighbourhood) are all sorts of enticing options, from simple tapas bars to top-class seafood. Gràcia is loaded with Middle Eastern, and to a lesser extent Greek, restaurants, which are chirpy and good value.

BOTAFUMEIRO Map p194   Seafood €€€

☎ 93 218 42 30; www.botafumeiro.es; Carrer Gran de Gràcia 81; meals €70-80; ⏱ 1pm-1am; Ⓜ Fontana; ✖

It is hard not to mention this classic temple of Galician shellfish and other briny delights, long a magnet for VIPs visiting Barcelona. You can bring the price down by sharing a few *medias raciones* to taste a range of marine offerings or a *safata especial del Mar Cantàbric* (seafood platter) between two. Try the *percebes,* the strangely twisted goose barnacles harvested along Galicia's north Atlantic coast, which many Spaniards consider the ultimate seafood delicacy.

RESTAURANT ROIG ROBÍ

Map p194   Catalan €€€

☎ 93 218 92 22; www.roigrobi.com; Carrer de Sèneca 20; meals €70-80; ⏱ lunch & dinner Mon-Fri, dinner Sat; Ⓜ Diagonal; ✖

This is an altar to refined traditional cooking. The *textures de carxofes amb vieires a la plantxa* (artichokes with grilled scallops) are like a whiff of artichoke wafting over the prized shellfish. It also does several seafood- and-rice dishes and offers half portions for those with less of an appetite.

IPAR-TXOKO Map p194   Basque €€

☎ 93 218 19 54; Carrer de Mozart 22; meals €40-50; ⏱ Tue-Sat Sep-Jul; Ⓜ Diagonal

Inside this Basque eatery, the atmosphere is warm and traditional. Hefty timber beams hold up the Catalan vaulted ceiling, and the bar (tapas available) has a garish green columned front. Getxo-born Mikel turns out traditional cooking from northern Spain, including a sumptuous *chuletón* (T-bone steak for two – look at the size of that thing!) or a less gargantuan *tortilla de bacalao* (a thick salted-cod

Outdoor cafe, Park Güell

RACHEL LEWIS

omelette). Then there are curiosities, like *kokotxas de merluza,* heart-shaped cuts from the hake's throat. The wine list is daunting but Mikel is on hand to explain everything – in English, too.

BILBAO Map p194   Northern Spanish €€

☎ 93 458 96 24; Carrer del Perill 33; meals €40; ⏰ Mon-Sat; Ⓜ Diagonal

It doesn't look much from the outside, but Bilbao is a timeless classic, where reservations for dinner are imperative. The back dining room, with bottle-lined walls, stout timber tables and a yellowing light evocative of a country tavern, will appeal to carnivores especially, although some fish dishes are also on offer. Consider opting for a *chuletón* (T-bone steak), washed down with a good Spanish red.

TIBET Map p186   Catalan €€

☎ 93 284 50 45; Carrer de Ramiro de Maetzu 34; meals €35; ⏰ lunch & dinner Wed-Sat & Mon, lunch Sun; Ⓜ Alfons X, 🚌 24 or 39

In a semirustic setting not far from Park Güell, this restaurant has as much to do with Tibet as the author of this review does with Eskimos. For 50 years it has been sizzling meat on the grill and dishing up snails, one of the house specialities. There's not an item of seafood in sight.

CAL BOTER Map p194   Catalan €€

☎ 93 458 84 62; Carrer de Tordera 62; meals €30-35; ⏰ Tue-Sun; Ⓜ Joanic

A classic eatery that draws families and noisy groups of pals for *cargols a la llauna* (snails sautéed in a tin dish), *filet de bou a la crema de foie* (a thick clump of tender beef drowned in an orange and foie gras sauce), and other Catalan specialities, including curious *mar i muntanya* (surf and turf) combinations like *bolets i gambes* (mushrooms and prawns). Finish with a *xarrup de llimona amb mar de cava* (lemon

sorbet drowned in *cava).* The *menú del día* (lunch Tuesday to Friday) comes in at a good-humoured €9.80.

O' GRÀCIA! Map p194   Catalan €€

☎ 93 213 30 44; Plaça de la Revolució de Setembre de 1868 15; meals €30-35; ⏰ Tue-Sat; Ⓜ Fontana; ⊗

This is an especially popular lunch option, with the *menú del día* outstanding value at €10.50. The *arròs negre de sepia* (squid-ink rice with cuttlefish) makes a good first course, followed by a limited set of meat and fish options with vegetable sides. Serves are decent, presentation careful and service attentive. There's a more elaborate tasting menu at €24.50.

ENVALIRA Map p194   Catalan €€

☎ 93 218 58 13; Plaça del Sol 13; meals €30; ⏰ lunch & dinner Tue-Sat, lunch Sun; Ⓜ Fontana

Surrounded by cool hang-outs, Lebanese eateries and grunge bars, you'd barely notice the modest entrance to this delicious relic. Head for the 1950s time-warp dining room out the back. Serious waiters deliver all sorts of seafood and rice dishes to your table, from *arròs a la milanesa* (savoury rice dish with chicken, pork and a light cheese gratin) to a *bullit de lluç* (slice of white hake boiled with herb-laced rice and a handful of clams).

LAC MAJÙR Map p194   Italian €€

☎ 93 285 15 03; Carrer de Tordera 33; meals €25; ⏰ Mon-Sat; Ⓜ Verdaguer

You could easily miss this cosy slice of northwest Italy while striding along the quiet and unusually leafy lane outside. Inside, all sorts of home-cooking delights await, including the house specials, gnocchi and *trofie.* The latter are twists of pasta, usually served with pesto sauce, from Liguria. Try the mascarpone and ham variant followed by, say, a *saltimbocca alla romana* (a veal slice cooked with ham, sage and sweet Marsala wine).

EL GLOP Map p194   Catalan €€

☎ 93 213 70 58; www.tavernaelglop.com; Carrer de Sant Lluís 24; meals €25; Ⓜ Joanic
Step inside this raucous eatery decked out in country Catalan fashion, with gingham tablecloths and no-nonsense, slap-up meals. The secret is hearty serves of simple dishes, such as *bistec a la brasa* (grilled steak), perhaps preceded by *albergínies farcides* (stuffed aubergines) or *calçots* in winter. Try the *tocinillo,* a caramel dessert, to finish. Open until 1am, it's a useful place to have up your sleeve for a late bite.

A CASA PORTUGUESA

Map p194   Portuguese €
☎ 93 368 35 28; www.acasaportuguesa.com; Carrer de Verdi 58; snacks €20; ☽ dinner Tue-Fri, lunch & dinner Sat, Sun & holidays; Ⓜ Fontana
As well as being a convivial halt for a glass or two of fine wine (ask waiters for advice) or a simple *vinho verde* ('green wine', a typical, simple Portuguese white wine), it is a good spot to fill up on snacks (cheeses, little pies and pastries), all in the name of getting to know the Iberian neighbours better. There is always a buzzing atmosphere and exhibitions are frequently held. Try a couple of *pastéis de Belém* (delightful little cream tarts) and stock up on goodies from Portugal, Brazil and other one-time Portuguese colonies.

LA LLAR DE FOC Map p194   Catalan €

☎ 93 284 10 25; Carrer de Ramón i Cajal 13; meals €20; Ⓜ Fontana
For a hearty sit-down meal at rock-bottom prices, the 'Hearth' is hard to beat. At lunch, it has a €9 *menú del día.* You could start with a mixed salad or *empanadita* (big slice of tuna pie), followed by chicken in a mild curry sauce or *costellas* (ribs). Go for flan for dessert, as the ice creams are on a stick.

NOU CANDANCHÚ Map p194   Tapas €

☎ 93 237 73 62; Plaça de la Vila de Gràcia 9; meals €15-20; ☽ Wed-Mon; Ⓜ Fontana

DIEGO LEZAMA

Restaurant in the Gràcia district

The liveliest locale on the square, Nou Candanchú is a long-time favourite for various reasons. Many flock to its sunny terrace just for a few drinks. Accompany the liquid refreshment with one of the giant *entrepans* (filled rolls) for which this place is famous. Otherwise, it offers a limited range of tapas and reasonable grilled-meat dishes.

LA NENA Map p194   Cafe & Chocolate €
☎ 93 285 14 76; Carrer de Ramon i Cajal 36; ☺ 9am-2pm & 4-10pm Mon-Sat, 10am-10pm Sun & holidays; Ⓜ Fontana

A French team has created this delightful chaotic space for indulging in cups of rich hot chocolate (known as *suïssos)* served with a plate of heavy homemade whipped cream and *melindros* (spongy sweet biscuits), fine desserts and even a few savoury dishes (including crêpes). The place is strewn with books and the area out back is designed to keep kids busy, making it an ideal family rest stop.

LA ZONA ALTA

Some of the grandest kitchens in the city are scattered across La Zona Alta, from Tibidabo across Sant Gervasi (as far down as Avinguda Diagonal, west of Gràcia) to Pedralbes. Plenty of places of all cuisines and qualities abound, often tucked in quiet, unassuming residential streets far from anything of interest to tourists.

VIA VENETO Map p186   Catalan €€€
☎ 93 200 72 44; www.viavenetorestaurant.com; Carrer de Ganduxer 10; meals €90-120; ☺ lunch & dinner Mon-Fri, dinner Sat, closed 3 weeks in Aug; Ⓡ FGC La Bonanova; ✗

Dalí used to regularly waltz into this high-society eatery after it opened in 1967. The vaguely art deco setting (note the oval mirrors), orange-rose tablecloths, leather chairs and fine cutlery may cater to more conservative souls, but the painter was here for the kitchen exploits. Catalan dishes dominate and the mouth waters at the mere mention of, say, *rodaballo al horno con espárragos blancos, alcachofas y navajas del Delta del Ebro* (oven-cooked turbot with white asparagus, artichokes and razor clams). The service is so good you barely notice the waiters' presence.

HOFMANN Map p194   Mediterranean €€€
☎ 93 218 71 65; www.hofmann-bcn.com; Carrer de Granada del Penedès 14-16; meals €80-100; ☺ Mon-Fri; Ⓡ FGC Gràcia; ✗

What's cooking here are the trainee chefs, helped along by their instructors. Dishes are generally elegant renditions of classic Mediterranean food, followed by such delicious desserts that some people prefer a starter and two sweets, skipping the main course altogether.

CAN TRAVI NOU off Map p186   Catalan €€
☎ 93 428 03 01; www.gruptravi.com; Carrer de Jorge Manrique, Parc de la Vall d'Hebron; meals €45-50; ☺ lunch & dinner Mon-Sat, lunch Sun; Ⓜ Montbau; Ⓟ ✗

This expansive 18th-century mansion has several dining areas that stretch across two floors. The warm colours, grandfather clock and a wholesome, rustic air make for a magical setting for a Catalan splurge. The *risotto de formatge* (cheese risotto) makes a hearty starter, but the generous mains will please you even more. The *arròs caldós amb llamàntol i cloïsses* (rice stew with lobster and clams) is irresistible, and the grilled steaks tender.

CAN CORTADA off Map p186   Catalan €€
☎ 93 427 23 15; www.gruptravi.com; Avinguda de l'Estatut de Catalunya; meals €40; Ⓜ Montbau; Ⓟ ✗

More than anything else, it is the setting and the hearty welcome that make this

11th-century estate (complete with the remains of a defensive tower) worth the excursion. Try for a table in the former cellars or on the garden terrace. Lots of Catalan fare, like *pollastre amb escamarlans* (chicken and crayfish), dominates the menu.

INDOCHINE Map p186 Pan-Asian €€
☎ 93 201 99 84; www.indochinebarcelona.com; Carrer d'Aribau 247; meals €35-40; ☺ Tue-Sun; ☒ FGC Molina; ☒

This uptown Asian eatery could almost pass for a florist. Once through the French doors and greenery you will be presented with a selection of Thai, Vietnamese and Cambodian dishes. Although somewhat Westernised, the food is enticing. You could start with a light green-papaya salad and follow with *pescado al estilo camboyano* (Cambodian-style fish, lightly steamed and done in a vegetable sauce). Those with flexible legs can sit on the floor.

CASA FERNÁNDEZ Map p186 Spanish €€
☎ 93 201 93 80; www.casafernandez.com; Carrer de Santaló 46; meals €30; ☺ 1pm-1am; ☒ FGC Muntaner

Immensely popular with bar hoppers suddenly aware they have skipped dinner when it's gone midnight, this bustling, cheerful eatery is a classic. Food is hearty and service hectic but pretty fast even when the place is brimful with carousers. There's plenty of choice of local and foreign beers and a reasonable wine selection.

DRINKING
GRÀCIA & PARK GÜELL

Gràcia is a quirky place. In many ways it's its own world, with rowdy young beer swillers who should probably be studying, trendy music bars and a couple of the city's big clubs.

ALFA Map p194 Bar
☎ 93 415 18 24; Carrer Gran de Gràcia 36; ☺ 11pm-3.30am Thu-Sat; ☒ Diagonal

Aficionados of good old-fashioned rock love this unchanging bar-cum-minidisco, a Gràcia classic. Records hang from the ceiling as if to remind you that most of the music comes from the pre-CD era, '60s to '80s and the occasional later intruder.

LA BAIGNOIRE Map p194 Bar
☎ 677 408993; Carrer de Verdi 6; ☺ 7pm-2.30am Sun-Thu, 7pm-3am Fri & Sat; ☒ Fontana

This inviting, tiny wine bar is always packed. Grab a stool and high table and order fine wines by the glass (beer and cocktails available too). It's perfect before and after a movie at the nearby Verdi cinema.

HIGH IN THE SKY

For a five-star dining experience beneath a transparent UFO-style dome, 105m above ground, grab a cab to Restaurant Evo (☎ 93 413 50 30; www.hesperia.com; Gran Via de les Corts Catalanes 144; ☺ dinner Mon-Fri, lunch & dinner Sat; ☒ Hospital Bellvitge; ☒ ☒), located in Hotel Hesperia Tower in L'Hospitalet de Llobregat. This is gourmet dining literally under the stars (of which one comes from Michelin). Lean lines dictate decor, with lacquer-finished tables, low white chairs and the inside of the dome lit up. The high point is the presentation of Mediterranean market cooking (say, the *consomé de faisà amb els seus raviolis de foie i tòfona negra* – a pheasant consommé with foie-gras ravioli and black truffle).

Casa-Museu Gaudí (p189)
KRZYSZTOF DYDYNSKI

LA CIGALE Map p194 — Bar
☎ 93 457 58 23; Carrer de Tordera 50;
🕙 6pm-2.30am Sun-Thu, 6pm-3am Fri & Sat;
Ⓜ Joanic

A very civilised place for a cocktail (or two for €8 before 10pm). Prop up the zinc bar, sink into a secondhand lounge chair around a teeny table or head upstairs. Music is chilled, conversation lively and you're likely to see Charlie Chaplin in action on the silent flat-screen TV. You can also snack on wok-fried dishes.

NOISE I ART Map p194 — Bar
☎ 93 217 50 01; Carrer de Topazi 26; 🕙 6pm-2.30am Tue & Wed, 7pm-3am Thu-Sat, 6pm-1.30am Sun; Ⓜ Fontana

Step into the 1980s in this retro den. Red, green and other primal colours dominate the decor in a place where you might encounter Boney M on the video music play. Drape yourself on the circular red lounge, have a light meal (served up on old LPs) at red-lit tables alongside floor-to-ceiling glass windows, or perch at the bar. The daiquiris may not be the best you've ever had, but they'll probably be the biggest!

SABOR A CUBA Map p194 — Bar
☎ 600 262003; Carrer de Francisco Giner 32;
🕙 10pm-2.30am Mon-Thu, 10pm-3am Fri & Sat;
Ⓜ Diagonal

Ruled since 1992 by the charismatic Havana-born Angelito is this home of *ron y son* (rum and sound). A mixed crowd of Cubans and fans of the Caribbean island come to drink mojitos and shake their stuff in this diminutive, good-humoured hang-out.

TAVERNA LA VIOLETA Map p194 — Bar
Carrer de Sant Joaquim 12; 🕙 9am-11pm Mon-Thu, 9am-2am Fri, 9am-1am Sat; Ⓜ Fontana

They just don't make bars like this anymore. A broad and sociable space with a pool room next door, this crumpled, cheerful bar was long something of a working-class meeting centre. Drinking goes on much as before at its mostly marble-topped tables, but the bulk of the punters are now of the student variety. The atmosphere is good-natured and rowdy, and you can pick up tapas and *bocadillos* (filled rolls).

LA ZONA ALTA

North of Avinguda Diagonal, the *pijos* (cashed-up mamma's boys and papa's girls) are in charge. Whether you sample the bars around Carrer de Marià Cubí (and surrounding streets) or try the clubs around Carrer d'Aribau or Tibidabo, expect to be confronted by perma-tanned Audi- and 4WD-driving folks in designer threads. What do you care? The eye candy more than compensates for the snobbery.

BOCAYMA Map p186   Bar

☎ 93 237 94 08; Carrer de l'Avenir 50; ☺ 11pm-2am Tue & Wed, 11pm-3am Thu-Sat; ⓡ FGC Muntaner

Bocayma starts in quiet fashion with patrons gathered around its low tables lined up on one side of the rear bar area. Two backlit bars also keep the drinks coming to this low-lit honey pot of good-looking 20- and 30-somethings. After 1am the music takes off and punters rev up for an outing to nearby clubs. It often opens beyond its official hours.

MARCEL Map p186   Bar

☎ 93 209 89 48; Carrer de Santaló 42; ☺ 10am-2am Mon-Thu, 10am-3am Fri & Sat; ⓡ FGC Muntaner

A classic meeting place, Marcel has a homey but classy old-world feel, with a timber bar, black-and-white floor tiles and high windows. It offers a few snacks and tapas as well. Space is somewhat limited and customers inevitably spill onto the footpath.

ENTERTAINMENT & ACTIVITIES

GRÀCIA & PARK GÜELL

MARTIN'S Map p194   Club

www.martins-disco.com; Passeig de Gràcia 130; admission Sat €12; ☺ 12.30-6am Tue-Sun; Ⓜ Diagonal

Under new management, Martin's is a gay club with a long history in Barcelona. The general dance floor is supplemented by a section for bears, a fetish zone and big, bad dark room for getting it on.

DIEGO LEZAMA

Elephant club

HELIOGÀBAL Map p194   Live Music
www.heliogabal.com; Carrer de Ramón i Cajal 80; ⊙ 9pm-2am Sun-Thu, 9pm-3am Fri & Sat; Ⓜ Joanic

This compact bar is a veritable hive of cultural activity where you never quite know what to expect. Aside from art exhibitions and poetry readings, you will often be pleasingly surprised by the eclectic live-music program. Jazz groups are often followed by open jam sessions, and experimental music of all colours gets a run. While many performers are local, international acts also get a look-in.

SALA BECKETT Map p186   Theatre
☎ 93 284 53 12; www.salabeckett.com; Carrer de Ca l'Alegre de Dalt 55bis; ⊙ box office 10am-2pm & 4-8pm Mon-Fri & 1hr before start of show; Ⓜ Joanic

One of the city's principal alternative theatres, the Sala Beckett is a smallish space that does not shy away from challenging theatre, contemporary or otherwise, and usually a heterodox mix of local productions and foreign drama.

VERDI Map p194   Cinema
☎ 93 238 79 90; www.cines-verdi.com; Carrer de Verdi 32; Ⓜ Fontana

A popular original-language movie house in the heart of Gràcia, handy to lots of local eateries and bars for pre- and post-film enjoyment.

LA ZONA ALTA

ELEPHANT Map p186   Club
☎ 93 334 02 58; www.elephantbcn.com, in Spanish; Passeig dels Til·lers 1; admission Fri & Sat €15; ⊙ 11.30pm-3am Wed, 11.30pm-5am Thu-Sun; Ⓜ Palau Reial; Ⓟ

Getting in here is like being invited to a private fantasy party in Beverly Hills. Models and wannabes mix with immaculately groomed lads who most certainly

didn't come by taxi. A big tentlike dance space is the main game here, but smooth customers slink their way around a series of garden bars in summer too.

OTTO ZUTZ Map p194   Club
☎ 93 238 07 22; www.grupo-ottozutz.com; Carrer de Lincoln 15; admission €15; ⊙ midnight-5.30am Tue-Sat; Ⓡ FGC Gràcia

Beautiful people only need apply for entry to this three-floor dance den. Downstairs, shake it all up to house, or head upstairs for funk and soul on the 1st floor. DJs come from the Ibiza rave mould and the top floor is for VIPs (although at some ill-defined point in the evening the barriers all seem to come down). Friday and Saturday it's hip hop, R&B and funk on the ground floor and house on the 1st floor.

BIKINI Map p194   Club & Live Music
☎ 93 322 08 00; www.bikinibcn.com; Carrer de Déu i Mata 105; admission €10-20; ⊙ midnight-6am Wed-Sun; Ⓜ Entença, 🚌 6, 7, 33, 34, 63, 67 or 68

This grand old star of the Barcelona nightlife scene has been keeping the beat since the darkest days of Franco. Every possible kind of music gets a run, depending on the night and the space you choose, from Latin and Brazilian hip jigglers to 1980s disco. It frequently stages quality local and foreign acts, ranging from funk guitar to rock. Performances generally start around 9pm or 10pm (the club doesn't happen until midnight).

RENOIR-LES CORTS Map p186   Cinema
☎ 93 490 55 10; www.cinesrenoir.com, in Spanish; Carrer de Eugeni d'Ors 12; Ⓜ Maria Cristina or Les Corts

With six cinemas, this is a somewhat distant alternative from central Barcelona for original versions.

PARK GÜELL & AROUND

ENTERTAINMENT & ACTIVITIES

RITUELS D'ORIENT Map p186 Spa
☎ 93 419 14 72; www.rituelsdorient.com, in Spanish; Carrer de Loreto 50; baths only €28; ☷ women only 1-9pm Tue, 10.30am-8pm Wed, 1-4pm Fri, mixed 1-10pm Thu, 4-10pm Fri, 10.30am-8pm Sat; Ⓜ Hospital Clínic
Luxuriating in hammams, indulging in massages, exfoliation and other treatments is the name of the game in this slice of what could be the Middle East. Dark woods, window grills, soft lighting and candles, cushion-covered sofas to relax on – all combine to evoke something of the mystery we all like to imagine for such a place. If you have time to hang about for four hours, try the 'Ritual Elixir de las Mil y una Noches' (Thousand and One Nights Ritual), which includes a facial, 40-minute massage, exfoliation and wrapping your body in a *ghassoul* mud pack.

SHOPPING

A wander along the narrow lanes of Gràcia turns up all sorts of surprises, mostly tiny enterprises producing anything from printed T-shirts to handmade table lamps. Carrer de Verdi has plenty of interesting threads shops.

HIBERNIAN Map p194 Books
☎ 93 217 47 96; Carrer de Montseny 17; ☷ 4-8.30pm Mon, 10.30am-8.30pm Tue-Sat; Ⓜ Fontana
The biggest secondhand English bookshop in Barcelona stocks thousands of titles covering all sorts of subjects, from cookery to children's classics.

RED MARKET Map p194 Fashion
☎ 93 218 63 33; Carrer de Verdi 20; Ⓜ Fontana
Several funky fashion boutiques dot this street, best known to locals for the queues outside the art-house cinema. Here you run into bright, uninhibited urban wear and accessories. Red dominates the decor more than the threads, and various brands of various things, from shoes to tops, are on offer.

JAMIN PUECH Map p186 Accessories
☎ 93 414 45 66; www.jamin-puech.com; Carrer de Calvet 44; Ⓡ FGC Muntaner
For beautiful quality bags and accessories designed by a Paris-based French couple who have forged an international reputation since the early 1990s (with shops in Paris, London, New York and Tokyo), it will be hard to resist a stop in this, their only store in Spain. They turn out 100 new models a year, with 'ingredients' ranging from silk to wood, and rattan to leather.

BEA BEA Map p186 Fashion
☎ 93 414 29 55; Carrer de Calvet 39; Ⓡ FGC Muntaner
In a bright and spacious locale, women find something to suit most generations and a range of tastes. Younger, carefree styles sit side by side with more classical skirts, jackets and accoutrements for uptown dames. Shoes and bags can also be had, making this a potential single stop for a full outfit refit.

LA BOTIGA DEL BARÇA
Map p186 Souvenirs
☎ 93 492 31 11; http://shop.fcbarcelona.com; Carrer de Arístides Maillol; ☷ 10am-9pm Mon-Sat; Ⓜ Collblanc
For some, football is the meaning of life. If you fall into that category, your idea of shopping heaven may well be this store at the football museum next to Camp Nou stadium. Here you will find shirts, key rings, footballs – pretty much anything you can think of, all featuring the famous red and blue colours.

MONTJUÏC, SANTS & EL POBLE SEC

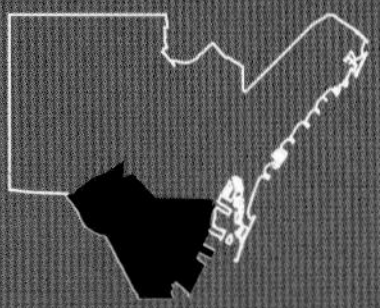

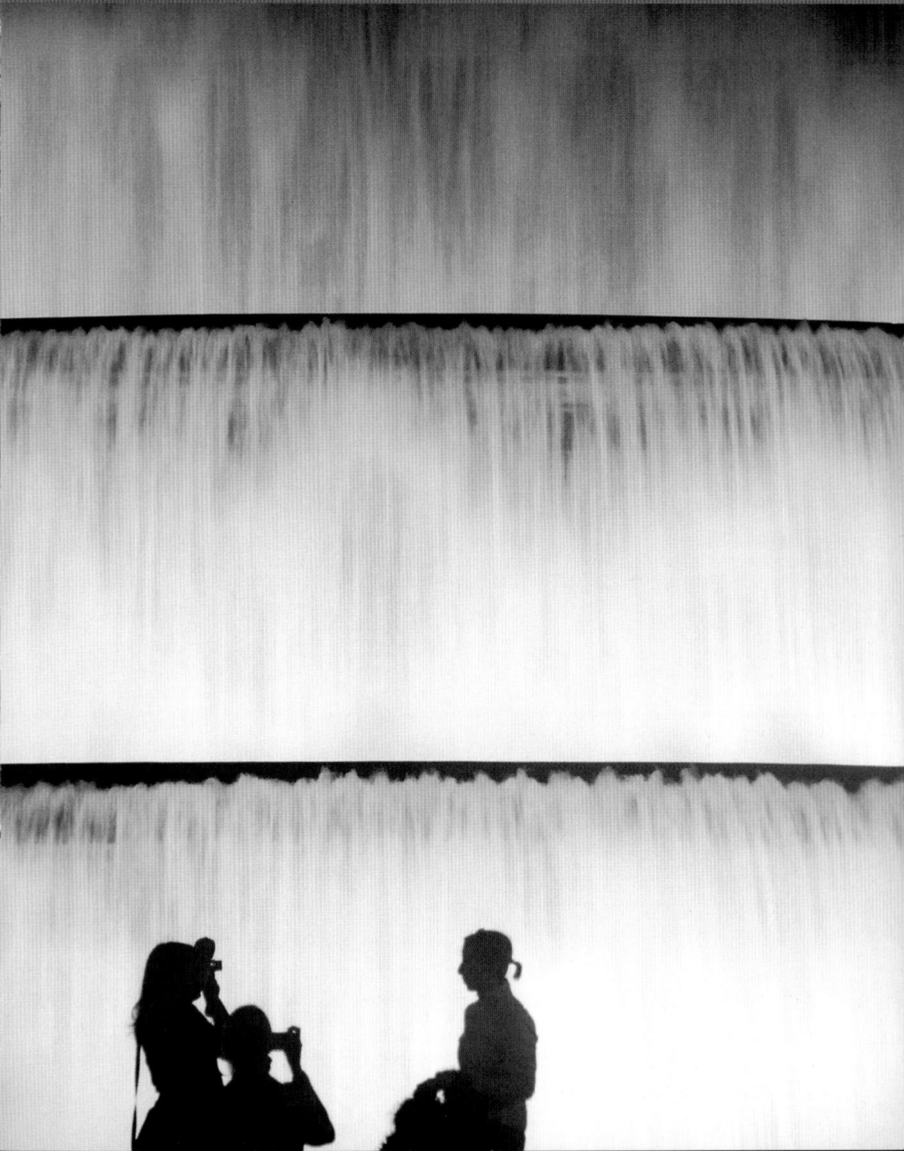

MONTJUÏC, SANTS & EL POBLE SEC

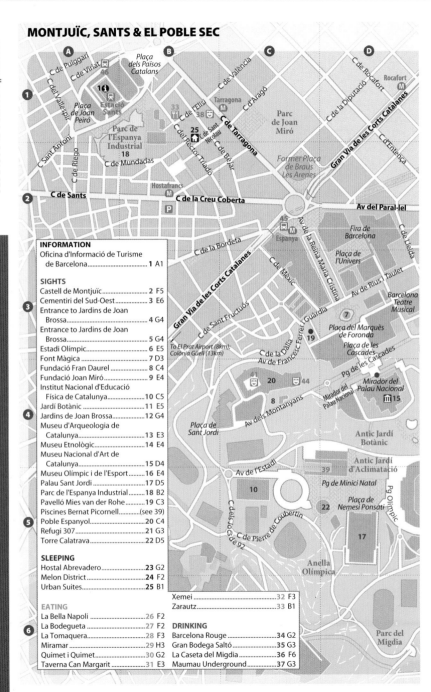

INFORMATION

Oficina d'Informació de Turisme
de Barcelona................................... **1** A1

SIGHTS

Castell de Montjuïc............................ **2** F5
Cementiri del Sud-Oest..................... **3** E6
Entrance to Jardins de Joan
Brossa... **4** G4
Entrance to Jardins de Joan
Brossa... **5** G4
Estadi Olímpic.................................... **6** E5
Font Màgica.. **7** D3
Fundació Fran Daurel......................... **8** C4
Fundació Joan Miró............................ **9** E4
Institut Nacional d'Educació
Física de Catalunya..................... **10** C5
Jardí Botànic.................................... **11** E5
Jardins de Joan Brossa.................... **12** G4
Museu d'Arqueologia de
Catalunya..................................... **13** E3
Museu Etnològic.............................. **14** E4
Museu Nacional d'Art de
Catalunya..................................... **15** D4
Museu Olímpic i de l'Esport........... **16** E4
Palau Sant Jordi............................... **17** D5
Parc de l'Espanya Industrial........... **18** B2
Pavelló Mies van der Rohe.............. **19** C3
Piscines Bernat Picornell..............(see 39)
Poble Espanyol................................ **20** C4
Refugi 307....................................... **21** G3
Torre Calatrava................................ **22** D5

SLEEPING

Hostal Abrevadero........................... **23** G2
Melon District.................................. **24** F2
Urban Suites..................................... **25** B1

EATING

La Bella Napoli................................. **26** F2
La Bodegueta................................... **27** F2
La Tomaquera................................... **28** F3
Miramar.. **29** H3
Quimet i Quimet.............................. **30** G2
Taverna Can Margarit....................... **31** E3

Xemei.. **32** F3
Zarautz... **33** B1

DRINKING

Barcelona Rouge.............................. **34** G2
Gran Bodega Saltó........................... **35** G3
La Caseta del Migdia........................ **36** F6
Maumau Underground..................... **37** G3

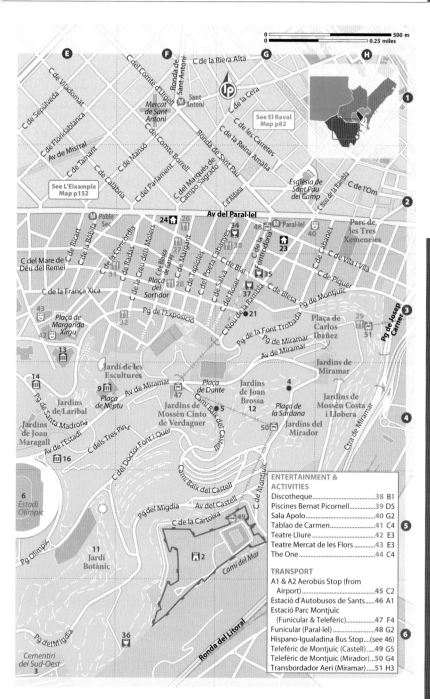

ENTERTAINMENT & ACTIVITIES

Discotheque	38 B1
Piscines Bernat Picornell	39 D5
Sala Apolo	40 G2
Tablao de Carmen	41 C4
Teatre Lliure	42 E3
Teatre Mercat de les Flors	43 E3
The One	44 C4

TRANSPORT

A1 & A2 Aerobús Stop (from Airport)	45 C2
Estació d'Autobusos de Sants	46 A1
Estació Parc Montjuïc (Funicular & Telefèric)	47 F4
Funicular (Paral·lel)	48 G2
Hispano-Igualadina Bus Stop	(see 46)
Telefèric de Montjuïc (Castell)	49 G5
Telefèric de Montjuïc (Mirador)	50 G4
Transbordador Aeri (Miramar)	51 H3

HIGHLIGHTS

1 GARDENS OF MONTJUÏC

Barcelona's Acropolis inhabits the high ground of Montjuïc, a hill covered in parkland that ends in steep cliffs overlooking Port Vell. You can break away from the urban clamour by taking a funicular or cable car to lofty vantage points utilised by the 1929 International Exhibition and 1992 Summer Olympics. In among the Grecian monuments, large pockets of greenery showcase parks, gardens and view-splattered lookouts. Almost all are free.

⤹ OUR DON'T MISS LIST

❶ JARDINS DE MOSSÈN CINTO DE VERDAGUER

Named for a romantic Catalan poet, these equally romantic gardens are famous for their high-maintenance bulbs – count on everything from tulips to narcissus and dahlias. Water terraces support many aquatic plants such as lotus and water lilies. Dirt paths and verdant lawns add to the dreamy ambience.

❷ JARDINS DE MOSSÈN COSTA I LLOBERA

Situated on the less-visited southern slopes of Montjuïc where the hill falls away steeply to the port, these gardens enjoy a microclimate that supports a wide range of desert vegetation, particularly cacti. Some of the plants are vaguely surreal, resembling prickly alien eggs. Handily located near the top of the Transbordador Aeri, the gardens make a pleasant alternative means of descent.

Clockwise from top: Jardins de Joan Brossa; Jardins de Mossèn Cinto de Verdaguer; Tropical plant ponds, Mossèn Cinto de Verdaguer; Gardens of Castell de Montjuïc (p223); Flower gardens, Mossèn Cinto de Verdaguer

CLOCKWISE FROM TOP: DIEGO LEZAMA; DIEGO LEZAMA; DIEGO LEZAMA; NEIL SETCHFIELD; DIEGO LEZAMA

❸ JARDINS DEL MIRADOR

While most cable-car users linger on the roof of the Transbordador Aeri Telefèric station to gawp at the view, the savvier few sidestep a few hundred metres to this landscaped cocoon where the views are equal but the surroundings a little more detached.

❹ JARDINS DE JOAN BROSSA

Regeneration reaches new heights in these salubrious gardens landscaped on the site of a former amusement park near Plaça de la Sardana. There are plenty of distractions here for kids (swings, slides etc) but also 5.2 hectares of Mediterranean vegetation punctuated by arty bronze statues of figures such as Charlie Chaplin and Carmen Amaya.

❺ JARDÍ BOTÀNIC

Where rubbish once festered, copious species bloom. This extensive botanic garden – very much the centrepiece of 'Parc de Montjuïc' – is the product of another late 1990s rejuvenation project that turned a dump into a lesson in Mediterranean botany. Amid the foliage are decent views of 1992 Olympic sites.

↘ THINGS YOU NEED TO KNOW

No charge Apart from the Jardí Botánic (€3.50), all the gardens are free **Getting there** Novel means of ascending the hill include outdoor escalators, a funicular and the Transbordador Aeri cable car **Rural past** Until the 1900s, Montjuïc was used for crop-growing and grazing **See p223 for more information**

HIGHLIGHTS

⚓ MUSEU NACIONAL D'ART DE CATALUNYA

Rising from its stately perch in Montjuïc, the first and most impressive exhibit of this popular **art museum** (p226) is the building itself, a stunning neobaroque palace known as the Palau Nacional, which was built for the 1929 International Exhibition and converted into a museum in 1995. Once inside, decipher the details of one of the best ensembles of Romanesque painting in Europe.

⚓ FUNDACIÓ JOAN MIRÓ

Contrarian, surrealist, experimentalist and, above all, Catalan, Miró was a local boy who went global with cutting-edge art that provoked and inspired yet rarely stood still. Barcelona can't claim Picasso as a native but it can gloat about Miró, a talented artistic conjurer who, along with Dalí, dragged surrealism into the mainstream. This **foundation** (p224) is the world's largest single collection of his work.

⤵ POBLE ESPANYOL

Architectural museum or over-indulgent dalliance in kitsch? The **Poble Espanyol** (p227) inspires many opinions, not all favourable. All the more reason to stop by this microcosmic Spanish 'village' – the brainchild of Modernist architect Josep Puig i Cadafalch – and make up your own mind. Every region of Spain is architecturally represented, from Andalucía to Galicia.

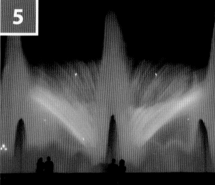

⤵ FONT MÀGICA

If you take the dictionary definition of 'magic' as 'something that seems to cast a spell' then the **Font Màgica** (p225) is aptly named. A grandiose aquatic feature built for the 1929 International Exhibition, the fountain forms the centrepiece of a series of terraces and waterfalls cascading from the Palau Nacional. For full psychedelic effect, catch a nightly sound and light show.

⤵ 1992 OLYMPIC SITES

Remember 1992? The first post–Cold War Olympics, a slew of fledgling sporting nations, and US basketball's incomparable 'Dream Team'? Relive what were arguably history's most spirited games amid the Hellenic grandiosity of the **Anella Olímpic** (p224), spread across the slopes of Montjuïc, with its refurbished stadium, abundance of parks, and Olympic museum.

2 GUY MOBERLY; 3 NEIL SETCHFIELD; 4 NEIL SETCHFIELD; 5 BETHUNE CARMICHAEL; 6 BILL WASSMAN

2 Museu Nacional d'Art de Catalunya (p226); 3 Fundació Joan Miró (p224); 4 Poble Espanyol (p227); 5 Font Màgica (p225); 6 Anella Olímpic (p224)

VIEWS & GARDENS WALK ON MONTJUÏC

When is a city not a city? When it allows you to stroll through the urban greenery on this 2.5km walk from the Castell de Montjuïc to the Font Màgica. Reserve an hour minimum; more if you feel inclined to wander. The general route is all downhill.

❶ CASTELL DE MONTJUÏC

Long synonymous with oppression, the dark history of **Castell de Montjuïc** (p223) is today overshadowed by the fine views it commands over the city and sea. The Telefèric is the perfect way to get up, and from there on it's all refreshingly downhill through amassing greenery.

❷ JARDINS DEL MIRADOR

A short stroll down the road or the parallel Camí del Mar pedestrian trail leads to another fine viewpoint over the city and sea, the **Jardins del Mirador** (p223). Take the weight off your feet on one of the park benches, or pick up a snack and grab some reflection time.

❸ JARDINS DE JOAN BROSSA

Further downhill is the multitiered **Jardins de Joan Brossa** (p224). The entrance is on the left just beyond Plaça de la Sardana, with the sculpture of people engaged in the classic Catalan folk dance. More fine city views can be had from among the many Mediterranean trees and plants.

❹ JARDINS DE MOSSÈN CINTO DE VERDAGUER

Exiting the Jardins de Joan Brossa at the other (west) side, cross Camí Baix del Castell to the painstakingly laid-out **Jardins de Mossèn Cinto de Verdaguer** (p223). This is a beautiful setting for a slow meander among tulip beds and water lilies that act as both relaxant and inspiration.

❺ FUNDACIÓ JOAN MIRÓ

Joan Miró left a broad collection of his works to the city in his specially designed hillside **foundation** (p224). You can discover his earliest, tentative artistic attempts and continue right through to the characteristic broad canvases for which he is known. Get close-up views of sculptures in the adjacent garden.

VIEWS & GARDENS WALK ON MONTJUÏC

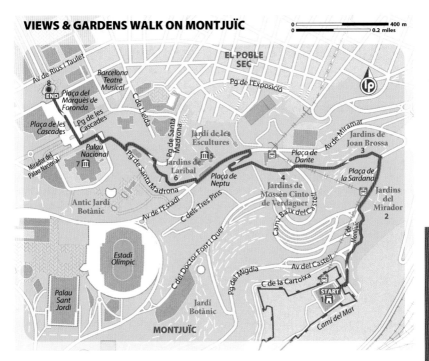

❻ JARDINS DE LARIBAL

Dropping away behind the Fundació Joan Miró, the Jardins de Laribal are a combination of terraced gardens linked by paths and stairways. The pretty sculpted watercourses along some of the stairways were inspired by Granada's Muslim-era palace of El Alhambra. Stop for a snack and contemplate a Moorish paradise.

❼ MUSEU NACIONAL D'ART DE CATALUNYA

Whichever direction you are coming from, it is worth making the effort to reach this huge ochre beast of a **museum** (p226) to see one of Europe's finest collections of Romanesque art, salvaged from countless churches and chapels sprinkled over northern Catalonia. Further collections range from Gothic to Modernisme.

❽ FONT MÀGICA

Descending from the Palau Nacional past the Plaça de les Cascades to the **Font Màgica** (p225) is as magic as the name suggests, particularly if you've stretched this walk long enough (easily done) to arrive here after dark – in time for the rather splendid sound and light show.

BEST...

⇘ GARDENS

- **Jardins de Mossèn Costa i Llobera** (p223) Tropical vegetation and desert plants.
- **Jardins de Mossèn Cinto de Verdaguer** (p223) Bulbs and aquatic plants.
- **Jardí Botànic** (p225) Gardens on an old municipal dump!
- **Jardins de Joan Brossa** (p224) Gardens on former amusement park.
- **Antic Jardí d'Aclimatació** (p224) Walk through Olympic site greenery.

⇘ VIEWS

- **Castell de Montjuïc** (p223) Strategically placed castle with commanding views.
- **Jardins del Mirador** (p223) More stupendous castle views.
- **Telefèric de Montjuïc** (p230) Cable car up to castle.
- **Miramar** (p232) Restaurant with Mediterranean views.
- **Transbordador Aeri** (p137 and p230) Panoramic cable car up from the beach.

⇘ 1929 WORLD EXHIBITION SITES

- **Pavelló Mies van der Rohe** (p228) Curious German pavilion.
- **Poble Espanyol** (p227) Microcosmic Spanish 'village'.
- **Estadi Olímpic** (p224) Stadium reborn for 1992 Olympics.
- **Palau Nacional** (p226) An art museum that is itself a piece of art.
- **Font Màgica** (p225) Astounding fountain with sound and light show.

⇘ MUSEUMS

- **Museu Olímpic i de l'Esport** (p224) Interactive look at the Olympics.
- **Refugi 307** (p229) Tunnels dug as air-raid shelters.
- **Fundació Joan Miró** (p224) Definitive word on surrealist master.
- **Museu Nacional d'Art de Catalunya** (p226) Europe's best collection of Romanesque Art.
- **Museu Etnològic** (p228) Esoteric look at societal organisation.

CLX/IMAGEBROKER

Torre de Jaume I (p137), Transbordador Aeri

DISCOVER MONTJUÏC, SANTS & EL POBLE SEC

Overlooking the sea, Montjuïc hill is a cornucopia of activities. Locals escape here for a breath of fresh air. A series of pretty gardens could occupy much of a lazy day, but there is plenty to see, from the Castell de Montjuïc at the hill's apex to the Fundació Joan Miró and majestic Museu Nacional d'Art de Catalunya. Nearby are more museums, the Olympic stadium, pools, concert venues and the Poble Espanyol, a composite of Spanish towns in miniature.

A varied and growing collection of inviting eateries and bars lines the higgledy-piggledy streets of Poble Sec, which slopes down the northeast face of the hill towards Avinguda del Paral·lel. You can also visit a civil war air-raid shelter.

To the northwest of Montjuïc sprawls the mostly working-class district of Sants, which also happens to be home to the city's main train station.

SIGHTS

CASTELL DE MONTJUÏC & AROUND

☎ 93 329 86 13; ☽ 9am-9pm Tue-Sun Apr-Sep, 9am-7pm Tue-Sun Oct-Mar; ☒ 193, Telefèric

The forbidding Castell (castle or fort) de Montjuïc dominates the southeastern heights of Montjuïc and enjoys commanding views over the Mediterranean. It dates, in its present form, to the late 17th and 18th centuries. For most of its dark history, it has been used to watch over the city and as a political prison and killing ground.

In the coming years, it is planned to establish an international peace centre in the castle, as well as a display on its history. There will also be an interpretation centre dedicated to Montjuïc. While waiting for this to happen, a modest temporary exhibition has been established in one of the castle's bastions, on the right as soon as you enter. Called **Barcelona Té Castell** (Barcelona Has a Castle), it explains something of the place's history as well as detailing plans for its future.

The views from the castle and the surrounding area looking over the sea, port and city below are the best part of making the trip up.

Catalan and Spanish speakers can join free guided tours of the castle on Saturdays and Sundays (11.30am in Catalan, 1pm in Spanish). Group tours (€65 to €80) can also be booked (also in English and French).

Around the seaward foot of the castle is an airy walking track, the **Camí del Mar**, which offers breezy views of city and sea. Towards the foot of this part of Montjuïc, above the thundering traffic of the main road to Tarragona, the **Jardins de Mossèn Costa i Llobera** (admission free; ☽ 10am-sunset) have a good collection of tropical and desert plants – including a veritable forest of cacti. Near the Estació Parc Montjuïc funicular/Telefèric station are the ornamental **Jardins de Mossèn Cinto de Verdaguer** (admission free; ☽ 10am-sunset).

From the **Jardins del Mirador**, opposite the Mirador Transbordador Aeri

(Telefèric) station, you have fine views over the port of Barcelona. A little further downhill, the **Jardins de Joan Brossa** (admission free; 🕙 10am-sunset) are charming, landscaped gardens on the site of a former amusement park near Plaça de la Sardana.

FUNDACIÓ JOAN MIRÓ

☎ 93 443 94 70; www.bcn.fjmiro.es; Plaça de Neptu; permanent exhibitions adult/senior & child €8.50/6, temporary exhibitions €4/3; 🕙 10am-8pm Tue, Wed, Fri & Sat, 10am-9.30pm Thu, 10am-2.30pm Sun & holidays Jul-Sep, 10am-7pm Tue, Wed, Fri & Sat, 10am-9.30pm Thu, 10am-2.30pm Sun & holidays Oct-Jun; 🚌 50, 55, 193 or funicular

This shimmering white temple to the art of one of the stars of the 20th-century Spanish firmament rests amid the greenery of its privileged position on the mountain.

Joan Miró, the city's best-known 20th-century artistic progeny, bequeathed this art foundation to his hometown in 1971. Its light-filled buildings, designed by close friend and architect Josep Lluís Sert (who also built Miró's Mallorca studios), are crammed with seminal works, from Miró's earliest timid sketches to paintings from his last years.

The foundation holds the greatest single collection of the artist's work, comprising around 220 of his paintings, 180 sculptures, some textiles and more than 8000 drawings spanning his entire life. Only a small portion is ever on display.

The museum library contains Miró's personal book collection.

Outside on the eastern flank of the museum is the **Jardí de les Esculptures** (admission free; 🕙 10am-dusk), a small garden with various pieces of modern sculpture (it is also a wi-fi zone).

ESTADI OLÍMPIC

Avinguda de l'Estadi; admission free; 🕙 10am-6pm Oct-Mar, 10am-8pm Apr-Sep; 🚌 50, 61 or 193

First opened in 1929, the 65,000-capacity stadium was given a complete overhaul for the 1992 Olympics. You enter from the northern end, in the shadow of the dish in which the Olympic flame burned. The stadium is used for occasional sporting events and major concerts (the Rolling Stones have played here).

Just east over the road, the **Museu Olímpic i de l'Esport** (☎ 93 292 53 79; www. fundaciobarcelonaolimpica.es; Avinguda de l'Estadi 60; adult/senior & under 14yr/student €4/free/2.50; 🕙 10am-8pm Tue-Mon Apr-Sep, 10am-6pm Tue-Sat, 10am-2.30pm Sun Oct-Mar) is an all-flashing, all-dancing, information-packed interactive museum dedicated to sport and the Olympic Games. After picking up tickets, you wander down a ramp that snakes below ground level and is lined with displays on the history of sport, starting with the ancients. On the basement floor is a special section devoted to Barcelona's 1992 Olympics, with another on the collection of Olympic stamps, art and more of the former head of the International Olympic Committee, Barcelona's Juan Antonio Samaranch.

West of the stadium is the **Palau Sant Jordi**, a 17,000-capacity indoor sports, concert and exhibition hall opened in 1990 and designed by Isozaki.

The **Anella Olímpic** (Olympic Ring; 🕙 8am-9pm Apr-Sep, 8am-7pm Oct-Mar) describes the whole group of sports installations created for the games to the west of the *estadi*. Westernmost is the **Institut Nacional d'Educació Física de Catalunya** (INEFC), a kind of sports university, designed by Ricard Bofill. Past a circular arena, the Plaça d'Europa, with the slender white **Torre Calatrava** communications tower

MONTJUÏC, SANTS & EL POBLE SEC

SIGHTS

GUY MOBERLY

Views across Barcelona from the Castell de Montjuïc

◥ IF YOU LIKE...

If you like the parks and garden surrounding the **Castell de Montjuïc** (p223) you may also enjoy the following green spaces:

- **Jardí Botànic** (☎ 93 426 49 35; www.jardibotanic.bcn.es; Carrer del Doctor Font i Quer 2; adult/under 16yr/student €3.50/free/1.70, free last Sun of month; ☉ 10am-8pm Jun-Aug, 10am-7pm Apr, May & Sep, 10am-6pm Feb, Mar & Oct, 10am-5pm Nov-Jan; 🚌 50, 61 or 193) Across the road to the south of the *Estadi Olímpic,* this botanic garden was created atop what was an old municipal dump. The theme is Mediterranean flora and the collection of some 40,000 plants includes 1500 species that thrive in areas with a climate similar to that of the Med, including the Eastern Mediterranean, Spain (including the Balearic and Canary Islands), North Africa, Australia, California, Chile and South Africa.

- **Parc de l'Espanya Industrial** Just south of Estació Sants, this park has ponds, little waterfalls, green spaces, trees, children's swings, a bar, and odd towers that look like they belong in a sci-fi prison camp.

behind it, is the **Piscines Bernat Picornell** building, where the swimming events were held (now open to the public; see p236). Separating the pool from the Estadi Olímpic is a pleasant garden, the **Antic Jardí d'Aclimatació**. You can wander (or skate) around this whole area, graced with little waterfalls and green areas.

FONT MÀGICA

Avinguda de la Reina Maria Cristina; admission free; ☉ **every 30min 7-9pm Fri & Sat** Oct-late Jun, 9-11.30pm Thu-Sun late Jun-Sep; Ⓜ **Espanya**

With a flourish, the 'Magic Fountain' erupts into a feast of musical, backlit liquid life. On hot summer evenings especially, this 15-minute spectacle (repeated several times throughout the evening) mesmerises onlookers. The main fountain of a series that sweeps up the hill from Avinguda de la Reina Maria Cristina to the grand facade of the Palau Nacional, Font Màgica is a unique

MARTIN HUGHES

Museu Nacional d'Art de Catalunya

⚓ MUSEU NACIONAL D'ART DE CATALUNYA

From vantage points across the city, the bombastic neobaroque silhouette of the so-called Palau Nacional (National Palace) can be seen halfway up the slopes of Montjuïc. Built for the 1929 World Exhibition and restored in 2005, it houses a vast collection of mostly Catalan art.

Head first to the Romanesque art section, considered the most important concentration of early medieval art in the world. It consists of frescos, wood-carvings and painted altar frontals (low-relief wooden panels that were the fore-runners of the elaborate altarpieces that adorned later churches), transferred from country churches across northern Catalonia early in the 20th century.

Opposite the Romanesque collection on the ground floor is the museum's Gothic art section. In these halls you can see Catalan Gothic painting (look out especially for the work of Bernat Martorell in Àmbit 32 and Jaume Huguet in Àmbit 34), and that of other Spanish and Mediterranean regions.

As the Gothic collection draws to a close, you pass through two separate and equally eclectic private collections, the Cambò bequest and works from the Thyssen-Bornemisza collections.

If you have any energy left, check out the photography section, which encompasses work from mostly Catalan snappers from the mid-19th century on. Coin collectors will enjoy the Gabinet Numismàtic de Catalunya, with coins from Roman Spain, medieval Catalonia and some engaging notes from the civil war days.

After all this, you can relax in the museum restaurant, which offers great views north towards Plaça d'Espanya.

Things you need to know: MNAC; ☎ 93 622 03 76; www.mnac.cat; Mirador del Palau Nacional; adult/senior & under 15yr/student €8.50/free/6, free 1st Sun of month; ⏲ 10am-7pm Tue-Sat, 10am-2.30pm Sun & holidays; Ⓜ Espanya

performance in which the water at times looks like seething fireworks or a mystical cauldron of colour.

POBLE ESPANYOL

☎ 93 508 63 00; www.poble-espanyol.com; Avinguda de Francesc Ferrer i Guàrdia; adult/4-12yr/senior & student €8.50/5.50/6.50; ☻ 9am-8pm Mon, 9am-2am Tue-Thu, 9am-4am Fri, 9am-5am Sat, 9am-midnight Sun; Ⓜ Espanya, 🚌 50, 61 or 193

Welcome to Spain! All of it! This 'Spanish Village' is both a cheesy souvenir hunters' haunt and an intriguing scrapbook of Spanish architecture built for the Spanish crafts section of the 1929 World Exhibition. You can wander from Andalucía to the Balearic Islands in the space of a couple of hours' slow meandering, visiting surprisingly good copies of characteristic buildings from all the country's regions.

You enter from beneath a towered medieval gate from Ávila. Inside, to the right, is an information office with free maps. Straight ahead from the gate is the Plaza Mayor (Town Square), surrounded with mainly Castilian and Aragonese buildings. It is sometimes the scene of summer concerts. Elsewhere you'll find an Andalucian *barrio* (neighbourhood), a Basque street, Galician and Catalan quarters and even a Dominican monastery (at the eastern end). The buildings house dozens of restaurants, cafes, bars, craft shops and workshops (such as glassmakers), and some souvenir stores.

Spare some time for the **Fundació Fran Daurel** (☎ 93 423 41 72; www.fundaciofrandaurel.com; admission free; ☻ 10am-7pm), an eclectic collection of 300 works of art including sculptures, prints, ceramics and tapestries by modern artists ranging from Picasso and Miró to more contemporary figures, including Miquel Barceló.

Children's groups can participate in the **Joc del Sarró** (admission €5; ☻ 10am-6pm). Accompanied by adults, the kids go around the *poble* seeking the answers to various mysteries outlined in a kit distributed to each group. Languages catered for include English.

DAMIEN SIMONIS

Building in the Poble Espanyol

INGOLF POMPE 52/ALAMY

Museu Etnològic

◥ IF YOU LIKE...

If you like the **Museu Nacional d'Art de Catalunya** (p226) you may also enjoy the following collections:

- **Museu d'Arqueologia de Catalunya** (☎ 93 423 21 49; www.mac.cat; Passeig de Santa Madrona 39-41; adult/under 16yr & senior/student €3/free/2.10; ☯ 9.30am-7pm Tue-Sat, 10am-2.30pm Sun; ☒ 55 or 193) This archaeology museum, housed in what was the Graphic Arts palace during the 1929 World Exposition, covers Catalonia and related cultures from elsewhere in Spain. Items range from copies of pre-Neanderthal skulls to lovely Carthaginian necklaces and jewel-studded Visigothic crosses.

- **Museu Etnològic** (☎ 93 424 64 02; www.museuetnologic.bcn.cat, in Catalan; Passeig de Santa Madrona 16-22; adult/under 12yr/senior & student €3.50/free/1.75, free 1st Sun of month; ☯ noon-8pm Tue-Sat, 11am-3pm Sun late Jun-late Sep, 10am-7pm Tue & Thu, 10am-2pm Wed & Fri-Sun late Sep-late Jun; ☒ 55) This curious museum explores how various societies have functioned down the centuries, as seen through collections of various ephemera.

PAVELLÓ MIES VAN DER ROHE

☎ 93 423 40 16; www.miesbcn.com; Avinguda de Francesc Ferrer i Guàrdia; adult/under 18yr/student €4.50/free/2.30; ☯ 10am-8pm; Ⓜ Espanya
Just to the west of Font Màgica is a strange building. In 1929 Ludwig Mies van der Rohe erected the Pavelló Alemany (German Pavilion) for the World Exhibition. Now known by the name of its architect, it was removed after the show. Decades later, a society was formed to rebuild what was in hindsight considered a key work in the trajectory of one of the world's most important modern architects. Reconstructed in the 1980s, it is a curious structure of interlocking planes – walls of marble or glass, ponds of water, ceilings and just plain nothing, a temple to the new urban environment.

CEMENTIRI DEL SUD-OEST

☎ 93 484 17 00; ⏱ 8am-6pm; 🚌 193

On the hill to the south of the Anella Olímpica stretches this huge cemetery, the Cementiri del Sud-Oest or Cementiri Nou, which extends down the southern side of the hill. It includes the graves of numerous Catalan artists and politicians. Among the big names are Joan Miró, Carmen Amaya (the flamenco dance star from La Barceloneta), Jacint Verdaguer (the 19th-century priest and poet to whom the rebirth of Catalan literature is attributed), Francesc Macià and Lluís Companys (nationalist presidents of Catalonia; Companys was executed by Franco's henchmen in the Castell de Montjuïc in 1940), Ildefons Cerdà (who designed L'Eixample) and Joan Gamper (the founder of the FC Barcelona football team, aka Hans Gamper). From the 193 bus stop, it's about an 800m walk southwest. Otherwise, bus 38 from Plaça de Catalunya stops close to the cemetery entrance.

REFUGI 307

☎ 93 256 21 22; www.museuhistoria.bcn.cat; Carrer Nou de la Rambla 169; admission incl tour €3; ⏱ tours 11am-2pm Sat & Sun; Ⓜ Paral·lel

Barcelona was the city most heavily bombed from the air during the Spanish Civil War and was dotted with more than 1300 air-raid shelters. Local citizens started digging this one under a fold of Montjuïc in March 1937. In the course of the next two years, the web of tunnels was slowly extended to 200m, with a theoretical capacity for 2000 people.

In the tough years of famine and rationing during the 1940s and 1950s, families from Granada took up residence here rather than in the shacks springing up all over the area, as poor migrants arrived from southern Spain. The half-hour tours (in Catalan or Spanish; book ahead for English or French) explain all this and more.

BAB/IMAGEBROKER

Pavelló Mies van der Rohe

TRANSPORT AROUND MONTJUÏC

Metro Línia 3 runs through El Poble Sec. The closest stops to Montjuïc are Espanya, Poble Sec and Paral·lel.

Bus

Bus 50 runs to Montjuïc along Gran Via de les Corts Catalanes via Plaça de l'Universitat and Plaça d'Espanya. Bus 61 runs (six times a day, Monday to Friday only) along Avinguda del Paral·lel to Montjuïc via Plaça d'Espanya. Bus 55 runs across town via Plaça de Catalunya and Carrer de Lleida past the Museu d'Arqueologia de Catalunya to terminate at the Estació Parc Montjuïc funicular station. The 193 (Parc de Montjuïc) line does a circle trip from Plaça d'Espanya to the Castell de Montjuïc. It operates every 20 minutes or so from 8am to 8pm on weekends and holidays.

The **Bus Turístic** (p283) also makes several stops on Montjuïc.

Metro & Funicular

Take the Metro (Línia 2 or 3) to the Paral·lel stop and pick up the **funicular railway** (⏱ 9am-10pm Apr-Oct, 9am-8pm Nov-Mar), part of the Metro fare system, to Estació Parc Montjuïc.

Transbordador Aeri

The quickest way to get to the mountain from the beach is this cable car that runs between Torre de Sant Sebastià in **La Barceloneta** (p137) and the Miramar stop on Montjuïc.

Telefèric de Montjuïc

From Estació Parc Montjuïc, this **cable car** (adult/child 1-way €6.30/4.80; ⏱ 10am-9pm Jun-Sep, 10am-7pm Mar-May & Oct, 10am-6pm Nov-Feb) carries you to the Castell de Montjuïc via the Mirador (a lookout point).

COLÒNIA GÜELL

☎ 93 630 58 07; www.coloniaguell.net; Carrer de Claudi Güell 6, Santa Coloma de Cervelló; adult/under 10yr/student & senior €5/free/3.50; ⏱ 10am-2pm & 3-7pm Mon-Fri, 10am-3pm Sat, Sun & holidays May-Oct, 10am-3pm daily Nov-Apr; 🚆 FGC lines S4, S7, S8 or S33

Apart from La Sagrada Família, Colònia Güell was Gaudí's last big project, the creation of a utopian textile workers' complex for his magnate patron Eusebi Güell outside Barcelona. Gaudí's main role was to erect the colony's church. Work began in 1908 but the idea fizzled eight years later and Gaudí only finished the crypt, which still serves as a working church.

This structure is a key to understanding what the master had in mind for his *magnum opus,* La Sagrada Família. The mostly brick-clad columns that support the ribbed vaults in the ceiling are inclined at all angles in much the way you might expect trees in a forest to lean. That effect was deliberate, but also grounded in physics. Gaudí worked out the angles so that their load would be transmitted from the ceiling to the earth without the help of extra buttressing. Similar thinking lay behind his plans for La Sagrada Família, whose Gothic-inspired structure would tower above any medieval building, without requiring a single buttress. Gaudí's hand is visible down to the wavy design of the pews. The primary colours in the curvaceous plant-shaped stained-glass windows are another reminder of the era in which the crypt was built.

Near the church spread the cute brick houses designed for the factory workers and still inhabited today. A short stroll away, the 23 factory buildings of a Modernista industrial complex, idle since the 1970s, were brought back to life in the early 2000s, with shops and businesses moving into the renovated complex.

In a five-room display with audiovisual and interactive material, the history and life of the industrial colony and the story of Gaudí's church are told in colourful fashion. Audioguides (€2) are available for visiting the site.

SLEEPING

Several options are strung out along and near the El Poble Sec side of Avinguda del Paral·lel, as well as near the train station in Sants.

URBAN SUITES Hotel & Apartments €€

☎ 93 201 51 64; www.theurbansuites.com; Carrer de Sant Nicolau 1-3; ste from €165; Ⓜ Sants Estació; Ⓟ ⊠ ▯ ☏

Directed largely at the trade fair crowd, this contemporary spot with 16 suites and four apartments makes for a convenient and comfortable home away from home. You get a bedroom, living room and kitchen, DVD player and free wi-fi, and the configuration is good for families. Prices fluctuate enormously.

MELON DISTRICT Hostal €

☎ 93 329 96 67; www.melondistrict.com; Avinguda Paral·lel 101; s €45-55, d €50-60; Ⓜ Paral·lel; Ⓟ ⊠ ▯ ☏

Whiter than white seems to be the policy in this student residence, where you can stay the night or book in for a year. Erasmus folks and an international student set are attracted to this hostel-style spot, where the only objects in the rooms that aren't white are the green plastic chairs. There are meeting lounges, kitchen facilities, a cafe and a laundrette on the premises.

DIEGO LEZAMA

El Poble Sec streetfront

HOSTAL ABREVADERO   Hostal €

☎ 93 441 22 05; www.hostalabrevadero.com; Carrer de Vila i Vilà 79; s/d €45/59; Ⓜ Paral·lel; Ⓟ ⌘ ▯

A bright *hostal,* with simple rooms (some quite spacious), this place is worth contemplating if you want to stay just outside the old centre and close to Montjuïc. Light-hued yellows and whites in the decor and spotless bathrooms are standard. There are lockers for left luggage too.

EATING

Montjuïc is largely bereft of notable eating options, for the obvious reason that it is mostly parks and gardens. In gruff old El Poble Sec you'll turn up all sorts of priceless nuggets, from historic taverns offering Catalan classics to a handful of smart, new-wave eateries.

MIRAMAR   Mediterranean & Asian €€

☎ 93 443 66 27; www.club-miramar.es; Carretera de Miramar 40; meals €40-50; Ⓨ lunch & dinner Tue-Sat, lunch Sun; ⊕ 50 & 193

With several terraces and a cool designer main dining area, this restaurant's key draw is the views it offers over Barcelona's waterfront. Hovering just above the Transbordador Aeri cable-car station, you can linger over a coffee or tuck into an elegant meal with a creative Catalan and Mediterranean slant, or opt for an extensive Asian menu.

XEMEI   Venetian €€

☎ 93 553 51 40; Passeig de l'Exposició 85; meals €45; Ⓨ Wed-Mon; Ⓜ Poble Sec; ✂

Xemei ('twins' in Venetian, because it is run by a pair of twins from Italy's lagoon city) is a wonderful slice of Venice in Barcelona. To the accompaniment of gentle jazz, you might try an entrée of mixed *cicheti* (Venetian seafood tapas), followed by *bigoi in salsa veneziana* (thick spaghetti in an anchovy and onion sauce).

ZARAUTZ   Basque €€

☎ 93 325 28 13; Carrer de l'Elisi 13; meals €30-35; Ⓨ 8am-11.30pm Mon-Sat Sep-Jul; Ⓜ Tarragona; ✂

A short hop away from the train station, you can take in some quality Basque tapas at the bar any time of the day, or retire to the restaurant for a full meal, such as *carpaccio de carn amb formatge Idiazábal* (beef carpaccio with a tangy Basque cheese). The owner is a dessert specialist, so save some room. It's a rough-and-tumble-looking joint, but don't let that put you off.

LA BODEGUETA   Catalan €€

☎ 93 442 08 46; www.labodeguetabcn.com; Carrer de Blai 47; meals €30; Ⓨ lunch Fri-Sun, dinner daily; Ⓜ Paral·lel

For a homey Catalan atmosphere (complete with wine barrels, an old Frigidaire and gingham tablecloths), pop by this cheery spot. Options are limited to classic local favourites, including an array of charcoal-grilled meat dishes, such as a thick *entrecot con Cabrales* (steak with strong northern Spanish cheese). Balance with a *graellada de verdures* (mixed grilled vegetables) and wash down with a generous ceramic jug of house red.

TAVERNA CAN MARGARIT   Catalan €€

☎ 93 441 67 23; Carrer de la Concòrdia 21; meals €25-30; Ⓨ dinner Mon-Sat; Ⓜ Poble Sec

For decades this former wine store has been dishing out dinner to often-raucous groups. Traditional Catalan cooking is the name of the game. Surrounded by aged wine barrels, take your place at old tables and benches and perhaps order the *conejo a la jumillana* (fried rabbit served with garlic, onion, bay leaves, rosemary, mint, thyme and oregano). Dishes are

DIEGO LEZAMA

Quimet i Quimet

abundant, wine flows freely and time seems to have stood still.

QUIMET I QUIMET   Tapas €€

☎ 93 442 31 42; Carrer del Poeta Cabanyes 25; meals €25-30; ☷ noon-4pm & 7-10.30pm Mon-Fri, noon-6pm Sat; Ⓜ Paral·lel; ✕

Quimet i Quimet is a family-run business that has been passed down from genera-tion to generation. There's barely space to swing a calamari in this bottle-lined, standing-room-only place, but it is a treat for the palate. Look at all those gourmet tapas waiting for you! Let the folk behind the bar advise you, and order a drop of fine wine to accompany the food.

LA TOMAQUERA   Catalan €

☎ 93 441 85 18; Carrer de Margarit 5; meals €20; ☷ Tue-Sat; Ⓜ Poble Sec

The waiters shout and rush about this classic, while carafes of wine are sloshed about the long wooden tables. You can't book, so it's first in, first seated (queues are the norm). Try the house speciality of snails or go for hearty meat dishes. The

occasional seafood option, such as *cas-sola de cigales* (crayfish hotpot), might also tempt. And cash is king.

LA BELLA NAPOLI   Pizza €

☎ 93 442 50 56; www.bellanapoli.net; Carrer de Margarit 14; pizza €7-21; ☷ daily; Ⓜ Paral·lel

There are pizza joints all over Barcelona. And then there's the real thing: the way they make it in Naples. This place even *feels* like Naples. The waiters are mostly from across the Med and have that cheeky southern Italian approach to food, cus-tomers and everything else. The pizzas are good, ranging from the simple *margherita* to a heavenly black-truffle number.

DRINKING

A couple of curious bars in El Poble Sec (literally 'Dry Town'!) make a good prelude to the clubs that hold sway up in the won-derfully weird fantasy world of the Poble Espanyol (p227). Some clubs on the lower end of Avinguda del Paral·lel are worth seeking out too.

BARCELONA ROUGE   Bar

☎ 93 442 49 85; Carrer del Poeta Cabanyes 21;
🕑 11pm-2am Tue-Thu, 11pm-3am Fri & Sat;
Ⓜ Poble Sec; 📶

Decadence is the word that springs to mind in this bordello-red lounge-cocktail bar, with acid jazz, drum and bass and other soothing sounds drifting along in the background. No, you're not addled with drink and drugs, the corridor leading out back to the bar really is that crooked. The walls are laden with heavy-framed paintings, dim lamps and mirrors, and no two chairs are alike. Stick to simple drinks, as the €10 glamour cocktails are on the watery side. It also offers sandwiches and snacks.

GRAN BODEGA SALTÓ   Bar

http://bodegasalto.net; Carrer de Blesa 36;
🕑 7pm-3am Wed-Sat, noon-2am Sun; Ⓜ Paral·lel

You can tell by the ranks of barrels that this was once an old-fashioned wine store. Now, after a little homemade psychedelic redecoration, with odd lamps, figurines and old Chinese beer ads, this is a magnet for an eclectic barfly crowd. Mohicans and tats abound, but the crowd is mixed and friendly.

LA CASETA DEL MIGDIA   Bar

☎ 93 301 91 77, 617 956572; www.lacaseta.org; Mirador del Migdia; 🕑 6pm-2.30am Thu-Sat, noon-1am Sun Jun-Sep, noon-7pm Sat & Sun Oct-May; Ⓜ Paral·lel, then funicular

The effort of getting to what is, to all intents and purposes, a simple *chiringuito* (makeshift cafe-bar) is well worth it. Walk below the walls of the Montjuïc castle along the dirt track or follow Passeig del Migdia (watch out for signs for the Mirador del Migdia). Stare out to sea over a beer or coffee by day. As sunset approaches the atmosphere changes, as lounge music (from samba to funk) wafts out over the hammocks.

MAUMAU UNDERGROUND   Bar

☎ 93 441 80 15; www.maumaunderground.com; Carrer de la Fontrodona 35; 🕑 11pm-2.30am Thu-Sat; Ⓜ Paral·lel

Funk, soul, hip hop – you never know what you might run into in this popular Poble Sec music and dance haunt, housed in a former factory. Above the backlit bar, a huge screen spews forth weird and wonderful images, which contribute to the relaxed lounge effect. On occasion it might transmit the latest Barça match instead.

ENTERTAINMENT & ACTIVITIES

DISCOTHEQUE   Club

☎ 902 023865; www.discotheque.info; Carrer de Tarragona 141; admission €15; 🕑 midnight-6am Fri & Sat, 7pm-1am Sun; Ⓜ Tarragona

Inspired by the megaclubs in Ibiza, this is one of Barcelona's big hitters. House is the main baseline in this sprawling designer club, where the nights can get rather hot and scantily clad. The Sunday Café Olé session is a mix of chill, dance music and suggestive stage dance shows to accompany DJs on the end-of-weekend blast.

THE ONE   Club

www.theonebarcelona.com, in Spanish; Avinguda de Francesc Ferrer i Guàrdia; admission €18; 🕑 midnight-6am Fri & Sat; Ⓜ Espanya

A new name for a classic dance place inside the fantasy land of Poble Espanyol has come with a new look. The main dance floor, with the latest in lighting effects and video screens, gets jammed with people from all over town as the night wears on. Friday nights has a house-Ibiza flavour, while Saturday nights tend to be more raucous. A lift and stairs lead up to a more chilled area with several VIP sections.

SALA APOLO
Club & Live Music

☎ 93 441 40 01; www.sala-apolo.com, in Catalan & Spanish; Carrer Nou de la Rambla 113; admission €6-12; ⏱ 12.30-6am Fri & Sat, midnight-5am Sun-Thu; Ⓜ Paral·lel

This is a fine old theatre, where red velvet dominates and you feel as though you're in a movie-set dancehall scene featuring Eliot Ness. 'Nasty Mondays' and 'Crappy Tuesdays' are aimed at a diehard, we-never-stop-dancing crowd. Earlier in the evening, concerts generally take place. Tastes are as eclectic as possible, from local bands to big-name international acts.

TABLAO DE CARMEN
Flamenco

☎ 93 325 68 95; www.tablaodecarmen.com; Carrer dels Arcs 9, Poble Espanyol; show only €35, with tapas/dinner €45/69; ⏱ shows 7.30pm & 10pm Tue-Sun; Ⓜ Espanya

Named after the great Barcelona *bailaora* (flamenco dancer) Carmen Amaya, the set-up here is similar to that at the Tablao Cordobés, although it is somewhat larger and the pseudo-Andalucian decor has a colder, more modern look.

TEATRE MERCAT DE LES FLORS
Contemporary Dance

☎ 93 426 18 75; www.mercatflors.org; Carrer de Lleida 59; admission €15-20; ⏱ box office 11am-2pm & 4-7pm Mon-Fri & 1hr before show; Ⓜ Espanya

Next door to the Teatre Lliure, and together with it known as the Ciutat de Teatre (Theatre City), this is a key venue for top local and international contemporary dance acts. Dance companies perform all over Barcelona but this spacious modern stage is number one.

TEATRE LLIURE
Theatre

☎ 93 289 27 70; www.teatrelliure.com; Plaça de Margarida Xirgu 1; admission €13-26; ⏱ box office 5-8pm; Ⓜ Espanya

Housed in the magnificent former Palau de l'Agricultura building on Montjuïc (opposite the Museu d'Arqueologia) and consisting of two modern theatre

VERONICA GARBUTT

Flamenco dancer

spaces (Espai Lliure and Sala Fabià Puigserver), the 'Free Theatre' puts on a variety of quality drama (mostly in Catalan), contemporary dance and music.

PISCINES BERNAT PICORNELL   Swimming

☎ 93 423 40 41; www.picornell.cat, in Catalan; Avinguda de l'Estadi 30-38; late Sep-late Jun adult/15-24yr/senior & 6-15yr/under 6 yr €9.65/6.50/5.95/free, outdoor pool only late Jun-late Sep adult/15-24yr/senior & 6-15yr/under 6yr €5.30/5.25/3.70/free; ☾ 6.45am-midnight Mon-Fri, 7am-9pm Sat, 7.30am-4pm Sun, outdoor pool hours vary; ☒ 50, 61 or 193

Included in the standard entry price to Barcelona's official Olympic pool on Montjuïc is use of the gym, saunas and spa bath. Membership costs €53.50 to join and €36.10 a month. Nude bathing is also possible here.

DAY TRIPS

DAY TRIPS

HIGHLIGHTS

1

⬎ MONESTIR DE MONTSERRAT

While others head to Lourdes and Fatima, penitent Catalans converge on an impos-ing Benedictine **monastery** (p240) set amid the saw-toothed Montserrat Mountains. Long a place of refuge and veneration, this religious shrine-cum–monastic retreat hides plenty of other curiosities, including the world's oldest functioning printing press, a museum filled with local artistic talent, and a dulcet boys' choir.

2

⬎ ROMAN RUINS IN TARRAGONA

Though usurped by Barcelona in medieval times, Tarragona had had its much heralded moment in the sun: it was once capital of a Roman province that stretched as far as Cantabria on the Atlantic coast. Vestiges of this early Latin flowering lie scattered all over the modern town in a raft of architectural **ruins** (p248), which have earned the city a Unesco World Heritage site listing.

DAY TRIPS

HIGHLIGHTS

⇲ WINE-TASTING

Let the French snigger haughtily into their champagne flutes. Catalonia has endowed the world with its own speciality, *cava*, a revered sparkling wine wrung from grapes grown in the fertile Penedès region (p245), west of Barcelona. In a country where Rioja is the self-proclaimed king, this refined but pleasantly affordable 'bubbly' acts as a credible dauphin.

⇲ SITGES CARNIVAL

Small towns can still deliver big festivals. Look no further than Sitges, a Costa Brava satellite resort that's happy to live in Barcelona's shadow for 95% of the year and even happier to step out of it for the cacophony of its debauched annual carnival (p46). Festivities start on 'Fat Tuesday', and include folk dancing, colourful floats and 'Extermination night'.

⇲ HIKING IN MONTSERRAT

If Montjuïc and Tibidabo barely get your pulse above 100, head northwest to the serrated mountains of Montserrat (p243), where pilgrims climb craggy peaks to watch the sun rise, and the rugged terrain quickly replaces the fuggy smokescreen of the city with something purer. The best paths connect from the top of the Sant Joan funicular.

1 BETHUNE CARMICHAEL; 2 BETHUNE CARMICHAEL; 3 DENNIS JOHNSON; 4 OSO MEDIA/ALAMY; 5 VINCENT LOWE/ALAMY

1 Monestir de Montserrat (p240); 2 Amfiteatre Romà (p248), Tarragona; 3 Freixenet winery (p246), Penedès; 4 Carnival in Sitges (p243); The mountains of Montserrat (p243)

DAY TRIPS

Barcelona is just the beginning. Break through the choking ring of satellite suburbs and dormitory towns surrounding the capital, and one of Spain's most diverse regions unfolds. Catalonia (Catalunya to the locals), a land with its own language and a proud history setting it apart from the rest of Spain, offers everything from golden beaches to wicked ski runs, medieval monasteries to the Roman ruins of Tarragona, top-quality wines to the art of Salvador Dalí.

Catalonia is not, however, all high culture. Myriad beaches, coves and seaside locales dot the rugged spectacle of the Costa Brava. Another fine strand southwest of town is Sitges, loaded with bars and an obligatory stop on the gay partygoer's European circuit. Those who take their hedonism with more restraint can trundle around the Penedès wine country, west of Barcelona. And the jagged mountain range of Montserrat makes the perfect antidote to a seaside hangover.

MONTSERRAT

Shimmering bizarrely in the distance as you drive the C-16 toll road between Terrassa and Manresa is the emblematic mountain range of Catalonia, Montserrat (Serrated Mountain). So dear is it to Catalan hearts that it has long been a popular first name for girls (Montse for short). Lying 50km northwest of Barcelona, the serried ranks of wind- and rain-whipped rock pillars (reaching a height of 1236m) were formed from a conglomeration of limestone, pebbles and sand that once lay beneath the sea. With the historic Benedictine monastery, one of Catalonia's most important shrines, perched at 725m on the mountain range's flank, it makes a great outing.

The **Monestir de Montserrat** (☎ 93 877 77 01; www.abadiamontserrat.net; ☾ 9am-6pm) was founded in 1025 to commemorate a vision of the Virgin on the mountain. Wrecked by Napoleon's troops in 1811, then abandoned as a result of anticlerical legislation in the 1830s, it was rebuilt from 1858. Today a community of about 80 monks lives here. Pilgrims come from far and wide to venerate **La Moreneta** (Black Madonna), a 12th-century Romanesque wooden sculpture of Mary with the infant

---

ORGANISED TOURS

The **Catalunya Bus Turístic** (☎ 93 285 38 32; Plaça de Catalunya) offers a series of day tours from Barcelona to various parts of the region. Routes include a day in Vic, north of Barcelona, visiting the old town and huge weekly market (€35; ☾ Tuesday); Girona and Figueres (€71; ☾ Tuesday to Sunday); a Penedès wine and *cava* jaunt with three winery tours and lunch (€59; ☾ Wednesday to Friday and Sunday); and Montserrat and Sitges (€69; ☾ Tuesday to Sunday). All tours leave at 8.30am from Plaça de Catalunya from late March to October.

DAY TRIPS

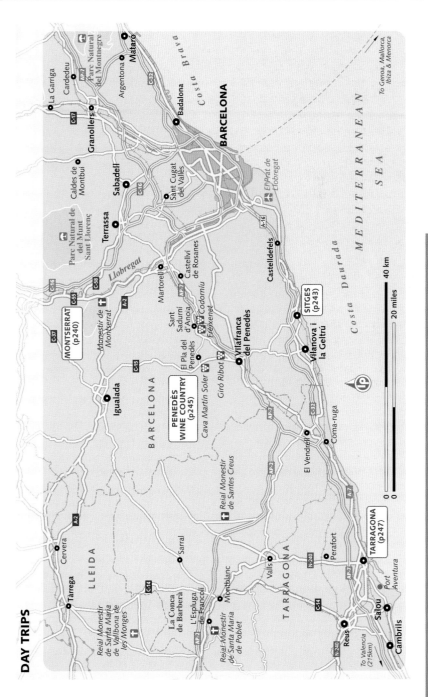

TRANSPORT: MONTSERRAT

Distance from Barcelona 46km

Direction Northwest

Travel time One hour

Bus A daily bus (€53) from Barcelona with Julià Tours (☎ 93 317 64 54; Ronda de la Universitat 5, Barcelona) leaves for the monastery at 9.30am (returning at 3pm). The price includes travel, all entry prices, use of funiculars at Montserrat and a meal at the self-service restaurant. Be at the office a quarter of an hour before departure.

Car Take the C-16. Shortly after Terrassa, follow the exit signs to Montserrat, which will put you on the C-58. Follow it northwest to the C-55. Head 2km south on this road to the municipality of Monistrol de Montserrat, from where a road snakes 7km up the mountain.

Train The R5 line trains operated by FGC (☎ 93 205 15 15) run from Plaça d'Espanya station in Barcelona to Monistrol de Montserrat up to 18 times daily starting at 5.16am. They connect with the cremallera (rack-and-pinion train; ☎ 902 312020; www .cremallerademontserrat.com; one way/return €5.15/8.20), which takes 17 minutes to make the upward journey. One way/return from Barcelona to Montserrat with the FGC train and *cremallera* costs €10.10/18.10. Alternatively, you can get off the train at the previous stop, Montserrat Aeri, and take the Aeri de Montserrat telecabin (☎ 93 237 71 56; www.aeridemontserrat.com; one way/return €5.40/8.50; ⓨ 9.40am-7pm Mar-Oct, 10.10am-5.45pm Mon-Sat, 10.10am-6.45pm Sun & holidays Nov-Feb), which takes five minutes. For various all-in ticket options, check out the above website or www .fgc.net.

Jesus that has been Catalonia's official patron since 1881.

The two-part Museu de Montserrat (☎ 93 877 77 77; Plaça de Santa Maria; adult/ student €6.50/5.50; ⓨ 10am-6pm) has a collection ranging from ancient artefacts, including an Egyptian mummy (the collection of Egyptian artefacts counts more than 1000 items, including a mummified crocodile), to occasional works by Caravaggio, Monet, Degas, Picasso and others (including an ample parade of Catalan painters). The Espai Audiovisual (adult/senior & student €2/1.50, free with Museu de Montserrat; ⓨ 9am-6pm) is a walk-through multimedia space that illustrates the monks' daily life.

From Plaça de Santa Maria you enter the courtyard of the 16th-century basilica (ⓨ 7.30am-8pm Jul-Sep, earlier closing rest of year). The facade, with its carvings of Christ and the 12 apostles, dates from 1901, despite its 16th-century plateresque style. For La Moreneta, follow the signs to the Cambril de la Mare de Déu (La Moreneta; ⓨ 8-10.30am & 12.15-6.30pm daily), to the right of the basilica's main entrance.

The Escolania (www.escolania.cat; admission free; ⓨ performances 1pm & 6.45pm Mon-Thu, 1pm Fri, noon & 6.45pm Sun late Aug-late Jun), reckoned to be Europe's oldest music school, has a boys' choir, the Montserrat Boys' Choir, which sings in the basilica once a day, Sunday to Friday. See the latest performance times (which can change) on the web page.

To see where the holy image of the Virgin was discovered, take the **Funicular de Santa Cova** (one way/return €1.80/2.90; ⏱ every 20min 10am-5.35pm Apr-Oct, 11am-4.25pm Nov-Mar) down from the main area. You can explore the mountain above the monastery by a network of paths leading to some of the peaks and to 13 empty and rather dilapidated little chapels. The **Funicular de Sant Joan** (one way/return €4.50/7.20; ⏱ every 20min 10am-5.40pm Apr-mid-Jul, Sep & Oct, 10am-7pm mid-Jul–Aug, 10am-4.30pm Mar & Nov, 11am-4.30pm Dec, closed Jan & Feb) will carry you from the monastery 250m up the mountain in seven minutes. You can also walk.

From the Sant Joan top station, it's a 20-minute stroll (signposted) to the **Sant Joan chapel**. Enjoy the views as you look west from the trail.

Check the monastery website for accommodation options. There are several places to eat.

SITGES

Jet-setters, honeymooners and international gay party-goers descend on this once-quiet fishing village from spring to autumn. Just 32km (a half-hour by train) southwest of Barcelona, Sitges boasts a long sandy beach, groovy boutiques for fashionistas, a handful of interesting sights and nightlife that thumps from dusk 'til dawn. In winter, Sitges can be dreary, but it wakes up with a vengeance for Carnaval (see p46) in February, when the gay crowd puts on an outrageous show.

The main landmark is the parish church, **Església de Sant Bartomeu i Santa Tecla**, atop a rocky elevation that separates the 2km-long main beach to the southwest from the smaller, quieter Platja de Sant Sebastià to the northeast.

Three **museums** (☎ 93 894 03 64; per museum adult/child/student €3.50/free/2; ⏱ 9.30am-2pm & 4-7pm Tue-Sat, 10am-3pm Sun mid-Jun–Sep, 9.30am-2pm & 3.30-6.30pm Tue-Sat, 10am-3pm Sun Oct–mid-Jun), which offer a combined ticket (adult/child/student €6.50/free/3.50),

ELAN FLEISHER/ALAMY

A restaurant in Sitges

TRANSPORT: SITGES

Distance from Barcelona 32km

Direction Southwest

Travel time 30 minutes

Car The best road from Barcelona is the C-32 toll road. More scenic is the C-31, which hooks up with the C-32 after Castelldefels, but it is often busy and slow.

Train Four *rodalies* trains an hour, from about 6am to 10pm, run from Barcelona's Passeig de Gràcia (€3, 38 to 46 minutes) and Estació Sants to Sitges.

serve as a timid counterweight to the hedonism. Closed for renovations at time of writing, the **Museu Cau Ferrat** (Carrer de Fonollar) was built in the 1890s as a house-cum-studio by artist Santiago Rusiñol. The house is full of his own art and that of his contemporaries. The interior, with its exquisitely tiled walls and lofty arches, is enchanting. Next door is the **Museu Maricel del Mar** (Carrer de Fonollar), with art and handicrafts from the Middle Ages to the 20th century.

The **Museu Romàntic** (Carrer de Sant Gaudenci 1), housed in late-18th-century Can Llopis mansion, recreates with its furnishings and dioramas the lifestyle of a 19th-century Catalan landowning family. It also has a collection of several hundred antique dolls – and some of them are mighty ugly!

At night, head down to the 'Calle del Pecado' (Sin St), actually Carrer del Marquès de Montroig, and its extension, Carrer del 1er de Maig, for wall-to-wall bars that will kick your Sitges nocturnal life off with many decibels.

INFORMATION

Policia Local (☎ 704 101092; Plaça d'Ajuntament)

Tourist office (☎ 93 894 50 04; www.sitges tur.com; Plaça d'Eduard Maristany 2; ☼ 9am-8pm daily mid-Jun–mid-Sep, 9am-2pm & 4-6.30pm Mon-Fri, 10am-2pm & 4-7pm Sat, 10am-2pm Sun mid-Sep–mid-Jun)

Tourist office (☎ 93 811 06 11; Passeig de la Ribera; ☼ 10am-2pm & 4-8pm daily mid-Jun–mid-Sep, 10am-2pm & 4-7pm daily mid-Sep–mid-Jun) A branch office.

SLEEPING & EATING

Romàntic Hotel (☎ 93 894 83 75; www.hotel romantic.com; Carrer de Sant Isidre 33; s/d from €86/119, without bathroom €72/102) Three adjoining 19th-century villas are sensuously restored in period style, and have a leafy dining courtyard. Prices rise a little for rooms with own terrace and/or facing the garden. If there are no rooms available in this gay-friendly spot, ask about its other boutique hotel, Hotel La Renaixença.

Al Fresco (☎ 93 894 06 00; Carrer de Pau Barrabeig 4; meals €30-40; ☼ dinner Tue-Sat mid-Jan–mid-Dec; ✂) Hidden along a narrow stairway that masquerades as a street, Al Fresco serves an array of food in a pleasant setting. You could try anything from an Indian-style chicken curry with green mango to a slab of Angus steak done in red wine and mustard and served with chips.

La Nansa (☎ 93 894 19 27; Carrer de la Carreta 24; meals €35; ☼ Thu-Mon, closed Jan) This seafood specialist is cast just back from the town's waterfront and up a little lane in a fine old house. It does a great line in paella and other rice dishes, including a local speciality, *cassola d'arròs a la sitgetana* (a brothy seafood-and-rice dish). There's a set menu for €24.

A Penedès vineyard

CEPHAS PICTURE LIBRARY/ALAMY

DAY TRIPS

PENEDÈS WINE COUNTRY

PENEDÈS WINE COUNTRY

Rivers of still white and bubbly, among Spain's best wines, spring forth from the area around the towns of Sant Sadurní d'Anoia and Vilafranca del Penedès. Sant Sadurní d'Anoia, a half-hour train ride west of Barcelona, is the capital of *cava*. Vilafranca del Penedès, 12km further down the track, is the heart of the Penedès DO region (*denominación de origen;* see p223), which produces light, still whites. Some good reds and rosés also gurgle forth here.

The epicentre of the Penedès wine-producing district is the large and somewhat straggly Vilafranca del Penedès. Spreading itself around the pleasant old town centre is a less captivating and sprawling new town.

The mainly Gothic Basilica de Santa Maria stands at the heart of the old town. Construction began in 1285 and, since then, it has been much restored. It is possible to arrange visits to the top of the bell

TRANSPORT: PENEDÈS WINE COUNTRY

Distance from Barcelona 48km (to Vilafranca del Penedès)
Direction West
Travel time 30 to 45 minutes
Car Head west along Avinguda Diagonal and follow the signs for the AP-7 freeway, then take either the Sant Sadurní d'Anoia or Vilafranca del Penedès exit.
Train Around two *rodalies* trains an hour run from Plaça de Catalunya and Estació Sants in Barcelona to Sant Sadurní (€3, 45 minutes from Plaça de Catalunya) and Vilafranca (€3.60, 55 minutes from Plaça de Catalunya).

PICTURE CONTACT BV/ALAMY

Cava-tasting at Freixenet

IN SEARCH OF THE PERFECT TIPPLE

To do a tour of the Penedès area, you will need your own transport. For suggestions on wine tourism, browse www.enoturismealtpenedes.net. Do not expect
to wander into any old winery; many only open their doors to the public at
limited times. The more enthusiastic ones will show you how wines and/or *cava*
(Catalan 'champagne') are made, and finish with a glass or two. Tours generally
last about 1½ hours and may only be in Catalan and/or Spanish. Groups must
book. You can search www.dopenedes.es for wineries but this list should get
you started:

Cava Martín Soler (☎ 93 898 82 20; www.cavamartinsoler.com; Puigdàlber; 🕙 9am-1pm
& 3-7pm Mon-Fri, 10am-1pm Sat, Sun & holidays) Located 8km north of Vilafranca in a
17th-century farmhouse surrounded by vineyards, this winery only makes *cava*.

Codorníu (☎ 93 891 33 42; www.codorniu.es; Avinguda de Jaume Codorníu, Sant Sadurní
d'Anoia; 🕙 9am-5pm Mon-Fri, 9am-1pm Sat, Sun & holidays) The Codorníu headquarters
is in a Modernista building at the entry to Sant Sadurní d'Anoia when coming
by road from Barcelona. One of the biggest names in *cava*, it made its first
bottle in 1872.

Freixenet (☎ 93 891 70 00; www.freixenet.es/web/eng; Carrer de Joan Sala 2, Sant Sadurní d'Anoia; adult/under 9yr/9-17yr/senior €6/free/2.20/4.50; 🕙 1½hr tours 10am-1pm &
3-4.30pm Mon-Thu, 10am-1pm Fri-Sun) Easily the best-known *cava* company inter-
nationally.

Giró Ribot (☎ 93 897 40 50; www.giroribot.es; Finca el Pont, Santa Fe del Penedès; 🕙 9am-
5pm Mon-Fri, 10am-2pm Sat & Sun) The magnificent farm buildings ooze centuries of
tradition. These vintners use mostly local grape varieties to produce a limited
range of fine *cava* and wines (including muscat). The times given are for the
shop. To visit the cellars, call ahead.

tower in summer at around sunset. Ask at the tourist office.

The basilica faces the **Vinseum** (☎ 93 890 05 82; www.vinseum.cat; Plaça de Jaume I 5, Vilafranca; adult/under 12yr/senior, student and 12-17yr €5/free/3; ☉ 10am-2pm & 4-7pm Tue-Sat, 10am-2pm Sun & holidays) across Plaça de Jaume I. Housed in a Gothic building, a combination of museums here covers archaeology, art, geology and bird life, along with an excellent section on wine.

INFORMATION

Tourist office (☎ 93 818 12 54; www.turisme vilafranca.com; Carrer de la Cort 14, Vilafranca; ☉ 4-7pm Mon, 9am-1pm & 4-7pm Tue-Sat, 10am-1pm Sun) A good source of information on wineries.

SLEEPING & EATING

Hostal del Castell Gimenelles (☎ 977 67 81 93; www.gimenelles.com; Sant Jaume dels Domenys; r €80-135; P) Eight rooms with antique furniture are arranged in a typical, 18th-century Penedès farmhouse and surrounded by vineyards, just west of the town of Sant Jaume dels Domenys. The restaurant offers hearty victuals (set meal €23.50).

Hotel Sol i Vi (☎ 93 899 32 04; www.solivi .com; Subirats; s/d €51/68; P 🖥 🍽) Occupying a renovated *masia* (Catalan country farm-house) in Subirats, 4km south of Sant Sadurní on the C-243a road to Vilafranca, Hotel Sol i Vi has spacious rooms, a res-taurant and country views.

Cal Ton (☎ 93 890 37 41; Carrer Casal 8, Vilafranca; meals €40; ☉ lunch & dinner Wed-Sat, lunch Tue & Sun) Hidden away down a narrow side street, Cal Ton has a crisp, modern decor and inventive Mediterranean chow, which tempts with anything from foie gras with apple to seafood and *cava* pancake.

TARRAGONA

A bustling port city, Tarragona was once Catalonia's leading light. Roman and me-dieval vestiges testify to its two greatest epochs. The Romans established the city as Tarraco in the 2nd century BC, and in 27 BC Augustus elevated it to the capital of his new Tarraconensis province (stretch-ing from Catalonia to Cantabria in the northwest and to Almería in the south-east). Abandoned when the Muslims arrived in AD 714, it was reborn as a Christian archbishopric in 1089.

TRANSPORT: TARRAGONA

Distance from Barcelona 96km

Direction Southwest

Travel time 55 minutes to 1¾ hours

Car Take the C-32 toll road along the coast via Castelldefels or the AP-7 (if following Avinguda Diagonal west out of town).

Train More than 40 regional and long-distance trains per day run to/from Bar-celona's Estació Sants (some also stop at Passeig de Gràcia). The cheapest fares (for Regional and Catalunya Express trains) cost €5.70 to €6.40 and the journey takes one to 1½ hours. Long-distance trains (such as Talgo, Alaris, Arco and Euromed trains) are faster but more expensive – as much as €19.80 in tourist (standard) class.

The superb **cathedral** (☎ 977 21 10 80; Pla de la Seu; adult/7-16yr/senior & student €3.80/1.20/2.80; ☺ 10am-7pm Mon-Sat Jun–mid-Oct, 10am-6pm mid-Mar–May, 10am-5pm mid-Oct–Nov, 10am-2pm Dec–mid-Mar) was built between 1171 and 1331 on the site of its Visigothic predecessor and a Roman temple (probably dedicated to Caesar Augustus), combining Romanesque and Gothic features, as typified by the main facade on Pla de la Seu. The rooms off the cloister house the **Museu Diocesà**, with an extensive collection ranging from Roman hairpins to some lovely 12th- to 14th-century polychrome woodcarvings of a breastfeeding Virgin. The interior of the cathedral, which is over 100m long, is Romanesque at the northeast end and Gothic at the southwest (a result of the prolonged construction period).

The so-called **Museu d'Història de Tarragona** (MHT, History Museum; ☎ 977 24 22 20; www.museutgn.com; adult/concession per attraction €3/1.50, all attractions €10/5; ☺ 9am-9pm Tue-Sat, 9am-3pm Sun Easter-Sep, 9am-7pm Tue-Sat, 10am-3pm Sun & holidays Oct-Easter) is actually an ensemble of elements that includes four separate Roman sites (which together with other Roman sites around the province constitute a Unesco World Heritage site).

For the Roman stuff, start with the **Fòrum Provincial** (Plaça del Rei), which is dominated by the **Torre del Pretori**, a multistoreyed building later reused by the city's medieval rulers. Stretching west from behind the Torre del Pretori is the **Circ Romà** (Roman circus), where chariots would thunder along in dangerous, and often deadly, races along a 300m-long track that extended just beyond the present Plaça de la Font. What remains of the vaults of the circus can be entered from Rambla Vella. Nearby, **Casa Canals** (Carrer d'en Granada) is a fine 19th-century

noble family's house abutting the Roman city wall and jammed with period furniture and *objets d'art*. Near the beach is the well-preserved **Amfiteatre Romà** (Plaça d'Arce Ochotorena; ☺ 9am-9pm Tue-Sat, 9am-3pm Sun Easter-Sep, 9am-5pm Tue-Sat, 10am-3pm Sun & holidays Oct-Easter), where gladiators hacked away at each other, or wild animals, to the death. In its arena are the remains of 6th- and 12th-century churches built to commemorate the martyrdom of the Christian bishop Fructuosus and two deacons, believed to have been burnt alive here in AD 259. There was certainly no lack of excitement in Roman Tarraco! East of Carrer de Lleida are remains of the **Fòrum Romà** (Carrer del Cardenal Cervantes), also known as Fòrum de la Colònia and dominated by several imposing columns. The **Passeig Arqueològic** is a peaceful walk around part of the perimeter of the old town between two lines of city walls; the inner ones are mainly Roman, while the outer ones were put up by the British in the War of the Spanish Succession.

The town beach, **Platja del Miracle**, is clean but crowded.

INFORMATION

Hospital Joan XXIII (☎ 977 29 58 00; Carrer del Dr Mallafre Guasch 4)
Tourist office (☎ 977 25 07 95; www.tarragonaturisme.es; Carrer Major 39; ☺ 10am-9pm Mon-Sat, 10am-2pm Sun Jul-Sep, 10am-2pm & 4-7pm Mon-Sat, 10am-2pm Sun & holidays Oct-Jun)

SLEEPING & EATING

Hotel Lauria (☎ 977 23 67 12; www.hlauria.es; Rambla Nova 20; s/d €55/75; ⚄ ⚄) Pleasant enough rooms with parquet floors, good location and a modest pool and sun deck.

Pensió Plaça de la Font (☎ 977 24 61 34; www.hotel pdelafont.com; Plaça de la Font 26;

IAN DAGNALL/ALAMY

Platja Llarga

⬎ IF YOU LIKE...

If you like **Platja del Miracle** you may also enjoy the fine yellow sand at these two beaches:

- **Platja Arrabassada** One kilometre northeast from the main town beach across the headland is this fine sandy beach whose name in Catalan means the 'beach of the uprooted field'. Nothing could be further from the truth. Wide and relatively uncrowded, Arrabassada is rather sublime.
- **Platja Llarga** Beginning 2km beyond Arrabassada, the rather more aptly named 'Long Beach' stretches for about 3km. Local bus 1 from the Balcó stop on Via Augusta goes to both here and Platja Arrabassada.

s/d €55/70; ☒) Reasonable *pensión* with its own restaurant on a characterful, busy old town square.

Toful (☎ 977 21 42 16; Plaça del Fòrum; meals €20-25; ☼ lunch Sun & Tue-Thu, lunch & dinner Fri & Sat) A classic tapas bar in the old town, this place serves up generous servings of old faves like *xipirons* (little battered cuttle-fish) and *aletes de pollastre* (oven-cooked chicken wings). During the week you could opt for the lunch menu at €9.80. It becomes a little more elaborate on the weekend (€17).

↘ BARCELONA IN FOCUS

ARCHITECTURE

KRZYSZTOF DYDYNSKI

Interior, Palau del Baró Quadras (p168), designed by Josep Puig i Cadafalch

Some cities ape architectural styles; others create them. Barcelona's architectural gift to the world was Modernisme, a flamboyant Catalan creation that erupted in the late 19th and early 20th centuries. Related but by no means religiously cloned to the art nouveau movement in France and the exponents of Jugendstil in Germany, Modernisme was personified by the prodigious architectural talent of Antoni Gaudí. Barcelona's other great contribution to global architecture was Catalan Gothic; the city's Barri Gòtic in the Old Town contains one of the finest surviving ensembles of Gothic buildings in Europe.

CATALAN GOTHIC

Barcelona's first great moment of creative electricity came when the city, grown rich on its Mediterranean trade and empire-building, transformed what is now the old city centre into the pageant of Gothic building that has survived in great part to this day.

Historically, Gothic sits between the Romanesque and Renaissance periods of medieval construction. It was an architectural style that emerged in France in the 1100s, but gradually spread throughout Europe, spawning numerous regional variations. The overlying themes, best exemplified in the ecclesial buildings of the day, were humungous scale (Gothic churches were the skyscrapers of their era), well-lit interiors, large windows, pointed arches, lofty pinnacles and spires, and majestic decoration.

Most of these themes were employed in medieval Barcelona in a raft of buildings that spanned the whole era and later inspired a small neo-Gothic revival in the mid-19th century. The Església de Santa María del Mar (p116) is a fairly unembellished example of Levantino (14th-century) Gothic style at its height and is usually considered the city's greatest Gothic achievement. The more decorative Catedral (p64) is the synthesis of a Levantino Gothic base overlaid with a neo-Gothic facade.

THE MODERNISTAS

The second wave of Catalan creativity, also carried on the wind of boom times, came around the turn of the 20th century. The urban expansion program known as L'Eixample (the Extension), designed to free the choking population from the city's bursting medieval confines, coincided with a blossoming of unfettered thinking in architecture that arrived in the back-draft of the 1888 International Exposition of Barcelona.

Leading the way was Antoni Gaudí i Cornet (1852–1926), but he was closely followed by Catalan nationalists, Lluís Domènech i Montaner (1850–1923) and Josep Puig i Cadafalch (1867–1957). Puig i Cadafalch was also a senior politician and president of the Catalan Mancomunitat (a shadow parliament that demanded Catalan autonomy) from 1916 to 1923. The political associations are significant as Modernisme became a means of expression for Catalan identity that barely touched the rest of Spain.

The vitality and rebelliousness of the Modernistas is best summed up in the epithets modern, new, liberty, youth and secession. A key uniting element was the sensuous curve, implying movement, lightness and vitality. But the movement never stood still. Gaudí, in particular, repeatedly forged his own path. As he became more adventurous he appeared a lone wolf. With age he became almost exclusively motivated by stark religious conviction and devoted much of the latter part of his life to what remains Barcelona's call sign – the unfinished La Sagrada Família (p161).

Paradoxically, Modernista architects often looked to the past for inspiration. Gothic, Islamic and Renaissance design all had something to offer. At its most playful, Modernisme was able to intelligently flout the rule books of these styles and create exciting new cocktails.

BARCELONA SINCE THE OLYMPIC GAMES

Barcelona's latest architectural revolution began in the 1980s, when in the run up to the 1992 Olympics the city set about its biggest phase of renewal since the heady days of L'Eixample.

⚓ ANTONI GAUDÍ

Few architects are as instantly recognisable in their buildings as Antoni Gaudí. Born in Reus in 1852, Gaudí personifies, and largely transcends, a movement that brought a thunderclap of innovative greatness to an otherwise middle-ranking European city.

Gaudí's inspiration in the first instance was Gothic. But he also sought to emulate the harmony he observed in nature. Straight lines were out. The forms of plants and stones were in. Gaudí used complex string models weighted with plumb lines to make his calculations. His work is at once a sublime reaching-out to the heavens, and yet an earthy appeal to sinewy movement.

⟫ THE BEST

KRZYSZTOF DYDYNSKI

Facade detail, Torre Agbar (p139)

CONTEMPORARY BUILDINGS

- **Torre Agbar** (p139)
- **Mercat de Santa Caterina** (p117)
- **W Barcelona** (p141)
- **Torre de Collserola** (p201)
- **Edifici Fòrum** (p140)

The Olympic makeover included the transformation of the Port Vell waterfront, the long road to resurrecting the 1929 International Exhibition sites in Montjuïc (including the refurbishment of the Olympic stadium), and the creation of landmarks such as Santiago Calatrava's (1951–) Torre Calatrava.

Post-1992, landmark buildings still went up in strategic spots, usually with the ulterior motive of trying to pull the surrounding area up by its bootstraps. One of the most emblematic of these projects was the gleaming white Museu d'Art Contemporani de Barcelona (Macba; p91), opened in 1995. Another big recent project is Diagonal Mar, a whole district built in the northeast coastal corner of the city where before there was a void. High-rise apartments, waterfront office towers and a gigantic photovoltaic panel that provides some of the area's electricity are the striking additions here.

The most visible addition to the skyline came in 2005. The shimmering, cucumber-shaped Torre Agbar (p139) is emblematic of the city's desire to make the developing hi-tech zone of 22@ (www.22barcelona.com) a reality.

FAMILY TRAVEL

ADINA TOVY AMSEL

Catalunya Square, L'Eixample district

Barcelona and kids ought to be a marriage made in heaven. First of all, the city has plenty of running-around space in the parks and gardens of Montjuïc and Tibidabo, and the ample beaches of La Barceloneta. Secondly it has quirks: fairy-tale Modernista architecture and the ever-revolving street theatre that is La Rambla. Thirdly, as a major European city, it has activities aimed specifically at children, including an aquarium, a chocolate museum, and an amusement park in the new Parc del Fórum. The long and short of it: neither adults nor children will battle tedium here.

OUT-OF-THE-BOX ACTIVITIES

One of the great things about Barcelona is the inclusion of children in what would normally be considered adult activities. Going out to eat or sipping a beer on a late summer evening at a *terraza* (terrace) needn't mean leaving children with minders. Locals take their kids out all the time and don't worry about keeping them up late.

If you're going to be in the metro area a while, try to adjust your child's sleeping habits to 'Spanish time' early on, or else you'll miss out on about three-quarters of what this city is all about. Also, be prepared to look for things 'outside the box'. Yes, there are beaches and amusement parks aplenty, but how about introducing your kids to other stuff. There's the childlike creativity of Picasso and Miró (give your children paper and crayons and take them around the museums), the Harry Potter meets Tolkein fantasy of Park Güell and La Pedrera, or the tribal passion of a game of football at Camp Nou.

GUY MOBERLY

Children with papier mâché heads at a festival

BABYSITTERS

Barcelona is an eternally romantic city and to enjoy it whine-free you may need the services of a babysitter. Most of the mid- and upper-range hotels in Barcelona can organise babysitting services. A company that many hotels use and that you can also contact directly is 5 Serveis (Map p82; ☎ 93 412 56 76; Carrer de Pelai 50). It has multilingual babysitters (canguros). Rates vary, but in the evening expect to pay around €10 an hour plus the cost of a taxi home for the babysitter. Tender Loving Canguros (☎ 647 605989; www.tlcanguros.com) offers English-speaking babysitters for a minimum of three hours (€7 an hour).

You could take younger kiddies (maximum age 11) to Happy Parc (☎ 93 317 86 60; www.happyparc.com, in Catalan; Carrer de Pau Claris 97; per hr €4; ☺ 5-9pm Mon-Fri, 11am-9pm Sat & Sun) for a play on the slides and other diversions.

☜ THE NITTY-GRITTY

- **Change facilities** Not as ubiquitous as in North America, but generally good and clean
- **Cots** Usually available in hotels; reserve ahead
- **Health** High health-care standards
- **High chairs** Many restaurants have at least one; bring your own crayons
- **Nappies (diapers)** Widely available
- **Strollers** Bring your own (preferably a fold-away)
- **Transport** Easily accessible without a car

KIDS & BIKES

Barcelona has excellent bike hire facilities, with some companies offering special kids' bicycles. **Trixi** (Map p52; ☎ 93 310 13 79; www.trixi.info; Plaça dels Traginers 4) hires out bicycles, kickbikes and 'trixi-kids', tricycles with a kind of front-end trolley for transporting young children. **Barnabike** (Map p136; ☎ 93 269 02 04; www.barnabike.com; Carrer del Pas de Sota la Muralla 3; per 2hr/24hr €6/15; ☼ 10am-9.30pm) rents out an assortment of bikes (including kick bikes) and karts, Trikkes (odd three-wheel contraptions), electric bikes and bikes for kids.

◥ THE BEST

NEIL SETCHFIELD

Children at La Barceloneta beach (p138)

KID-SPECIFIC SIGHTS

- **Beaches** (p138)
- **L'Aquàrium** (p135)
- **Museu de la Xocolata** (p118)
- **Museu Marítim** (p89)
- **Tibidabo & Parc d'Atraccions** (p200)
- **Transbordador Aeri** (p137)

FOOD & DRINK

DIEGO LEZAMA

A *tortilleria* in the Gràcia district

Not two decades ago, to suggest that Spanish chefs could compete favourably with the French would have been to utter the ultimate dinner party *faux pas*. Then, along came the great Catalan culinary revolution, with Michelin stars flying around like *cava* at a wedding and Catalan restaurants such as elBulli hitting numerous 'world's best' lists. As the centre of all things Catalan, Barcelona has played an integral role in this gastronomic alchemy, with its restaurant scene enjoying a prolonged renaissance. Basque loyalists may protest, but herein lies some of the kookiest *comida* (food) on the peninsula – nay, planet.

A RICE BASE

Barcelona may have become a cauldron of culinary wackiness of late with the foams and froths of elBulli master chef Ferran Adrià and his disciples but, lest we forget, this is Spain, where certain dishes – paella, tortilla and tapas, to name but three – are as timeless as the well-trodden streets of the Barri Gòtic.

Paella's main ingredient, rice, is grown not far from the city limits, in the Delta de l'Ebre area of southern Catalonia, and used widely. Mixed with fish from the Mediterranean and meat from the nearby mountains, Barcelona's paella concoctions are some of the best in Spain, save, of course, Valencia. *Arròs a la cassola* or *arròs a la catalana* is the moniker given to Catalan paella. It's cooked in an earthenware pot without saffron, whereas *arròs negre* is rice cooked in squid ink – much tastier than it sounds. *Fideuà* is similar to paella, but uses noodles rather than rice. You should also receive a little side dish of *allioli* (a mayonnaise-style sauce of pounded garlic with olive oil) to mix in.

WHERE THE MOUNTAINS MEET THE SEA

As Spain's biggest coastal city, Barcelona, not surprisingly, produces excellent seafood, but the meat from the metropolitan area's peripheral mountains also spills liberally onto the city's dinner plates. This mountain-meets-sea ethos is best summed up in local combo dishes such as *llangosta i pollastre* (lobster with chicken in a nutty tomato sauce) and the hybrid paellas, which sometimes shun Valencia purism by including fish *and* chicken.

Botifarra (sausages) are popular and come in many shapes and sizes. They are best served grilled *amb mongetes,* ie with white haricot beans. Others prefer more substantial meat such as a sizzling *solomillo* (sirloin) of *vedella* (beef) prepared *a punto* (medium rare).

Catalans are similarly passionate about *calçots* (large, sweet spring onions), which are barbecued over hot coals, dipped in tangy romesco sauce (a finely ground mixture of tomatoes, peppers, onions, garlic, almonds and olive oil) and eaten voraciously when in season – from January until March. This is most traditionally done as a Sunday lunch outing in which the *calçots* are the first course, followed by copious meat and sausage dishes as the main.

Typical desserts include *crema catalana,* a delicious version of crème brûlée, but you might also be offered *mel i mató,* honey and fresh cream cheese.

CAFES & RESTAURANTS

In Barcelona, new restaurants and cafes open (and close) with astounding rapidity, although brand spanking new is not always synonymous with good. Never fear, for the choice of good places is overwhelming.

A few old-guard restaurants specialise in traditional Catalan cooking, while other equally venerable establishments, often run by Basques or Galicians, offer a mix of regional specialties and what can loosely be termed 'Spanish cooking'. Such places are scattered across the Barri Gòtic, El Raval and L'Eixample areas. Seafood is also prominent, especially in La Barceloneta. Booking is advisable at midrange and expensive places, especially from Thursday to Saturday.

⚜ CAVA

Welcome to *cava* country. That's sparkling wine to the uninitiated, or wine with significant levels of carbon dioxide either added after fermentation or produced during a second process of fermentation. Catalonia produces 95% of Spain's *cava* and the grapes are grown almost exclusively in the grape-rich Penedès region (p245), most notably in the village of Sant Sadurni d'Anoia. Its most famous brand is Freixenet, a black-bottled sparkling wine that has long been the cheap supermarket stand-in for what purists consider the real McCoy – French champagne.

BARCELONA IN FOCUS

FOOD & DRINK

THE BEST

PASCALE BEROUJON

Tapas

TAPAS

- **Tapaç 24** (p177)
- **Taktika Berri** (p177)
- **Bar Celta** (p74)
- **Cal Pep** (p121)
- **Vaso de Oro** (p144)

Cafes and bars abound. Locals tend to take their coffee on the hop at the bar but there's no shortage of places to sit over a hot cuppa and the paper. To satisfy a sweet tooth, head for a *granja,* where thick hot chocolate is the go.

TAPAS

Although tapas, Spain's quintessential bar snacks, were invented in Andalucía and weren't originally part of the Catalan eating tradition, they have been enthusiastically imported. Particularly popular are the Basque Country tapas known as *pintxos,* most of which come in the form of canapés. On slices of baguette are perched anything from *bacalao* (cod) to *morcilla* (black pudding). These are most refreshingly washed down with a slightly tart Basque white wine, *txacoli,* which is served like cider to give it a few (temporary) bubbles. Each *pintxo* comes with a toothpick, and payment is by the honour system – keep your toothpicks and present them for the final count when you ask for the bill.

In some gourmet spots, tapas have become something of an art form, while in many straightforward, beery bars you might just get a saucer of olives to accompany your tipple.

FOOTBALL

BARCELONA IN FOCUS

FOOTBALL

PAUL SHAWCROSS/ALAMY

Boys playing football in Park Güell

To understand a country – any country – you must first decipher its sporting rituals. In Barcelona that means football. Challenging the cathedral as the city's primary place of worship is Camp Nou, home of FC Barcelona – football club, international brand and fervent bastion of Catalan identity, whose blue-and-red stripes can be seen on everyone from football-mad Thai schoolkids to goat herders in the African bush.

A CULTURAL FORCE

The story starts on 29 November 1899, when Swiss Hans Gamper founded FC Barcelona, four years after English residents had first played the game here. His choice of club colours – the blue and maroon of his home town, Winterthur – has stuck. By 1910 FC Barcelona was the premier club in a rapidly growing league, and had picked up its first Spanish Cup. When Spain's La Liga was founded in 1929, Barcelona ran away with the first title, though its playing record became patchier as the decades wore on and the Franco regime suppressed all manifestations of Catalan-ness.

Barça's reemergence as a footballing and cultural force coincided with the death of Franco and an influx of foreign players, starting with Dutch midfield ace Johann Cruyff in 1973. More legends followed, with Diego Maradona arriving in 1982, the Brazilian Ronaldo in 1996, and Ronaldinho in 2003. Fortunes went from good to better. Barça won La Liga four years in a row in the early '90s, took the Champions League in 2006, and in 2009 won an unprecedented 'treble' of La Liga, Spanish Cup and Champions League, spurred by vertically challenged midfield maestro, Lionel Messi, 67kg of pure footballing genius.

⚓ THE OTHER TEAM

The pub-quiz question pretty much guaranteed to stump all but the most in-the-know football geeks is: what is Barcelona's other team? The answer: RDC Espanyol, the city's perennial underachievers based at the brand new **Estadi RCD Espanyol** (**www.rcdespanyol.com; Avinguda del Baix Llobregat, Cornellà;** Ⓜ **Cornellà Centre**). The Barça-Espanyol rivalry is one of the most one-sided and divisive in football. While FC Barcelona is traditionally associated with Catalan nationalism, Espanyol is usually identified with Spanish immigrants from other parts of the country. Then there's the trophy haul: currently standing at Barcelona 69, Espanyol 4.

Portuguese midfielder Luís Figo invited ridicule in the early 2000s when he moved from Barça to cursed rivals Real Madrid.

GETTING TO SEE A GAME

A match at Camp Nou (p196), the largest stadium in Europe, can be breathtaking.

Tickets are available at Camp Nou, as well as by phone and online. You can also purchase them through the ServiCaixa ticketing service. To purchase tickets by phone or online, nonclub members must reserve at least 15 days before the match. Tickets can cost anything from €31 to €225, depending on seat and match. The ticket windows open on Saturday morning and in the afternoon until the game starts. If the match is on Sunday, the ticket windows open Saturday morning only and then on Sunday until the match starts. Usually tickets are *not* available for matches with Real Madrid.

HISTORY

JOHN ELK III

Ajuntament (city hall; p66), on Plaça de Sant Jaume

The history of Barcelona hasn't always been married intrinsically to the history of Spain. In fact, on balance this fiercely independent Catalan city has looked east as much as it west for its inspiration, resulting in culture peculiarities coloured with influences from Mallorca, Sardinia and Greece, as well as Madrid and Seville.

WILFRED THE HAIRY & MEDITERRANEAN EXPANSION

It was the Romans who first etched Barcino onto Europe's map in the 3rd century BC, though the nascent settlement long played second fiddle to their provincial capital in Tarragona. The Visigoths came next, followed by the Moors, whose relatively brief occupation was usurped when the Franks put the city under the control of local counts in 801 as a buffer zone against the still Muslim-dominated caliphate to the south.

Eccentrically named Wilfred the Hairy (Count Guifré el Pelós) moulded the entity we now know as Catalonia in the 9th century by wresting control over several neighbouring territories and establishing Barcelona as its key city. The hirsute one founded

circa AD 15	717	1137
Settlement of Barcino first mentioned in Roman chronicles under control of Tarraco (Tarragona).	Barcelona captured by the Moors, who rule until the arrival of the Franks in 801.	Barcelona becomes an integral part of the Kingdom of Aragon through royal marriage.

a dynasty that lasted nearly five centuries and developed almost independently from the Reconquista wars that were playing out in the rest of Iberia.

The counts of Barcelona gradually expanded their territory south and, in 1137, Ramon Berenguer IV, the Count of Barcelona, married Petronilla, heir to the throne of neighbouring Aragón. Thus, the combined Crown of Aragón was created.

In the following centuries the regime became a flourishing merchant empire, seizing Valencia and the Balearic Islands from the Muslims, and later taking territories as far flung as Sardinia, Sicily and parts of Greece.

CASTILIAN DOMINANCE

Overstretched, racked by civil disobedience and decimated by the Black Death, Catalonia began to wobble by the 14th century. When the last count of Wilfred the Hairy's dynasty expired without leaving an heir, the Crown of Aragón was passed to a noble of Castile. Soon these two Spanish kingdoms merged, with Catalonia left as a very junior partner. As business shifted from the Mediterranean to the Atlantic after the discovery of the Americas in 1492, Catalans were increasingly marginalised from trade.

DECLINE & FALL

The region, which had retained some autonomy in the running of its own affairs, was dealt a crushing blow when it supported the wrong side in the War of the Spanish Succession (1702–14). Barcelona, under the auspices of British-backed archduke Charles of Austria, fell after a stubborn siege on 11 September 1714 (now celebrated as National Catalan Day) to the forces of Bourbon king Philip V, who established a unitary Castilian state. Barcelona now faced a long backlash as the new king banned the writing and teaching of Catalan, swept away the remnants of local legal systems and tore down a whole district of medieval Barcelona in order to construct an immense fort (on the site of the present-day Parc de la Ciutadella; p118), whose sole purpose was to watch over Barcelona's troublemakers.

THE RENAIXENÇA & THE ROAD BACK

Buoyed by the lifting of the ban on its trade with the Americas in 1778, Barcelona embarked on the road to industrial revolution, based initially on textiles but spreading to wine, cork and iron in the mid-19th century.

It soon became Spain's leading city. As the economy prospered, Barcelona outgrew its medieval walls, which were demolished in 1854–56. Work on the grid-plan L'Eixample (Extension) district began soon after. The so-called Renaixença (Renaissance) brought a revival of Catalan culture, as well as political activism, and sowed the seeds of growing

1380s	1714	1860s
The Aragonese Empire extends as far as Sardinia, Sicily and Greece.	Under siege, Barcelona falls to King Philip V in the War of the Spanish Succession.	Barcelona outgrows its medieval city walls and work begins on L'Eixample (the extension).

GUY MOBERLY

Parlament de Catalunya (p118)

political tension in the early 20th century, as demands for autonomy from the central state became more insistent.

THE MASSES AGAINST THE CLASSES

Adding to the fiery mix was growing discontent among the working class. The grand Catalan merchant-bourgeois families grew richer, displaying their wealth in a slew of whimsical private mansions built with verve and flair by Modernista (Catalan art nouveau) architects such as Antoni Gaudí. At the same time, the industrial working class, housed in cramped quarters such as La Barceloneta and El Raval, and oppressed by poverty and disease, became organised and, on occasion, violent. Spain's neutrality during WWI had boosted Barcelona's economy, and from 1900 to 1930 the population doubled to one million, but the postwar global slump hit the city hard. Waves of strikes, organised principally by the anarchists' Confederación Nacional del Trabajo, brought tough responses. Left- and right-wing gangs took their ideological conflict to the streets. Tit-for-tat assassinations became common currency and the death toll mounted.

When the Second Spanish Republic was created under a left-wing government in 1931, Catalonia declared independence. Later, under pressure, its leaders settled for devolution, which it then lost in 1934, when a right-wing government won power in Madrid. The election of a left-wing popular front in 1936 again sparked Catalan

1888	1929	1937
The first International Exposition in Barcelona paves the way for two decades of Modernisme architecture.	The International Exhibition leads to further urban development in Montjuïc, and a new Metro system.	During the civil war Barcelona is controlled by anarchists then communists and, finally, Spain's Republican government.

autonomy claims but also led General Franco to launch the Spanish Civil War (1936–39), from which he emerged the victor.

REVOLUTIONARY FERVOUR

The acting capital of Spain for much of the civil war, Barcelona was run by anarchists and the Partido Obrero de Unificación Marxista (Marxist Unification Workers' Party) Trotskyist militia until mid-1937. Unions took over factories and public services, hotels and mansions became hospitals and schools, everyone wore workers' clothes, bars and cafes were collectivised, trams and taxis were painted red and black (the colours of the anarchists), and one-way streets were ignored as they were seen to be part of the old system.

The more radical anarchists were behind the burning of most of the city's churches and the shooting of more than 1200 priests, monks and nuns. The anarchists in turn were shunted aside by the communists (directed by Stalin from Moscow) after a bloody internecine battle in Barcelona that left 1500 dead in May 1937. Later that year the Spanish Republican government fled Valencia and made Barcelona the official capital (the government had left besieged Madrid early in the war).

The Republican defeat at the hands of the Nationalists in the Battle of the Ebro in southern Catalonia in summer 1938 left Barcelona undefended. It fell to the Nationalists on 25 January 1939, triggering a mass exodus of refugees to France, where most were long interned in makeshift camps. Purges and executions under Franco continued until well into the 1950s. Former Catalan president Lluís Companys was arrested in France by the Gestapo in August 1940, handed over to Franco, and shot on 15 October on Montjuïc. He is reputed to have died with the words 'Visca Catalunya!' ('Long live Catalonia!') on his lips.

THE CITY REBORN

The Francoist Josep Maria de Porcioles was mayor from 1957 until his death in 1973, a grey time for Barcelona, marked by regular demonstrations against the regime, always brutally put down. When Franco himself died two years later, the city rejoiced. In 1977 Catalonia was granted regional autonomy.

In 1980, in the first free regional elections since before the civil war, wily Catalan nationalist Jordi Pujol was elected president of Catalonia at the head of the Convergència i Unió coalition. He remained at the controls until 2003, when he stepped down and was succeeded by the former socialist mayor of Barcelona, Pasqual Maragall. Maragall's rocky three-party coalition stumbled in 2006, and he was replaced by socialist colleague José Montilla, who remains at the head of an uneasy coalition government today.

1939	1977	1992
After nearly three years of bitter fighting, the city falls to Franco's fascist forces.	After one million demonstrate peacefully on Barcelona's streets, Catalonia is granted regional autonomy.	Barcelona hosts a highly lauded Summer Olympics, ushering in another prolonged period of urban renewal.

Torre Calatrava (p224), Montjuïc

CLX/IMAGEBROKER

The 1992 Olympics marked the beginning of a long process of urban renewal. The waterfront, beaches and Montjuïc were in the first wave, but the momentum hasn't been lost since. The Ciutat Vella (Old City) continues to be spruced up, and a determined campaign to repair the city's facades is lending Barcelona a brighter feel. Ambitious projects such as the 22@ hi-tech zone in the once-industrial El Poblenou district, the major development around new trade-fair grounds between the city and the airport, and the fancy Diagonal Mar waterfront development around the Parc del Fòrum at the northeast tip of the city are just a few examples of Barcelona's urban dynamism.

1994	2000s	2010
The Gran Teatre del Liceu, Barcelona's opera house, burns to the ground. It is rebuilt and reopens in 1999.	Fresh immigration and slick modern buildings along the waterfront bring Barcelona into the 21st century.	The mayor of Barcelona, Jordi Hereu, announces that the city will be a candidate for the 2022 Olympic Winter Games.

MODERN ART

DIEGO LEZAMA

Sculpture by Fernando Botero, El Raval district

Barcelona is to modern art what Greece is to ruined temples. Three of the figures at the vanguard of 20th-century avant-gardism were either born or spent their formative years here. First came Málaga-born Pablo Picasso, who lived in Barcelona from 1896 to 1904 during his melancholic Blue Period. Second was Joan Miró, an early surrealist and avid questioner of asphyxiating contemporary mores. Lastly came Salvador Dalí, from nearby Figueres, as wacky and twisted as his twirly waxed moustache suggested. The now-deceased trilogy's gigantic legacy is stamped all over Barcelona in museums, sculptures and a nothing-is-too-weird artistic zeitgeist.

THE CRUCIAL THREE

Spain has been a giant in world art ever since Velázquez etched his haunting *meninas* and ushered in the glittery Siglo de Oro (c 1492–1680), though Catalonia was a little late to the ball. It wasn't until the late 19th century that truly great artists began to emerge in Barcelona and its hinterland, led by dandy portraitist Ramón Casas (1866–1932). Casas, an early Modernista, founded a Barcelona bar known as Els Quatre Gats, which became the nucleus for the city's growing art movement, holding numerous shows and expositions. An early host was a young then unknown Malagueño named Pablo Picasso (1881–1973). Picasso lived sporadically in Barcelona between the innocence-losing ages of 16 and 24, and the city heavily influenced his early painting. This was the period in which he amassed the raw materials for his Blue Period. In 1904 the then-mature Picasso moved to Paris where he found fame, fortune and Cubism, and went on to become one of the greatest artists of the 20th century.

Continuing the burst of brilliance was the Barcelona-born experimentalist Joan Miró (1893–1983), best remembered for his use of symbolic figures in primary colours. Declaring he was going to 'assassinate art', Miró wanted nothing to do with the constricting labels of the era, although he has often been called a pioneering surrealist, Dadaist and automatist.

Rising on Miró's coattails was the extravagant Catalan surrealist and showman, Salvador Dalí, from nearby Figueres, who mixed imaginative painting with posing, attention-seeking and shameless self-promotion. Dalí is hard to avoid anywhere in the world, especially Barcelona.

PUBLIC ART

The streets, squares and parks of Barcelona are littered with the signatures of artists past and present, famous and unknown. They range from Modernista sculptors, such as Josep Llimona, to international star sculptors, such as Roy Lichtenstein and Fernando Botero. Picasso and Joan Miró both left lasting reminders in the city.

Since the return of democracy in the late 1970s, the town hall has not been shy about encouraging the placement of sometimes grandiose and often incomprehensible contemporary works in the city's public spaces. Reactions range from admiration to perplexity.

Justly proud of its rich street-art heritage, the council has created an extensive archive of it all on the internet at www.bcn.cat (click on Art Públic, under Blog Barcelona). The site is rich in description of hundreds of items scattered across the city, and includes commentary on the history of the city through its street art. You can search particular items by district, period and key word.

The best thing about art in the streets is that it is open to all comers.

CONTEMPORARY ART

In the wake of the big three, Barcelona has been a minor cauldron of activity, dominated by the figure of Antoni Tàpies (b 1923). Early in his career (from the mid-1940s onwards) he seemed keen on self-portraits, but also experimented with collage using all sorts of materials, from wood to rice.

A poet, artist and man of theatre, Joan Brossa (1921–98) was a cultural beacon in Barcelona. His 'visual poems', lithographs and other artworks in which letters

⚓ ART GOES INFORMAL

Picasso, Miró and Dalí were hard acts to follow. Few envied the task of Catalan Antoni Tàpies in reviving the red hot Modernista flame. An early admirer of Miró, Tàpies soon began pursuing his own esoteric path embracing 'art informal' (a Jackson Pollack–like use of spontaneity) and inventing painting that utilised clay, string and even bits of rubbish. In April 2010 King Juan Carlos I elevated Tàpies to the Spanish nobility for his contribution to postwar art with the hereditary title the 1st Marquess of Tàpies. He remains, arguably, Spain's greatest living painter.

THE BEST

DIEGO LEZAMA

Museu d'Art Contemporani de Barcelona (p91)

PLACES TO SEE MODERN ART

- Museu Picasso (p113)
- Fundació Joan Miró (p224)
- Fundación Antoni Tàpies (p167)
- Museu d'Art Contemporani de Barcelona (p91)

generally figure, along with all sorts of objects, make his world accessible to those who can't read his Catalan poetry.

Joan Hernández Pijuan (1931–2005), one of Barcelona's most important 20th-century abstract painters, produced work concentrating on natural shapes and figures, often using neutral colours on different surfaces.

Jaume Plensa (b 1955) is possibly Spain's best contemporary sculptor. His work ranges from sketches, through sculpture, to video and other installations that have been shown around the world.

Susana Solano (b 1946), one of Barcelona's best painters and sculptors, also works with video installations, collages and jewellery.

SHOPPING

DIEGO LEZAMA

Fashion on Carrer d'Avinyó (p78)

Mixing old junk with top name brands, and bohemian ethnicity with a penchant for Euro-chic, Barcelona does quirky shops like novelist Carlos Luís Zafón does Gothic thrillers. Whether you're an extravagant prince or a thrifty pauper matters not a jot. Hit the Passeig de Gràcia to tear metaphoric chunks out of your credit card. For bargain-hunting, ephemera and indie boutiques, gravitate towards shabby-chic El Raval or the über-trendy La Ribera district.

THE CUTTING EDGE

Prêt-à-porter giant Mango is one of Barcelona main success stories. Emerging as one of the hippest local names on the world fashion catwalks is the youthful Custo Dalmau (aka Custo Barcelona), with a rapidly growing chain of stores in Spain and abroad. Other local names or Barcelona-based designers include Antonio Miró, Joaquim Verdú, David Valls, Josep Font, Armand Basi, Purificación García, Konrad Muhr, Sita Murt and TCN. All the big names of Spanish couture, from Adolfo Domínguez to Zara, are also present and there's barely an international brand that doesn't have outlets in Barcelona.

Twice a year the exclusive urban fashion salon Bread & Butter attracts hundreds of fashion producers and buyers from around the world to Barcelona. Born in Berlin, the salon transferred to Barcelona in 2006 and is going from strength to strength.

NEIGHBOURHOOD BY NEIGHBOURHOOD

In Barcelona, different enclaves offer different shopping experiences.

For high fashion, design, jewellery and many department stores, the main shopping axis starts on Plaça de Catalunya, proceeds up Passeig de Gràcia and turns left (west) into Avinguda Diagonal, along which it proceeds as far as Plaça de la Reina Maria Cristina. The densely packed section between Plaça de Francesc Macià and Plaça de la Reina Maria Cristina is good hunting ground.

The heart of L'Eixample – known as the Quadrat d'Or (Golden Sq) – is jammed with all sorts of glittering shops. La Rambla de Catalunya (p183) is lined with chic stores, and it's not just about fashion. Carrer del Consell de Cent (p183) bursts with art galleries and the nearby streets are also busy with shopping options, from specialist wine purveyors to bookstores.

Shopkeepers in the Barri Gòtic think of their area as 'Barnacentre' (from Barna – slang for Barcelona). Some of the most curious old stores, whether milliners or candle-makers, lurk in the narrow lanes around Plaça de Sant Jaume (p78). The once-seedy Carrer d'Avinyó has become a minor fashion boulevard, with creations by up-and-coming designers for a young (and young at heart) clientele. Antique stores abound on and around Carrer de la Palla and Carrer dels Banys Nous.

Over in La Ribera there are two categories of shops to look out for: some fine old traditional stores dealing in speciality foodstuffs; and a new crop of fashion and design stores (particularly along the stretch of Carrer del Rec between Passeig del Born and Avinguda del Marquès de l'Argentera, catering to the young professionals who have moved into the *barri*). Old-time stores abound in El Raval, where you'll also discover a cluster of preloved-clothes shops on Carrer de la Riera Baixa.

THE BEST

El Rey de la Magia (p128)

DIANA BIER BARCELONA ES/ALAMY

SHOPPING SECRETS

- **El Rey de la Magia** (p128)
- **La Portorriqueña** (p102)
- **Sala Parés** (p79)
- **El Ingenio** (p80)
- **L'Arca de Àvia** (p80)
- **Old Curiosity Shop** (p126)

REFUNDS

Non-EU residents are entitled to a refund of the 16% IVA (the Spanish equivalent of VAT or GST) on purchases of more than €90.16 from any shop if they take the goods out of the EU within three months. Ask the shop for a Cashback (or similar) refund form, which you present (with goods, prior to check-in) at the customs booth for IVA refunds when you leave Spain. At Barcelona airport, look for the customs booth opposite the bar on the ground floor of Terminal A.

BARCELONA IN FOCUS

🔰 TO MARKET, TO MARKET

One of the greatest sound, smell and colour sensations in Europe is Barcelona's most central produce market, the Mercat de la Boqueria (p62). It spills over with all the rich and varied colour of plentiful fruit and vegetable stands, seemingly limitless varieties of sea critters, sausages, cheeses, meat and sweets. It is also sprinkled with half a dozen or so unassuming places to eat well, at lunchtime stalls. According to some chronicles, there has been a market on this spot since 1217. Nowadays it's no easy task getting past the gawping tourists to get to the slippery slab of sole you're after.

THE URGE TO RUMMAGE

Lovers of old books, coins, stamps and general bric-a-brac can indulge their habits uninhibited at several markets. They generally get going from 9am and wind down around 8pm. The coin and stamp collectors' market and the old-book peddlers around the Mercat de Sant Antoni usually pack up by 2pm.

The Barri Gòtic is enlivened by an art and crafts market (Plaça de Sant Josep Oriol; Ⓜ Liceu) on Saturday and Sunday, the antiques-filled Mercat Gòtic (Plaça Nova; Ⓜ Liceu or Jaume I) on Thursday, and a coin and stamp collectors' market (Plaça Reial; Ⓜ Liceu) on Sunday morning.

Just beyond the western edge of El Raval, the punters at the Modernista Mercat de Sant Antoni (Map p82; Ⓜ Sant Antoni) dedicate Sunday morning to old maps, stamps, books and cards.

Once a fortnight, gourmands can poke about the homemade honeys, sweets, cheeses and other edible delights at the Fira Alimentació (Plaça del Pi; Ⓜ Liceu) from Friday to Sunday.

SHOPPING

SUSTAINABLE TRAVEL

GAB/IMAGEBROKER

Interior, Estació de Francia

Certain aspects of Barcelona's layout and background make sustainable choices easy. Forget car hire. Touring the city without an automobile is a breeze thanks to a comprehensive public transport system. The variety of public transportation here is astonishing and supersedes many other European cities. You can choose from a far-reaching bus system, trains, a Metro, a funicular railway or a cable car.

To go one step further you can walk. Laid out long before the invention of the motor car, Barcelona's Old Town was designed with medieval walkers in mind. Strolling is made more pleasant, thanks to numerous pedestrian-only streets, a redeveloped waterfront, and the parks and gardens of Montjuïc and Tibidabo.

Bikes are another option but, although cycle lanes have been laid out along many main arteries, the city centre is no Amsterdam – yet.

It's not hard to find local food and wine on the menus. With vineyards not far from the urban periphery there's no flying miles on the *cava* – most of it comes from the nearby Penedès region along with many other wines. Furthermore, plenty of the fish in the sea-faring quarter of La Barceloneta will have originated within shouting distance of your plate. Markets are excellent places to see and buy into the local economy and small independent food shops litter La Ribera district specialising in products such as chocolate and olive oil. El Raval is another alternative shopping area with some interesting antiques and secondhand clothes shops.

⬛ DIRECTORY & TRANSPORT

DIRECTORY

ACCOMMODATION

There has been little let-up in Barcelona's hotel-building boom since the early 2000s. Some fine, up-to-the-minute hotels in a broad price bracket have opened in historic buildings and key locations, the number of options near the sea has increased, and high-end digs have popped up in various strategic spots.

Hotels cover a broad range. At the bottom end there is often little to distinguish them from better *pensiones* and *hostales,* and they run up the scale to five-star luxury. If you are looking for a budget deal, check around the many *pensiones* and *hostales* – family-run, small-scale hotels, often in sprawling apartments. Some are fleapits, others immaculately maintained gems.

For more accommodation recommendations by Lonely Planet authors, check out the online booking service at www.lonelyplanet.com. You'll find the insider lowdown on the best places to stay, and reviews are thorough and independent.

CONSULATES

Most countries have an embassy in Madrid. Look them up under Embajada in that city's *Páginas Amarillas (Yellow Pages).* Various countries also maintain consulates in Barcelona:

Australia (Map p186; ☎ 93 490 90 13; Plaça de Gal·la Placídia 1-3; Ⓡ FGC Gràcia)

Canada (Map p162; ☎ 93 412 72 36; Plaça de Catalunya 9; Ⓜ Catalunya)

France (Map p162; ☎ 93 270 30 00; www.consulfrance-barcelone.org; Ronda de la Universitat 22B; Ⓜ Universitat)

Germany (Map p186; ☎ 93 292 10 00; www.barcelona.diplo.de; Passeig de Gràcia 111; Ⓜ Diagonal)

Ireland (Map p186; ☎ 93 491 50 21; Gran Via de Carles III 94; Ⓜ Maria Cristina)

New Zealand (Map p186; ☎ 93 209 03 99; Travessera de Gràcia 64; Ⓡ FGC Gràcia)

UK (Map p152; ☎ 93 366 62 00; Avinguda Diagonal 477; Ⓜ Hospital Clínic)

US (Map p186; ☎ 93 280 22 27; http://barcelona.usconsulate.gov; Passeig de la Reina Elisenda de Montcada 23-25; Ⓡ FGC Reina Elisenda)

CUSTOMS

People entering Spain from outside the EU are allowed to bring one bottle of spirits, one bottle of wine, 50mL of perfume and 200 cigarettes into Spain duty free. There are no duty-free allowances for travel between EU countries. For duty-paid items bought in one EU country and taken into another, the allowances are 90L of wine, 10L of spirits, unlimited quantities of perfume and 800 cigarettes.

DANGERS & ANNOYANCES

It cannot be stressed enough that newcomers to Barcelona must be on their guard. Petty theft is a problem in the city centre, on public transport and around main sights. Report thefts to the national police. You are unlikely to recover your goods but you will need to make this formal *denuncia* (police report) for insurance purposes. To avoid endless queues at the *comisaría* (police station), you can make the report by phone (☎ 902 102 112) in various languages or on the web at www.policia.es (in Spanish; click on 'Denuncias'). The following day you go to the station of your choice to pick up and sign the report, without queuing. You can also report losses to the Catalan police, the Mossos d'Esquadra (www.gencat.net/mossos, in Catalan). There's a handy (and busy) **police station** (Map p82; Carrer Nou de la Rambla 80; Ⓜ Paral·lel) near La Rambla and you can also report petty crime online at www.policia.es/denuncias.

DISCOUNT CARDS & TICKETS

If you want to get around Barcelona fast and visit multiple museums in the blink of an eye, the **Barcelona Card** (www.barcelona card.com) might come in handy. It costs €26/31.50/36/42 (a little less for children aged four to 12) for two/three/four/five days. You get free transport (and 20% off the Aerobús), and discounted admission prices (up to 30% off) or free entry to many museums and other sights, as well as minor discounts on purchases at a small number of shops, restaurants and bars. The card is available at the tourist offices and online.

GAY & LESBIAN TRAVELLERS

Barcelona has a busy gay scene, but the region's gay capital is the saucily hedonistic Sitges (p243), a major destination on the international gay party circuit. The gay community takes a leading role in the wild Carnaval celebrations there in February/March. In Barcelona, the bulk of the nocturnal goings happen in what is known as the 'Gaixample', the part of L'Eixample bounded by Gran Via de les Corts Catalans, Carrer de Balmes, Carrer del Consell de Cent and Carrer de Casanova.

HOLIDAYS

The following are national public holidays:
New Year's Day (Any Nou/Año Nuevo) 1 January
Epiphany/Three Kings' Day (Epifanía or El Dia dels Reis/Día de los Reyes Magos) 6 January
Good Friday (Divendres Sant/Viernes Santo) March/April
Easter Monday (Dilluns de Pasqua Florida) March/April

Labour Day (Dia del Treball/Fiesta del Trabajo) 1 May
Day after Pentecost Sunday (Dilluns de Pasqua Granda) May/June
Feast of St John the Baptist (Dia de Sant Joan/Día de San Juan Bautista) 24 June
Feast of the Assumption (L'Assumpció/La Asunción) 15 August
Catalonia's National Day (Diada Nacional de Catalunya) 11 September
Festes de la Mercè 24 September
Spanish National Day (Festa de la Hispanitat/Día de la Hispanidad) 12 October
All Saints Day (Dia de Tots Sants/Día de Todos los Santos) 1 November
Constitution Day (Día de la Constitución) 6 December
Feast of the Immaculate Conception (La Immaculada Concepció/La Inmaculada Concepción) 8 December
Christmas (Nadal/Navidad) 25 December
Boxing Day/St Stephen's Day (El Dia de Sant Esteve) 26 December

INTERNET ACCESS

Barcelona is full of internet centres. Some offer student rates and also sell cards for several hours' use at reduced rates. Look also for *locutorios* (public phone centres), which often double as internet centres.
Bornet (Map p104; ☎ 93 268 15 07; Carrer de Barra Ferro 3; per hr/10hr €2.80/20; ☾ 10am-11pm Mon-Fri, 2pm-11pm Sat, Sun & holidays; Ⓜ Jaume I)
Internet MSN (Map p194; Carrer del Penedès 1; per min €0.02; ☾ 10am-midnight; Ⓜ Fontana)

MEDICAL SERVICES

All foreigners have the same right as Spaniards to emergency medical treatment in public hospitals. EU citizens are entitled to the full range of health-care services in public hospitals, but must present a European Health Insurance Card

DIRECTORY

(enquire at your national health service) and may have to pay up front.

Non-EU citizens have to pay for anything other than emergency treatment. Most travel-insurance policies include medical cover.

For minor health problems you can try any *farmàcia* (pharmacy), where pharmaceuticals tend to be sold more freely without prescription than in places such as the USA, Australia or the UK.

Hospitals include the following:

Hospital Clínic i Provincial (Map p152; ☎ 93 227 54 00; Carrer de Villarroel 170; Ⓜ Hospital Clínic)

Hospital de la Santa Creu i de Sant Pau (Map p152; ☎ 93 291 90 00; Carrer de Sant Antoni Maria Claret 167; Ⓜ Hospital de Sant Pau)

Hospital Dos de Maig (Map p152; ☎ 93 507 27 00; Carrer del Dos de Maig 301; Ⓜ Hospital de Sant Pau)

Some 24-hour pharmacies:

Farmàcia Castells Soler (Map p162; ☎ 93 487 61 45; Passeig de Gràcia 90)

Farmàcia Clapés (Map p52; ☎ 93 301 28 43; La Rambla 98)

Farmàcia Torres (Map p162; ☎ 93 453 92 20; www.farmaciaabierta24h.com, in Spanish; Carrer d'Aribau 62)

MONEY

As in 15 other EU nations (Austria, Belgium, Cyprus, Finland, France, Germany, Greece, Ireland, Italy, Luxembourg, Malta, the Netherlands, Portugal, Slovakia and Slovenia), the euro is Spain's currency.

Increasingly, the subject of how to take your money abroad, especially within Europe, has only one answer – plastic. Though some people still like to take some cash and travellers cheques. If you wish to be sure to have some ready euros on arrival, fine, but only take in enough to cover needs over the first day or two.

Having a little cash at all times is a good idea, just in case cards are stolen and you find yourself in a jam.

Barcelona abounds with banks, many with ATMs, including several around Plaça de Catalunya and more on La Rambla and Plaça de Sant Jaume in the Barri Gòtic.

The foreign-exchange offices that you see along La Rambla and elsewhere are open for longer hours than banks.

NEWSPAPERS & MAGAZINES

A wide selection of national daily newspapers from around Europe (including the UK) is available at newsstands all over central Barcelona and at strategic locations such as train and bus stations.

El País includes a daily supplement devoted to Catalonia, but the region also has a lively home-grown press. *La Vanguardia* and *El Periódico* are the main local Spanish-language dailies. The latter also publishes a Catalan version. The more conservative and Catalan-nationalist-oriented daily is *Avui. El Punt* concentrates on news in and around Barcelona.

The most useful publication for expats is *Barcelona Metropolitan* (www.barcelona -metropolitan.com), with news, views, ads and listings information. *Pilote Urbain* (www.piloteurbain.com) is a French equivalent. *Catalonia Today* is a slim newssheet put out by the owners of *El Punt*.

ORGANISED TOURS

Organised tours range from walking tours of the Barri Gòtic or Picasso's Barcelona to organised spins by bicycle.

The Oficina d'Informació de Turisme de Barcelona organises a series of guided walking tours under the name of **Barcelona Walking Tours** (Map p162; ☎ 93 285 38 34; Plaça de Catalunya 17-S; Ⓜ Catalunya). One explores the Barri Gòtic (adult/child

DIRECTORY

€12.50/5; ⊗ 10am daily in English, noon Saturday in Spanish and Catalan), another follows in Picasso's footsteps and winds up at the Museu Picasso, to which entry is included in the price (adult/child €19/7; ⊗ 4pm Tuesday, Thursday and Sunday in English, 4pm Saturday in Spanish and Catalan) and a third takes in the main jewels of Modernisme (adult/child €12.50/5; ⊗ 4pm Friday and Saturday in English, 4pm Saturday in Spanish, all tours in both English and Spanish at 6pm June to September). It also offers a 'gourmet' tour of traditional purveyors of fine foodstuffs across the old city (adult/child €19/7; ⊗ 10am Friday and Saturday in English, 10.30am Saturday in Spanish and Catalan).

Bus Turístic (p283; ☎ 010; www.tmb.net) is a hop-on hop-off service that links virtually all the major tourist sights.

For a trip around the harbour, board a **Golondrina Excursion Boats** (☎ 93 442 31 06; www.lasgolondrinas.com; Moll de les Drassanes; adult/under 4yr/4-10yr/student & senior €13.50/free/5/11; Ⓜ Drassanes) golond-rina (swallow) from Moll de les Drassanes in front of Mirador de Colom. The one-hour round trip takes you to Port Olímpic, the Fòrum and back again. The number of departures depends largely on the season

and demand. If you just want to discover the area around the port, you can opt for a 35-minute excursion to the breakwater and back (adult/under four years/four to 10 years €6.50/free/2.60).

Barcelona Segway Fun (Map p130; ☎ 670 484000; www.barcelonasegwayfun.com) offers urban and even country tours on two-wheel people-movers! A one-hour tour costs €30 and leaves from in front of the Torre Mapfre at 12.30pm daily. Segway-mounted guides wait about in front of the Torre Mapfre from 10am daily.

My Favourite Things (☎ 637 265405; www.myft.net; tours from €26-32) offers tours for no more than 10 participants based on numerous themes: anything from design to food. Other activities include flamenco and salsa classes and cycle rides in and out of Barcelona.

Barcelona Scooter (Map p130; ☎ 93 285 38 32; €45; ⊗ 10.30am Sat), run by Cooltra, offers a three-hour tour around the city by scooter (€50) in conjunction with the city tourism office. Departure is from the Cooltra rental outlet at 3.30pm on Thursdays and 10.30am on Saturdays.

TAXES

TAXES

Value-added tax is otherwise known as IVA (*impuesto sobre el valor añadido,*

🚲 BICYCLE TOURS

Barcelona is awash with companies offering bicycle tours. Tours typically take two to four hours and generally stick to the old city, the Sagrada Família and the beaches. Operators include the following:

Bike Tours Barcelona (Map p104; ☎ 93 268 21 05; www.biketoursbarcelona.com; Carrer de l'Esparteria 3)

Barcelona By Bike (☎ 93 268 81 07; www.barcelonabybike.com)

CicloTour (Map p82; ☎ 93 317 19 70; Carrer dels Tallers 45; tours €21; ⊗ 11am daily, 4.30pm mid-Apr–Oct, 7.30pm Thu-Sun Jun-Sep) Three-hour tours starting in Plaça de Catalunya. Just turn up in front of the Hard Rock Café (Map p52) 10 minutes before.

pronounced 'EE-ba') in Spain. IVA is 7% on accommodation and restaurant prices and is usually – but not always – included in quoted prices. On most retail goods the IVA is 16%. IVA-free shopping is available in duty-free shops at all airports for people travelling between EU countries.

Non-EU residents are entitled to a refund under certain conditions. For more information check out p273 and the Euro Refund website (www.eurorefund.com).

TELEPHONE

The ubiquitous blue payphones are easy to use for international and domestic calls. They accept coins, *tarjetas telefóni-cas* (phonecards) issued by the national phone company Telefónica and, in some cases, credit cards. *Tarjetas telefónicas* come in €6 and €12 denominations and are sold at post offices and tobacconists.

Locutorios (call centres) are another option. You'll mostly find these scattered about the old town, especially in and around El Raval. Check rates before making calls. Increasingly, these double as internet centres.

To call Barcelona from outside Spain, dial the international access code, followed by the code for Spain (☎ 34) and the full number (including Barcelona's area code, ☎ 93, which is an integral part of the number).

The access code for international calls from Spain is ☎ 00. To make an international call, dial the access code, country code, area code and number.

You can dial an operator to make reverse-charge calls to your own country for free – pick up the number before you leave home. You can usually get an English-speaking Spanish international operator on ☎ 1408. For international directory enquiries, dial ☎ 11825. A call to this number costs €2.

Dial ☎ 1409 to speak to a domestic operator, including for a domestic reverse-charge call *(llamada por cobro revertido)*. For national directory inquiries, dial ☎ 11818.

Mobile-phone numbers start with 6 (from 2011 new ones will begin with 7). Numbers starting with 900 are national toll-free numbers, while those starting with numbers between 901 and 905 come with varying conditions.

TIME

Spain is one hour ahead of GMT/UTC during winter, and two hours ahead during daylight saving, or summer time (the last Sunday in March to the last Sunday in October). Most other western European countries are on the same time as Spain year-round. The UK, Ireland and Portugal are one hour behind. Spaniards use the 24-hour clock for official business (timetables etc) but generally switch to the 12-hour version in daily conversation.

TOURIST INFORMATION

Several tourist offices operate in Barcelona. A couple of general information numbers worth bearing in mind are ☎ 010 and ☎ 012. The first is for Barcelona and the other is for all Catalonia (run by the Generalitat). In addition to what follows, check out www.turisme total.org for info on Barcelona province.

Oficina d'Informació de Turisme de Barcelona Plaça de Catalunya (Map p162; ☎ 93 285 38 32; www.barcelona turisme.com; Plaça de Catalunya 17-S, underground; ☉ 9am-9pm; ⓂCatalunya); Ajuntament (Map p52; Carrer de la Ciutat 2; ☉ 9am-8pm Mon-Fri, 10am-8pm Sat, 10am-2pm Sun & holidays; ⓂJaume I); Estació Sants (Map p214; Estació Sants train station; ☉ 8am-8pm late Jun-late Sep, 8am-8pm Mon-Fri, 8am-2pm Sat, Sun & holidays Oct-May; ⓂSants Estació); El Prat airport (**Terminal 1**

arrivals, Terminal 2B arrivals hall, Terminal 2A arrivals hall; ☺ 9am-9pm) The Plaça de Catalunya tourist information office concentrates on city information and can help book accommodation. Expect to queue.

TRAVELLERS WITH DISABILITIES

Some hotels and public institutions have wheelchair access. All buses in Barcelona are wheelchair accessible and a growing number of Metro stations are theoretically wheelchair accessible (generally by lift, although there have been complaints that they are only any good for parents with prams). Ticket vending machines in Metro stations are adapted for the disabled and have Braille options for the blind.

You can order special taxis. Most street crossings in central Barcelona are accessible to wheelchair users.

For more information on what the city is doing to improve accessibility, click on 'Barcelona Accessible' at the city council website (www.bcn.cat).

VISAS

Spain is one of 25 member countries of the Schengen Convention, under which 22 EU countries (all but Bulgaria, Cyprus, Ireland, Romania and the UK) plus Iceland, Norway and Switzerland have abolished checks at common borders.

EU nationals require only their ID cards to visit Spain. Nationals of many other countries, including Australia, Canada, Israel, Japan, New Zealand and the USA, do not require visas for tourist visits to Spain of up to 90 days. Non-EU nationals who are legal residents of one Schengen country do not require a visa to visit another Schengen country.

All non-EU nationals entering Spain for any reason other than tourism (such as study or work) should contact a Spanish consulate, as they may need a specific visa and will have to obtain work and/or residence permits. Citizens of countries not mentioned above should check whether they need a visa with their Spanish consulate.

TRANSPORT

AIRPORTS

Barcelona's **El Prat Airport** (☎ 902 404704; www.aena.es) lies 12km southwest of the city at El Prat de Llobregat. The airport has two main terminal buildings, the new T1 terminal and the older T2, itself divided into three terminal areas (A, B and C).

In T1, the main arrivals area is on the 1st floor (with separate areas for EU Schengen Area arrivals, non-EU international arrivals and the Barcelona-Madrid corridor). Boarding gates for departures are on the 1st and 3rd floors.

The main **tourist office** (☺ 9am-9pm) is on the ground floor of Terminal 2B. Others on the ground floor of Terminal 2A and in Terminal 1 operate the same hours. Lockers (which come in three sizes) can be found on the 1st floor of Terminal 1 and at the car park entrance opposite Terminal 2B. You pay €3.80/4.40/4.90 for 24 hours. Lost luggage offices can be found by the arrivals belts in Terminal 1 and on the arrivals floor in Terminals 2A and 2B.

Girona-Costa Brava airport (☎ 902 404704; www.aena .es) is 12km south of Girona and about 90km north of Barcelona. **Reus airport** (☎ 902 404704; www.aena.es) is 13km west of Tarragona and 108km southwest of Barcelona.

BICYCLE

Some 156km of (often discontinuous) bike lanes have been laid out across the

TRANSPORT

city, making it possible to get around on two environmentally friendly wheels. A waterfront path runs northeast from Port Olímpic towards Riu Besòs. Scenic itineraries are mapped for cyclists in the Collserola parkland, and the *ronda verda* is a still incomplete 72km cycling path that extends around the city's outskirts.

You can transport your bicycle on the Metro on weekdays (except between 7am and 9.30am or 5pm and 8.30pm). On weekends and holidays, and during July and August, there are no restrictions. You can use FGC trains to carry your bike at any time and Renfe's *rodalies* trains from 10am to 3pm on weekdays and all day on weekends and holidays.

For information on all aspects of cycling in Barcelona, take a look at the city's website, www.bcn.cat/bicicleta (in Catalan/Spanish).

Countless companies around town offer bicycles (and anything remotely resembling one, from tandems to tricycle carts and more). They include the following:

BICYCLE

↘ GETTING INTO TOWN

The A1 Aerobús (☎ 93 415 60 20) runs from Terminal 1 at Barcelona El Prat Airport to Plaça de Catalunya (Map p162; €5, 30 to 40 minutes depending on traffic) via Plaça d'Espanya (Map p214), Gran Via de les Corts Catalanes (corner of Carrer del Comte d'Urgell, Map p162) and Plaça de la Universitat (Map p162) every five to 10 minutes (depending on the time of day) from 6.05am to 1.05am. Departures from Plaça de Catalunya are from 5.30am to 12.30am and stop at the corner of Carrer de Sepúlveda and Carrer del Comte d'Urgell, and Plaça d'Espanya. The A2 Aerobús from Terminal 2 (stops outside terminal areas A, B and C) runs from 6am to 12.30am with a frequency of between eight and 15 minutes and follows the same route as the A1. Buy tickets on the bus or from machines at the airport (if they are working!). Considerably slower local buses (such as the No 46 to/from Plaça d'Espanya and a night bus, the N17, to/from Plaça de Catalunya) also serve Terminals 1 and 2.

Train operator Renfe (www.renfe.es) runs the R2 Nord line every half an hour from the airport (from 6.08am to 11.38pm) via several stops to Estació Sants (the main train station) and Passeig de Gràcia in central Barcelona, after which it heads northwest out of the city. The first service from Passeig de Gràcia leaves at 5.28am and the last at 11.02pm, and about five minutes later from Estació Sants. The trip between the airport and Passeig de Gràcia takes 25 minutes. A one-way ticket costs €3.

The airport railway station is about a five-minute walk from Terminal 2. Regular shuttle buses run from the station and Terminal 2 to Terminal 1 – allow for an extra 15 to 20 minutes.

Barcelona HotelBus (www.barcelonahotelbus.com) offers small buses designed for people with luggage a door-to-door service to a series of hotels in central Barcelona and to the Fòrum area.

A taxi between either terminal and the city centre – about a half-hour ride depending on traffic – costs €20 to €25.

BarcelonaBiking.com (Map p52; ☎ 656 356300; www.barcelonabiking.com; Baixada de Sant Miquel 6; per hr/24 hr €5/15; ☷ 10am-8pm) City, road and mountain bikes.

BEB (Map p162; ☎ 93 451 50 31; www.beb .com.es; Carrer d'Enric Granados 61; rental per day from €20; ☷ 10am-2pm & 4.30-8.30pm) Offers more relaxed cyclists the option of renting motorised bikes. You are provided with bike, battery and charger. Discounts are available for longer periods. Bookings must be made a day in advance.

Un Cotxe Menys (Map p104; ☎ 93 268 21 05; www.bicicletabarcelona.com; Carrer de l'Esparteria 3; per hr/full day/week €5/15/55; ☷ 9am-7pm daily Easter-Nov, 11am-2pm Dec-Easter; Ⓜ Jaume I) This business also organises bike tours.

BUS
BARCELONA

Transports Metropolitans de Barcelona (TMB; ☎ 010; www.tmb.net) buses run along most city routes every few minutes from between 5am and 6.30am to between around 10pm and 11pm.

Bus Turístic, the hop-on hop-off service (audioguides in 10 languages) run by TMB, operates from Plaça de Catalunya (Map p162) and Plaça del Porta de la Pau, and covers three circuits (44 stops) linking virtually all the city's main sights. Tickets are available online (www.tmb .net) and on the buses, and cost €22 (€14 for children from four to 12 years) for one day of unlimited rides, or €29 (€18 for children) for two consecutive days. Buses run from 9am to 7.30pm and the frequency varies from every five to 25 minutes.

CATALONIA
Much of the Pyrenees and the entire Costa Brava are served only by buses, as train services are limited to important railheads such as Girona, Figueres, Lleida, Ripoll and Puigcerdà. Various bus companies operate across the region. Most operate from **Estació del Nord** (Map p152; ☎ 902 260606; www.barcelonanord.com; Carrer d'Ali Bei 80; Ⓜ Arc de Triomf), but Hispano-Igualadina and TEISA do not.

A subsidiary of Alsa **Alsina Graells** (☎ 902 422242; www.alsa.es) runs buses from Barcelona to destinations west and northwest, such as Vielha, La Seu d'Urgell and Lleida.

Barcelona Bus (☎ 902 130014; www. sagales.com, in Catalan & Spanish) runs buses from Barcelona to Girona (and Girona–Costa Brava airport), Figueres, parts of the Costa Brava and northwest Catalonia.

Hispano-Igualadina (Map p214; ☎ 902 447726; www.igualadina.net; Estació Sants & Plaça de la Reina Maria Cristina) serves central and southern Catalonia.

LONG-DISTANCE
Long-distance buses leave from Estació del Nord. A plethora of companies operates to different parts of Spain, although many come under the umbrella of **Alsa** (☎ 902 422242; www .alsa.es). For other companies, ask at the bus station. There are frequent services to Madrid, Valencia and Zaragoza (20 or more a day) and several daily departures to distant destinations such as Burgos, Santiago de Compostela and Seville.

Eurolines (www.eurolines.com), in conjunction with local carriers all over Europe, is the main international carrier. Its website provides links to national operators; it runs services across Europe and to Morocco from Estació del Nord, and **Estació d'Autobusos de Sants** (Map p214; Carrer de Viriat; Ⓜ Sants Estació), next to Estació Sants Barcelona.

◤ TICKETS & TARGETES

The Metro, FGC trains, *rodalies/cercanías* (Renfe-run local trains) and buses come under one zoned-fare regime. Single-ride tickets on all standard transport within Zone 1, except on Renfe trains, cost €1.40.

METRO & FGC

The easy-to-use **TMB Metro** (☎ 010; www.tmb.net) system has seven numbered and colour-coded lines (one, the new Line 9, only partially completed). It runs from 5am to midnight Sunday to Thursday and holidays, from 5am to 2am on Friday and days immediately preceding holidays, and 24 hours on Saturday. Line 2 has access for people with disabilities and a handful of stations on other lines also have lifts.

TAXI

Taxis charge €2 flag fall plus meter charges of €0.86 per kilometre (€1.10 from 8pm to 7am and all day on weekends). A further €3.10 is added for all trips to/from the airport, and €1 for large luggage. The trip from Estació Sants to Plaça de Catalunya, about 3km, costs about €10. You can call a **taxi** (☎ 93 225 00 00, 93 300 11 00, 93 303 30 33, 93 322 22 22) or flag them down.

Trixis (Map p52; ☎ 93 310 13 79; www.trixi.info; Plaça dels Traginers 4), three-wheeled cycle taxis, operate along the waterfront and around much of the centre (noon to 8pm daily between March and November). They can take two passengers and cost €6/10/18 per 25 minutes/30 minutes/one hour.

TRAIN

Train is the most convenient overland option for reaching Barcelona from major Spanish centres such as Madrid and Valencia. Information on travel within Spain is available at train stations or travel agents. A network of *rodalies/cercanías* serves towns around Barcelona (and the airport). Contact **Renfe** (☎ 902 320320; www.renfe.es). For information on travelling from the UK, contact the **Rail Europe Travel Centre** (☎ in the UK 0844 848 4064; www.raileurope.co.uk; 1 Lower Regent St, London SW1).

Eighteen high-speed Tren de Alta Velocidad Española (AVE) trains between Madrid and Barcelona run daily in each direction, nine of them in under three hours. A typical one-way price is €114.

The main train station in Barcelona is **Estació Sants** (Map p214; Plaça dels Països Catalans; Ⓜ Sants Estació), 2.5km west of La Rambla. Direct overnight trains from Paris, Geneva, Milan and Zurich arrive here.

◤ CLIMATE CHANGE & TRAVEL

Every form of transport that relies on carbon-based fuel generates CO_2, the main cause of human-induced climate change. Modern travel is dependent on aeroplanes, which might use less fuel per kilometer per person than most cars but travel much greater distances. The altitude at which aircraft emit gases (including CO_2) and particles also contributes to their climate change impact. Many websites offer 'carbon calculators' that allow people to estimate the carbon emissions generated by their journey and, for those who wish to do so, to offset the impact of the greenhouse gases emitted with contributions to portfolios of climate-friendly initiatives throughout the world. Lonely Planet offsets the carbon footprint of all staff and author travel.

⬎ BEHIND THE SCENES

THE AUTHORS
BRENDAN SAINSBURY
Coordinating author

Brendan has logged many achievements while in Spain, including meeting his future wife, learning to play flamenco guitar and holding down a job as a travel guide writer. He first visited Barcelona in the late 1980s on an inter-rail card and returned many years later – on a bicycle. A native Brit, Brendan now lives in Vancouver, Canada, with his wife, Liz, and five-year-old son, Kieran.

Author thanks Thanks to Joe Bindloss for offering me the gig, Sasha Baskett and Dora Whitaker for their help along the way, and Damien Simonis for his inspiring text.

DAMIEN SIMONIS
In 1990, during a continental foray from a rain-sodden London, Damien found himself in pre-Olympics Barcelona. He had never before set foot in Spain. What was it about this town? The crowded produce markets, the dimly lit *colmados* (treasure caverns of all sorts of weird and wonderful foods), the gaily noisy terraces where chatter mixed so easily with wine, the Gaudí colours, the mysterious narrow lanes of the Barri Gòtic, the seaside? Perhaps it was all this and some unifying, indefinable quality that got under his skin. Eight years later, Damien turned up in a Rambla-side pensión on assignment for Lonely Planet. And that old magic started doing its work again. A chat with a fellow in a bar and he had a room in a top-floor flat in Gran Via. Barcelona was for years a second home for Damien and is now our restless correspondent's main base.

THE PHOTOGRAPHER
Based in Madrid, professional photographer Diego Lezama Orezzoli spends a large part of the year travelling abroad and within Spain. Since discovering his passion for photography on a trip to Morocco in 1989, he has travelled extensively on assignment

for numerous clients. His favourite subject is architecture – especially the ancient Mayan sites in Central America. Diego considers his best photo to be one he took at the ruins of Tikal, the mighty jaguar temple of the Mayas. It took five days and nights to find the perfect moment to illuminate this monument with artificial light right before sunrise.

THIS BOOK

This 1st edition of *Discover Barcelona* was coordinated by Brendan Sainsbury, and researched and written by him and Damien Simonis. The La Sagrada Família highlight was written by Anthony Ham. This guidebook was commissioned in Lonely Planet's London office and produced by the following:

Commissioning Editors Joe Bindloss, Dora Whitaker
Coordinating Editor Kirsten Rawlings
Coordinating Cartographer Andy Rojas
Coordinating Layout Designer Lauren Egan
Managing Editors Sasha Baskett, Bruce Evans
Managing Cartographers Alison Lyall, Herman So
Managing Layout Designers Celia Wood, Indra Kilfoyle
Assisting Editor Alison Ridgway
Assisting Cartographer Brendan Streager
Assisting Layout Designers Paul Iacono, Kerrianne Southway
Cover Research Naomi Parker
Internal Image Research Aude Vauconsant
Language Content Annelies Mertens

Thanks to Glenn Beanland, Jessica Boland, Ryan Evans, Fayette Fox, Joshua Geoghegan, Michelle Glynn, Brice Gosnell, Charlotte Harrison, Wayne Murphy, Darren O'Connell, Trent Paton, Rebecca Skinner, Lyahna Spencer, Marg Toohey, Gerard Walker, Juan Winata

Internal photographs p4 La Sagrada Família, Christopher Groenhout; pp10–11 El Raval district, Martin Hughes; pp12–13 Sala Hipóstila, Park Güell, Rachel Lewis; p31 La Sagrada Família, Jean-Pierre Lescourret; p39 Plaça del Rei, Krzysztof Dydynski; p3, pp50–1 *Castellers* at Festes de la Mercè, Barri Gòtic, Martin Hughes; p3, p81 Museu d'Art Contemporani de Barcelona, Richard Cummins; p3, p103 Palau de la Música Catalana, Krzysztof Dydynski; p3, p129 La Barceloneta, Neil Setchfield; p3, p151 Casa Batlló, John Banagan; p3, p185 Casa-Museu Gaudí, Krzysztof Dydynski; p3, p213 Waterfalls in front of Museu Nacional d'Art de Catalunya, Krzysztof Dydynski; p3, p237 Tarragona cathedral, Damien Simonis; pp250–1 City street and Torre Agbar, John Hay; p275 El Born District, Diego Lazama Orezzoli

ACKNOWLEDGMENTS

Many thanks to the following for the use of their content: Barcelona Metro Map © TMB Metro 2010

BEHIND THE SCENES

NOTES

NOTES

↘ INDEX

See also separate indexes for Drinking (p298), Eating (p298), Entertainment & Activities (p299), Shopping (p300), Sights (p301) and Sleeping (p303).

INDEX

INDEX

INDEX

INDEX

ENTERTAINMENT & ACTIVITIES

INDEX

INDEX

INDEX

MAP LEGEND

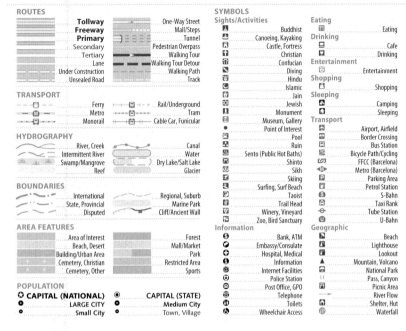

ROUTES
- Tollway
- Freeway
- Primary
- Secondary
- Tertiary
- Lane
- Under Construction
- Unsealed Road
- One-Way Street
- Mall/Steps
- Tunnel
- Pedestrian Overpass
- Walking Tour
- Walking Tour Detour
- Walking Path
- Track

TRANSPORT
- Ferry
- Metro
- Monorail
- Rail/Underground
- Tram
- Cable Car, Funicular

HYDROGRAPHY
- River, Creek
- Intermittent River
- Swamp/Mangrove
- Reef
- Canal
- Water
- Dry Lake/Salt Lake
- Glacier

BOUNDARIES
- International
- State, Provincial
- Disputed
- Regional, Suburb
- Marine Park
- Cliff/Ancient Wall

AREA FEATURES
- Area of Interest
- Beach, Desert
- Building/Urban Area
- Cemetery, Christian
- Cemetery, Other
- Forest
- Mall/Market
- Park
- Restricted Area
- Sports

POPULATION
- ✪ CAPITAL (NATIONAL)
- ● LARGE CITY
- ● Small City
- ◉ CAPITAL (STATE)
- ● Medium City
- ● Town, Village

SYMBOLS

Sights/Activities
- Buddhist
- Canoeing, Kayaking
- Castle, Fortress
- Christian
- Confucian
- Diving
- Hindu
- Islamic
- Jain
- Jewish
- Monument
- Museum, Gallery
- Point of Interest
- Pool
- Ruin
- Sento (Public Hot Baths)
- Shinto
- Sikh
- Skiing
- Surfing, Surf Beach
- Taoist
- Trail Head
- Winery, Vineyard
- Zoo, Bird Sanctuary

Information
- Bank, ATM
- Embassy/Consulate
- Hospital, Medical
- Information
- Internet Facilities
- Police Station
- Post Office, GPO
- Telephone
- Toilets
- Wheelchair Access

Eating
- Eating

Drinking
- Cafe
- Drinking

Entertainment
- Entertainment

Shopping
- Shopping

Sleeping
- Camping
- Sleeping

Transport
- Airport, Airfield
- Border Crossing
- Bus Station
- Bicycle Path/Cycling
- FFCC (Barcelona)
- Metro (Barcelona)
- Parking Area
- Petrol Station
- S-Bahn
- Taxi Rank
- Tube Station
- U-Bahn

Geographic
- Beach
- Lighthouse
- Lookout
- Mountain, Volcano
- National Park
- Pass, Canyon
- Picnic Area
- River Flow
- Shelter, Hut
- Waterfall

LONELY PLANET OFFICES

Australia
Head Office
Locked Bag 1, Footscray, Victoria 3011
☎ 03 8379 8000, fax 03 8379 8111

USA
150 Linden St, Oakland, CA 94607
☎ 510 250 6400, toll free 800 275 8555,
fax 510 893 8572

UK
2nd fl, 186 City Rd,
London EC1V 2NT
☎ 020 7106 2100, fax 020 7106 2101

Contact
talk2us@lonelyplanet.com
lonelyplanet.com/contact

Published by Lonely Planet Publications Pty Ltd
ABN 36 005 607 983

Printed in Singapore

MIX
Paper from
responsible sources
FSC™ C021741
www.fsc.org